MW00463194

UNGODLY

A True Story of Unprecedented Evil

Bill Osinski

Indigo Publishing Group, LLC

Publisher	Henry S. Beers
Associate Publisher	Richard J. Hutto
Executive Vice President	Robert G. Aldrich
Operations Manager	Gary G. Pulliam
Editor-in-Chief	Joni Woolf
Art Director/Designer	Julianne Gleaton
Designer	Daniel Emerson
Director of Marketing and Public Relations	Mary D. Robinson
Distribution	Nick Malloy

Printed in the USA.

Library of Congress Control Number: 2007923959

ISBN: (13 digit) 978-1-934144-13-8
         (10 digit) 1-934144-13-4

Indigo books are available at quantity discounts with bulk purchase for educational, business, or sales promotional use. For information, please write to:
Indigo Publishing Group, LLC., SunTrust Bank Building, 435 Second Street, Suite 320, Macon, GA 31201, or call 866-311-9578.

www.ungodlybook.com

Photo by W.A. Bridges, *Atlanta Journal-Constitution*

TABLE OF CONTENTS

PREFACE

I had come to the big city and helped to crack a twenty-year-old murder case. I deserved a steak and a scotch, both rare. I was also on expense account.

I shouldered my way through the crowd at the Gramercy Tavern in Manhattan and found a seat at the bar. I wanted badly to share my story with someone, so the bartender and the stranger at the next stool became my audience.

I'd hit town with some suspicions and a secret federal investigative report. It blamed a 1979 killing on a psychotic thug formerly associated with a strange group with an even stranger leader, a man with many names, the only verifiably valid of which was Dwight York. His group had transplanted itself from some of the meanest streets in Brooklyn, where it was a Black Muslim outfit known as Ansaru Allah Community, to a four hundred-acre farm in Putnam County, Georgia, where its base was an Egyptian-style theme park called Tama-Re. That county was right in the middle of my beat, "The Other Georgia," which is what many people in my city, Atlanta, call everything in the state outside Atlanta.

The biggest revelation in the report was that one of York's enforcers, who called himself Hashim the Warrior, real name Roy Savage, had assassinated Horace Green, a well-known neighborhood activist, in broad daylight and in front of a small group of witnesses on a sidestreet off Bushwick Avenue. Nearly twenty years later, the case remained officially unsolved and inactive. By my pica ruler, this looked like news.

My copy of the federal report proved to be an effective entrée to the homicide detectives' offices on the second floor of an NYPD precinct house in Brooklyn. Some of the older detectives remembered the Green case quite well; the investigation had gone cold almost as fast as the body. I shared the report with them, and as soon as they read it, they re-opened the inactive case and declared Savage a suspect.

In return, the detectives pulled out a couple of dusty boxes that contained the files on the murder investigation. They put me and the boxes in an empty office and allowed me to dig for a couple of hours. I struck a reporter's gold mine.

From the files, I discovered that the victim's widow still lived on Bushwick Avenue, just across the street from York's old headquarters. Not only that, I found the name of one of the original detectives on the case; he had retired and moved to Los Angeles, but incredibly, he happened to be in New York on that day. When I contacted him, he told me that not only did he remember the case well, he was eager to talk to me about it. It had always bothered him that restrictive policies in effect at the time had prevented him from finding Horace Green's killer.

The information I had gained confirmed the bombshell in the FBI report: the leader of the group that had moved to rural Georgia had quite likely gotten away with murder back in Brooklyn.

Moments like this are why I'd become a reporter twenty-seven years earlier. The quiet sense of triumph that comes when you know you're sitting on a great story – and it's all yours – is every bit as delicious as getting a big award or picking up your paper before dawn and seeing your story plastered across page one.

I thought I had everything I needed to start writing a hard-edged investigative exposé. As it turned out, however, I had only set myself up for the first of a series of disappointments and struggles. I exasperated my editors, who generally thought I was pressing too hard. I must have been doing something right, though, because York thought the same thing.

Along the way, several of my stories were diluted. My name was placed on a sort of hit list circulated by the Nuwaubians, who offered $500 for any information they could use to discredit me. I later learned that York sometimes led his followers in praying for great misfortune to befall me. When that failed, his minions wrote letters to my bosses implying that I should be fired. When that failed, I received a few thinly-veiled threats.

I wish I could say that my dogged pursuit was a key factor in ultimately bringing York to justice. It wasn't.

My problems were minor compared to those of some dedicated lawmen, who were simply trying to do their jobs but who received little but antagonism and resistance from their superiors at the state and federal levels.

And all those problems were miniscule, compared to what the children of the cult were suffering.

I offer this account of how I didn't break the big story, because it is symptomatic of the political and societal conditions that allowed a monster to operate with virtual impunity for more than three decades.

Simply put, no one wanted to look for the criminal behind the clerical robes.

INTRODUCTION

The girl was as lovely as she was quiet – and she wasn't making a sound. Her height and long-muscled limbs suggested she should be on her way to junior-high basketball practice; yet she stood motionless in the middle of a cheap Athens, Georgia, apartment being used as a safe house. Her eyes kept darting toward the door, as if she expected it to be broken down at any moment.

The terror I saw in the eyes of the girl I'll call Yasmin had not come from any adolescent campfire story but from the reality of what she had endured for the past two years.

Yasmin's older brother had only a few days earlier rescued her from Tama-Re, the Egyptian-style theme park that had been built on a fallow farm a few counties away and that served as the home base of a con man extraordinaire and sexual predator nonpareil named Dwight York. For the past two or three years, York had used Yasmin as one of his harem of sex slaves. At that time, York was in his mid-fifties, and he was the founder and unquestioned leader of a cult he called the United Nuwaubian Nation of Moors.

Why was this girl silent? Where were her parents? Where were the agents of the law? Why did only her brother seem outraged?

And why was I so helpless to do anything about it? I was a reporter for a

At left is Hathor, the recording studio that York set up at Tama-Re.

major regional newspaper in the presence of the victim of an unspeakable crime. But all I could do then was to offer her some awkward and insufficient words of comfort, words to the effect of, "Your brother will take care of you now." I left the apartment, and outside I gave Yasmin's brother the name and phone number of a federal agent, whom I could only hope might be able to help.

Race and religion were the two main reasons no one seemed to want to hear or do anything about the girl's plight. First, the girl was black, as is York and as were nearly all his followers. Second, she was a member of York's purportedly religious community. At that time, no one wanted to be seen as persecuting, harassing, or discriminating against a black religious leader.

York was eventually exposed as a criminal, but he was also proven to be a master at playing the race and religion cards. Throughout his decades-long run – extending from the late 1960s on the streets of Brooklyn until 2002 at Tama-Re – York used those cards to trump all sorts of people who should have been able to stop him, including politicians, police officials, educators, academics, civil rights activists, and journalists.

Essentially, what he had done to Yasmin was just an extension of what he had been doing to his followers and their children for the previous thirty years or so.

Religious tolerance was written into the Constitution. After the Civil War and the tumult of the Civil Rights Movement, racial equality has been written

Pyramids dominate the landscape at Tama-Re.

into the laws of the land.

But now, the courage that ultimately won those cherished rights has been replaced in cases like this one by fear. No one in a position of power in modern-day America can afford to be perceived as racist or intolerant of anyone else's religion. The fear of even being accused of racial or religious bigotry can become paralysis in the guise of sensitivity.

Dwight York expertly exploited these fears and enjoyed a lucrative, long-lasting criminal career. And all the while he was flaunting all sorts of authorities, accusing those who opposed him of being racists, and portraying himself as a victim or racial injustice and religious persecution, he was preying perhaps on scores of children like Yasmin.

I cannot undo any of the damage done to them. But now I can, at the least, use this book to tell their story. In a broader sense, it is also a story about how our society deals with, or fails to deal with, issues of race and religion.

An amateur magician, York played his tricks of religious and racial subterfuge for more than twenty years in the nation's largest city and for nearly another decade from a farm in the rural South.

During his Brooklyn-based years, York purported to be an Imam, the leader of a devout community of Black Muslims. That claim gained his Ansaru Allah Community designation as a "sensitive site," which effectively meant that police investigations stopped at York's front gate, even when the crime

This archway leads to the central plaza at Tama-Re.

was murder.

Then York and a select group of his followers took the midnight train to Georgia. They shed all their Islamic trappings and morphed a few times, first into cowboys, then to Masons. His final costume change was into the role of Dr. Malachi Z. York, the Master Teacher of the United Nuwaubian Nation of Moors. This motif worked so well that York fleshed it out by building Tama-Re, a cheesy re-creation of the ancient City of the Dead, complete with plywood pyramids and a fake stucco sphinx, on his farm in Putnam County. This slice of the Old South also happens to be the breeding ground for some of the best writing on race-related topics in the history of American literature (i.e., Flannery O'Connor, Alice Walker, and Joel Chandler Harris).

When local officials dared to enforce the law against him – something that had rarely happened in the big city – York responded with a vicious racial smear campaign, falsely labeling his opponents as racists. He never produced evidence to support his accusations, but then, he didn't need to. His political allies and some nationally-known civil rights activists carried his cause to the highest levels of state government and to the general public. The reluctance to act against a black religious leader who was claiming to be the victim of Deep-South rednecks also extended to the top tier of the federal law enforcement pyramid.

All the while, York was helping himself to the vast sums of cash that his followers brought to him. He used the money primarily to indulge his lavish tastes and his sexual depravities. He fathered and abandoned an estimated two hundred or more children, and over the years, repeatedly molested dozens of the children of some of his most loyal followers. That much was proven in court; one can only make a soul-shuddering estimate of York's crimes that fell outside the scope of the criminal investigation.

It was only after some of the most seriously abused children grew up and stepped up to the witness stand to tell their stories that York's religious and racial charades were ended.

This book is not a biography of Dwight York. He may be the central character, but he is not what makes this story worth telling in book length. In chronicling his rise and fall, this author seeks to answer the most obvious question that arises in connection with York's, or anyone else's, cult or cults. Why? Why would anyone forfeit their possessions, their faculties of reason and independent judgment, and, in this case, their children, to the whims of a demented character like Dwight York?

The easy answer is that they were duped, that they had desperate needs to belong somewhere, even to a community where they were literally treated like slaves.

Yet, there is much more to that part of the story. Interviews with dozens of former Nuwaubians have convinced me that a significant percentage of those who joined York's cult were articulate, intelligent, African-Americans who were seeking something similar to the dream many of their ancestors had followed.

They wanted a place they could collectively call their home. They wanted to create a community where they could feel like they, or at least the leaders they chose, would make the rules, and where those rules did not have to be sanctioned by whites. They wanted to create a community where they could raise their children in an atmosphere not tainted by the evils of the outside world. They wanted a spiritual belief system that was more than an adaptation of a "white" faith.

They wanted to build something good. They wanted a Black Utopia.

In that light, the Nuwaubian phenomenon can be seen as a recent continuation of an enduring tradition, one that has had several other expressions in Georgia history. The Nuwaubians, like the other black utopian communities from outside Georgia, were people who thought they had found a place in Georgia to live out their dreams. The utopian allure seems to glow more brightly in the heart of the Deep South.

The Nuwaubian nation was clearly a religious cult, but more to the point, it was a cult run by a crook. York's followers may have believed in him, but he definitely did not believe what he was telling them to believe. He considered his followers to be fools for being so devoted to him. Further, he made it quite clear to several sources for this book that his only gods were sex and money.

At its dark heart, then, this is a crime story. I am, at heart, an investigative crime reporter. I have collected the raw material for this book by using the tools of my craft – persistence and persuasion. Many of the former cult members were reluctant to talk to me about their experiences. Some were still traumatized, some were afraid, some were ashamed, while others just wanted to forget everything that happened to them while they were held in York's sway.

To those who overcame their fears to share their stories with me, I have the responsibility to tell the tale as truthfully and as fully as I can.

That means delving into the ugly depths of what happened to the children. There is simply no way to soften the harsh reality that Dwight York repeatedly raped dozens of children, some of them on a daily basis, and some of those assaults continued over a period of years. Some of the girls who were adolescents when he started to molest them grew up to be women who bore him children; and, in a few cases, they groomed younger children to be receptive to be his next generation of victims. In some cases, the adult concubines participated in the sex crimes.

The victims necessarily had to relate their stories in graphic detail to investigators and to the court where they testified against York. I obtained access to the investigative and court documents, so for the most part, I did not ask the victims I interviewed to re-tell the most painful parts of their stories. I only sought confirmation that what they had told the authorities was the truth. In the text of this book, I have used only as much of the victims' stories as was necessary to convey those essential truths, while eliminating some of the more lurid parts.

York was offered the opportunity to be interviewed for this book, but through two different attorneys, he declined.

For all the victims and their parents, I have used fictitious names. They deserve a chance to bury those parts of their past.

They also deserve more help than they have received to date. I have made a commitment to donate half of any royalties I receive from this book to a fund to aid the victims, the lambs who brought down the wolf.

CHAPTER 1
Pyramids in the Cow Pasture (1998)

"Welcome to the Most Holy Land...Egypt of The West" ...from the cover of the program for Savior's Day.

Down Shadydale Road, in the heart of Georgia's dairy country, lay Tama-Re, the home base of a strange empire built on lies and drivit.

Drivit is a cheap, plasticized form of stucco, used on this four hundred-acre former cotton farm and former hunting preserve to create a fake sandstone effect for the exteriors of a collection of structures that formed a sort of downscale theme-park envisioning of the Land of the Pharaohs. Some of the largest of the assorted sphinxes, pyramids, obelisks, and dog-headed deities had been built by a New Orleans firm that specializes in designing Mardi Gras floats.

The lies had long been the basic construction material for a series of communal enterprises headed by the Pharaoh of Tama-Re, a black man named Dwight York, or, as he preferred to be called then, Dr. Malachi Z. York. A slight, short man with eyes that could seemingly hold a stare forever, York had for decades changed identities almost as easily as he changed costumes. He loved to play dress-up as a Muslim Imam, an Indian chief, a semi-Jewish rabbi, a disco/

rock 'n' roll singer, a cowboy, and most lately, a reincarnated Egyptian god, and a guest savior from another galaxy.

This particular day, June 26, 1998, happened to be his fifty-third birthday. Thousands of people were coming from all over the country and from several foreign nations to celebrate the occasion. The name for the event was Savior's Day.

Shadydale Road, or GA 142, cuts a gently curving swath through Jasper and Putnam Counties. There are a few working dairy farms, at least one front yard auto salvage center, and some well-tended but modest residences. Mostly though, the land is pine woods and cotton fields gone fallow.

Around one of those non-descript curves, the travelers driving Shadydale Road that day got their first sight of Tama-Re. Right alongside the highway, two forty-foot-high pyramids, one black and one gold, had been constructed. Nearby there was an obelisk, a ten-foot-high ziggeraut, and gilt-painted statues of various Egyptian deities. In a picnic area, plastic palm trees were meant to suggest a desert ambience, though the ground was covered in grass, not sand. The Georgia summer nearly matched Egypt in terms of heat, though.

The crowds of people could be seen milling pleasantly about the land, eating, shopping, exploring. The children could ride the Little Egypt Choo Choo around the public part of the property. Many of the women wore flowing white robes, edged in royal blue.

A few yards from the highway, visitors approached a twenty-foot-high arched entrance gate, with a guard shack inside. The arch was coated with sandstone-colored drivit surface, practically every inch of which was covered with Egyptian pictograms and paintings.

In the center of the arch was a depiction of a fan in the shape of a bird wing. On the left side of the arch was a painting of a large blue bird, with a red crest on its head. Around the bird were depictions of a crescent, a Star of Rafiq, and an ankh. On the right side was a painting of an Egyptian male, probably royalty, holding a scepter.

On the walls extending from the arch were more elaborate paintings of the type of scenes that could have been copied from a museum display of ancient papyrus scrolls. The scene on the left wall was of a man holding a jar and two women presenting birds to a seated woman with a boy on her lap. On the right wall was a painting of four males engaged in different forms of study.

Each person entering Tama-Re received a program of the weekend's festivities, as he or she passed through the gate. Inside each program was a free-will donation envelope. The outside flap was inscribed "Our Savior's Day," with a picture of York in ceremonial garb. On the inside front of the envelope, the giver was supposed to circle the amount of the gift -- $50, $100, $500, $1,000, or more. The money pitch also included a pre-inscribed good-will wish from the giver: "For all he has given and done for me this year. As well as many years before. Thank you and have a very happy and prosperous birthday."

One woman who came to Tama-Re that day had no intention of making any kind of contribution to Dwight York. She was rather hoping things might work the other way around.

She was called Alima, the name York had given her about eighteen years earlier, when she was seventeen. After making her one of his many concubines, York had also given her three children. He had neglected, however, to give her any means of supporting them. Instead, he had expelled her from his community when she was pregnant with their third child.

Alima was no longer the teenager who had embraced York and his teachings with a sense of awe and then given a decade of her life to him. She was still pretty and slim, with full eyebrows and large dark eyes; but she was also in desperate need.

In the years since her expulsion, Alima had maintained contact with York, writing him about the growth of their two healthy children. The third had been born profoundly retarded and had been made a ward of the State of Florida. A year or so before the 1998 Savior's Day festival, she learned that York had moved his community to Georgia, and she moved to Atlanta. York assigned her and the children space in what she called a "dump" of an apartment in a complex he controlled. York also "mated" her with a man who was affiliated with his community at Tama-Re. Alima and this man had recently had another child together.

She and her new mate agreed that York should be doing more to support his children, whom they were raising. They had York's two children with them as they drove onto the compound. While just about everyone else driving through the decorated gates of Tama-Re that day saw York as a god, or at least a holy man, Alima saw a Deadbeat Dad.

That did not stop her from being impressed, and then angered, by the lavishness of the scene. "He's gotten so powerful," Alima recalled thinking, as she entered Tama-Re, "but I'm not getting anything."

All the visitors drove their cars through the gate and up a driveway lined with a few dozen ten-foot-high statues of various deities, including the dog-faced god and the bird-headed god. At the top of the driveway was a ten-foot-high ziggeraut, a religious ceremonial platform. The cars were directed to parking places along a grassy hillside, and then the visitors were free to roam.

Inside one of the pyramids was a gift shop stocked with some of the

Entrance to Club Rameses, the nightclub at Tama-Re.

hundreds of books York claimed to have authored. The full-color covers were printed on slick paper stock, while most of the inside pages were printed on paper similar to that found in comic books, but their price tags ranged from $5 to $25. Cheaply made tee shirts sold for around $15. Doll figures of York in Nuwaubian garb went for $50.

All these things, plus whatever else was on sale, could be purchased with "Tama-Re money." This was scrip that the visitors could obtain by changing real money at the rate of $500 U.S. currency for $550 in Tama-Re money. All the Tama-Re bills were adorned with a picture of Dwight York.

"The face on the Tama-Re dollars is none other than the Pharaoh of Tama-Re, Egypt of the West, Neter A'aferte Atum-Re," proclaimed the flyer that explained the 'novelty money program.' "We are honoring our pharaoh's life-long dedication to helping others and truly appreciate all that he has given. Thus it would only be right for us to show our love and admiration for our pharaoh by engraving his image on our money that will be passed on for years to come."

The upper floors of the pyramid had been set up as a café, but it was not in use, probably due to the heat.

The other pyramid, the black one, was the religious centerpiece of Tama-Re. It was surrounded by a concrete plaza, on which a wooden maze had been constructed. The faithful could meditate or pray as they navigated the maze. To enhance the meditative atmosphere, loudspeakers played music that seemed to be a blend of New Age and Buddhist chant.

Food was being sold at a café near the picnic grounds along the highway, and near a large wooden stage set further back from the road. It may not have been anywhere near as grand as the real pyramids, but it was certainly closer than anything else in that part of Georgia.

Years later, an FBI agent would testify that the 1998 Savior's Day festival brought in about $500,000 cash to York.

During the 1998 festival, however, no one could visit what had been Tama-Re's major tourist attraction, the Club Rameses. It had been shut down about two months earlier by Putnam County Sheriff Howard Sills, acting on a court injunction. For at least six months, the nightclub had attracted 1,000 to 1,500 customers on weekend nights, each paying a $25 cover charge.

There was certainly nothing like Club Rameses in Middle Georgia. The exterior of the building had a sandstone drivit surface, decorated with murals of pharaohs in their chariots and on the hunt.

Inside, most of the 50x100 building was a red cement dance floor, covered in some sections with a white pergo flooring. There was a circular, red-velvet-covered divan in the middle of the dance floor, where the dancers could sit; a velvet cone rose from its center, and atop the cone was a statue of King Tut.

On the wall behind the main stage was a mural depicting the ancient city of Thebes. In the middle of the wall was a wheel with red lights running around the perimeter and along the spokes. The ceiling was painted black and scattered with day-glow stars.

During its limited run, the club was packed with what police estimated to be hundreds of thousands of dollars worth of state-of-the-art electronic gear. Generators were needed to supply enough power. The wiring for all this gear ran amidst tarpaper and particle board within the walls – a fire disaster in waiting.

The building had been given a construction permit only as a storage facility. It had never been inspected, and York had no liquor license, though beer was sold.

Next to the club was the Hathor Recording Studio, another drivit-covered building. It was the latest testament to York's persistent but unrealized dream of becoming a music mogul. In New York, he had been Dr. York, a wavy-haired R&B singer, record producer, and talent agent. Here, he had equipped the Hathor Studio to try the same sort of thing. But in both places, his state-of-the art studios belied the fact that the state of his art was poor.

Scattered behind these buildings were the dozen or so trailers, coated in sandstone drivit, where the approximately one hundred to one hundred-fifty full-time residents of Tama-Re lived. Most of them had no air-conditioning.

Branching off from the main street was a driveway that curled down a hill and led to the property's main house. With its exterior of fieldstone and dark brown wood, it looked like what it had been, a hunting lodge and country retreat.

Most of that house had been converted to offices, where York's most trusted concubines worked sixteen-hour days keeping his mail-order business and his network of satellite bookstores and schools operating smoothly.

Alima went to those offices and found some women she remembered from the old days, when she had done what they were doing. She told them about the hard times she was having, but they didn't seem interested. Instead, they questioned her complaints. After all, Dr. York had fixed her up with a man to help her, hadn't he? If the children were too much for her, maybe she should leave them at Tama-R for awhile.

"Nobody cared, as long as I didn't cry too loud," Alima said.

York's quarters were in an addition he'd built onto the main house. On the main level was a large glass window, through which York could observe the women in the office area. On the second level was the largest of his private chambers. The décor was Sheherezade on a bad acid trip. The floor of the octagon-shaped room was carpeted wall-to-wall with a leopard-skin pattern, beige with black stripes. There was a large four-poster bed with a canopy adorned with an intricate, Moorish-style pattern molding coated with gilt. The curtains were black and gold, made of a cheap cotton-and-synthetic blend.

The adjoining bathroom had a large black marble Jacuzzi, and there was a black ceramic fireplace in the bedchamber.

In the corner of the room, a spiral staircase carpeted in the same leopard pattern led to another, smaller private chamber. At the base of the stairway was a sign that stated, "DO NOT GO UPSTSAIRS."

The spiral staircase led to a small, green-carpeted room, whose space was largely taken up by a bed and a large plasma television. Years later, young women and men who'd grown up on Tama-Re would testify about many terrible things that happened in that room.

In an adjoining building, York maintained another private rest area.

That room was furnished with a Jacuzzi and a bed. The walls were painted black, and police found a tripod for a video camera in one corner of the room. Most of the ceiling was covered with mirrors. This room is where police found a life-sized stuffed animal resembling the cartoon character the Pink Panther. The panther had a plastic male sex organ sown into the appropriate place. The stuffed animal would later become evidence displayed in a federal courtroom.

Alima was able to meet briefly with York in the office area. Practically as soon as she saw him, though, all her resolve about confronting him disintegrated. She had intended to demand money from him, but she couldn't get the words out.

York disarmed her and frightened her by flirting with her, as if he'd never discarded her and their children. "When you coming back?" he asked her. It was clear to her that the invitation to rejoin his harem would not include the man she was then living with.

Something else Alima saw made her fearful of saying anything that might anger York. There was a clutch of young girls around York, some of whom she recognized from the days she lived in the community York had ruled in Brooklyn. "All those young girls I had helped to raise now all seemed so devoted to him," she said. "I told myself something was wrong."

She was especially disturbed to see the interactions between York and one of his daughters, now a woman in her early twenties. "She was putting her arms around him, in a way that a daughter shouldn't be touching her father," Alima said.

Though she did not get what she came for, her visit to Tama-Re was a turning point for Alima – and ultimately for Dwight York. Before she left, she made up her mind to do something. This time, she would not lose her resolve, and what she did would start a chain of events that would ultimately lead to the ruin both of Tama-Re and of Dwight York.

On that day, though, the prevailing mood on Tama-Re was mellow. York wanted to show the world what he had created in the Georgia countryside. Toward that end, television crews and newspaper reporters and photographers were invited to the festival. It was the most open York had ever been to the media – and the most open he would ever be.

The program for "Spiritual Day" called for a Procession of Osiris, which York would lead, arrayed in a blue-and-white-striped headdress fit for any pharaoh. York marched at the head of a troop of two hundred or more fabulously-costumed extras, from the Tama-Re version of the Temple of Imhotep to the Maguraj, or ceremonial, site. According to the program, this was "the second Opening of the Maguraj Ceremony in America from Egypt in over ten thousand years."

On that day, many of the Nuwaubian festival-goers were more than happy to talk with the outsiders about their community. They patiently explained how they were not a cult.

When they were asked about what had drawn them to Tama-Re, most cited racial pride. They responded to the Nuwaubian belief that blacks should reclaim their heritage as the descendants of the ancient rulers of African empires.

There was also total agreement that York was the Master Teacher. Everything he taught was Right Knowledge, and anything else was simply wrong.

Then there was the matter of the spaceship and the Man from Planet Rizq. You could read it right in the Holy Tablets. York was a divine being, and those who followed him loyally and truly enough would be able to board that big spaceship that was coming to shuttle them all away, while Armageddon consumed the Earth.

York was feeling so fine that he even deigned to give an audience to the press.

Looking like a ghetto pasha, York appeared to a small group of newspaper and television reporters. He wore a black, loose-fitting pajama-like ensemble, heavily accented with gold jewelry. His sharply-trim beard traced his jawline. His hair was plaited close to his scalp, and his eyes were hidden behind sunglasses that were suspended on a chain encrusted with sparkly stones.

For this occasion, York was positively fulsome, almost to the point

York as leader of his rock band, Passion.

of bragging. He dropped the names of several black stars from the music and movie world, claiming that they were somehow affiliated with his community.

He said it was necessary for the Nuwaubians to form and administer a sovereign government, due to the racism that surrounded them. They would run their own schools, their own fire department, and whatever else they needed.

It was necessary to keep the children close and protected, he said. There were about fifty children living on Tama-Re at the time. Officially, they were being home-schooled, but that turned out to be a scam as well.

York made it all sound so idyllic. The children could grow up free on Tama-Re, free from the crime and drugs that had polluted the surrounding world.

"It's all about the children," he said. "It's always been about the children."

Some of the children on Tama-Re would have begged to differ with him. One was a little girl who went directly from playing with Barbies to being subjected to pornography as a way of being prepped for York's sexual advances. Another was an adolescent girl who was trying to intercept her younger sister's love letters to York, so that the younger girl wouldn't become one of York's playthings, as the older sister had. Then there was the young boy who'd been pimped to York by his mother.

But in the broader though deeply perverted sense, when he said he was "all about the children," Dwight was right.

CHAPTER 2
A Cult Grows in Brooklyn (Late 1960s to early 1980s)

So it doesn't bother me to be called a cult, and I thank you for the compliment. That's right, we're a cult. – Dwight York, *Rebuttal To The Slanderers*

The children deserved a better life than what the man called Karim saw around him.

In Brooklyn of the late 1960s, he saw many children growing up in an environment plagued by drugs and crime. "The children should not be the victims of the crimes of their parents' ignorance," Karim said.

Karim's plan for building that better world was to become a pediatrician. A recent convert to Islam, he had received an undergraduate degree in biology, and he had been accepted to medical school.

Then he met Dwight York, who was calling himself Imam Isa at the time. Karim heard York preach about his vision of starting a community where the members were free to practice what he call "pure, unadulterated Islam." It would be a community where the children could grow up devout and safe and be prepared to become spiritual and secular leaders.

York's vision seemed so close to his own, Karim said, and he was able to express that vision so eloquently. "He was extremely intelligent, sincere, and profound," Karim said. York's group, then called the Nubian Islamic Hebrews, did not advocate the militancy of other Black Muslim groups, nor did it engage in the hostile sectarian and political rhetoric used by some groups of Islamic Arabs.

"We got along fine with the Jews, the Christians," Karim said. Following Islamic traditions, they adopted the teachings of many Jewish prophets and of Jesus, who is revered as a major prophet by most Muslims. "The message was purity and simplicity; it wasn't political," Karim said.

York was able to tap into a fertile niche market on the safe side of the spectrum of black separatist groups. His son, Malik, said the strongest appeal was to blacks who wanted their own community but weren't interested in militancy. "Once he (York) said, 'I got this brand new thing – Black Power mixed with clean living.'" Malik said.

He and the other children who grew up inside Ansaru Allah Community believed they were part of a devout religious community dedicated to their moral and intellectual growth. "We were going to be doctors and lawyers, a black master race," Malik said. "We were building a Black Utopia."

York credited his success in the early years to his own natural gifts of salesmanship, which he used to sell his own quasi-religious tracts on the streets of black neighborhoods from Brooklyn to Harlem. "I was blessed with the gift of gab, combined with a sense of humor and charisma that draws people of all walks of life to me," York wrote in his self-published manifesto, *The Holy Tablets*.

Karim joined York's community, which at that time was small enough for most of the male followers to sleep on the floor of the apartment of York and his wife, Zubaida. "He lived with us, prayed with us," Karim said. "If there was a nail to be driven, he would work with us." Often, he said, York would make sure that the children ate first; then his followers would eat before he would.

York never told Karim to discontinue his medical studies, but becoming a doctor started to be less important to him than helping York build a "pure" Islamic community. Karim said he recalled being in a neurology lab, when the instructor said that despite all the advances of modern medicine, medical science still understood very little about the inner workings of the human brain.

Why spend so much time studying to enter a field where the professionals admitted that they knew so little? Why not instead follow this man who spoke with such authority and certainty? So, Karim decided to abandon his plans to become a physician; instead, he would remain a loyal and devoted follower of Dwight York for the next thirty years.

When the group moved to the Bushwick district of Brooklyn in the early 1970s, the name was changed to Ansaru Allah Community (AAC). Strong relationships were quickly forged with local authorities, who were happy to have a non-confrontational, non-violent Muslim group in the neighborhood.

"We basically had carte blanche, because we were in with the police department," Karim said. Outwardly, York's arrival had transformed the Bushwick neighborhood, he said.

"When we came into Bushwick, it was infested with crime and drugs," Karim said. But once AAC moved in, their area became known as an oasis of safety. "People would come from outside the neighborhood to park their cars on our streets, because they knew they were safe," he said.

According to Karim, the local police were amenable to having to make appointments before entering AAC, and to allowing the men of AAC to conduct armed security patrols of their properties. Things were the same with the Fire Department. "We policed ourselves. If there was a fire, we put it out," Karim said.

The authorities welcomed what appeared to be a group devoted to neighborhood improvement, because in those days, that section of Bushwick needed all the improvement it could get. The center of AAC was in the 400 block of Bushwick Avenue, a few blocks from the intersection of Bushwick and Broadway, a major thoroughfare hooded by elevated train tracks and cluttered with low-rent shops. Along Bushwick Avenue was a residential area trying to fight off serious decline. Newspaper articles of the time compared the area to the South Bronx.

Karim believed he could live out his dream of helping children by helping to build AAC. In those years, York imported highly qualified teachers for the children of the community. Arabic was taught as the children's first language.

Most of the children in the community went to local public schools, but the administrators made special allowances for them. They wore Muslim robes to their classes, and twice during the school day, the robed children marched in groups segregated by age and gender back to the AAC mosque for prayers.

To many outsiders, the quiet, well-behaved children were a sign that AAC was a place where children were cared for. In the early years, that perception was valid, Karim said.

"The children were denied nothing," Karim said. "Everything was about the children."

Throughout the 1970s, Ansaru Allah Community flourished, expanding beyond Brooklyn to satellite communities in at least a dozen major American cities, as well as to a like number of foreign countries. According to federal investigators, as many as five hundred people lived in the twenty or so Bushwick Avenue townhouses that York gradually acquired. Once he obtained a new building, he had it painted white with green trim to match his other holdings. The growth and health of AAC was obvious.

A primary source of revenue for that growth was street sales of incense and of paperback books that York produced and printed within his community. Most of the men of the AAC were assigned street peddling duty. Originally, they were given a sales quota of fifty dollars per day, and later that was raised to one hundred dollars, according to former group members.

Selling the books and promoting AAC went hand in hand. The books contained advertisements touting the programs, services, and shopping opportunities at AAC. They also included glowing depictions of York and invitations to come hear him preach or to come learn more about the beautiful community he was building.

When the curious came to York's part of Bushwick, they saw a village of Muslim commerce and spirituality.

At the Ansar Needle Trades shop, people could purchase "the garb of the righteous," including Moroccan robes, fabric, jalabyas (men's tunics), kaftans, prayer caps, scarves, and draperies.

At the Sum Things gift shop and bookstore, there were items like Arabic-numeral watches, plants, games, leather goods, plus, of course, a wide selection of York's books.

The Turban Jewel shop offered a selection of pendants, earrings, broaches, bracelets, and nose rings (most members of AAC wore those adornments then). Your Community Market stocked groceries such as Halal pizza (prepared according to Islamic standards), Philly-style hoagies, and Islamic and Hispanic pastries.

Many outsiders could not help but be impressed.

In 1989, *Newsday* columnist Jimmy Breslin wrote a column contrasting the surrounding areas of crime and violence with the apparent peacefulness of York's community: "Outside, the street was tranquil, the carnations and roses turning the air sweet. The men in white watched. The women walked by with their faces covered. Agree with how they live or not, they run the only sidewalks in the City of New York where there is no such thing as drugs."

As Karim put it, "It was a beautiful community."

The peaceable kingdom of Ansaru Allah Community thrived in a time and place when other similar-looking Muslim communities were rife with turmoil. This was New York of the '60s and '70s. It was a time when racial consciousness and racial tensions were both decidedly on the rise.

One of the recurring themes of black protest was police brutality. In New York, this was not an abstract issue. An incident in April 1972 made it particularly acute. A patrol officer named Phillip Cardillo responded to a 911 call made from a Black Muslim mosque in Harlem. The caller identified himself as a police officer, giving a name and precinct number, and said he was on the second floor of Muhammad's Temple No. 7, and he was in trouble.

The call later turned out to be a hoax, but Cardillo didn't know that when he raced into the mosque, looking for a fellow cop in distress. What he found was his own violent death. There was an exchange of gunfire between Cardillo and some men inside the mosque, and Cardillo was killed.

The way this killing played out on the street, the main issue was the police officer's violation of the sanctity of the mosque. There were protest rallies and demonstrations around the city. Officials of the Nation of Islam demanded an apology for the actions of the police. There were also demands that the NYPD pull all its white officers out of Harlem.

A member of the mosque, a man named Louis X. Dupree, was arrested for the killing of the police officer. His trial was the occasion of more protests. When he was acquitted, the calls for a police apology grew louder.

That strain of protest was countered by officials of the police union, who publicly charged that city officials were meddling in police business.

Apparently, politics won out.

Police Chief Patrick Murphy issued a public apology for the police intrusion into the mosque. Also, the police department instituted a set of policies spelling out the extra care that would have to be taken in dealing with the Black Muslims. One high-ranking police official resigned in protest over the new policies.

As outlined in an internal police memo that became public, the policies were a big step up in restricting police actions. The memo stated, "The events of April 19, 1972, reveal that the department must exercise greater care when responding to mosques or other locations where militant groups are located. It is imperative that this department do everything possible to prevent a misunderstanding of our actions or prevent any abrasive or irritating action by members of the department."

The new policies included an order that no patrol officer enter a mosque unless a commanding officer was present. Also, commanders were ordered to coordinate personally with those in charge of the mosques, in order to establish guidelines for police behavior, when there was police business inside a mosque.

By policy, seventeen Muslim mosques and offices around New York were designated as "sensitive sites," where these new policies were to be observed. Besides the mosques, the sensitive sites included offices of groups like the Black Panther Party, the Young Lords, and the Black Liberation Army. By 1979, Ansaru Allah Community had, in practice, been added to the list. This author could not determine precisely when and how that happened.

In a 2006 interview, Ed Koch, who had begun his first term as Mayor of New York in 1978, said he did not recall Ansaru Allah Community, but he did remember how real the tensions were between the police and the Muslims back then. "There's no question that there was a civil war going on," Koch said.

Koch added that he thought the restrictions on police investigations of the Muslims – restrictions which had been put into place by a prior administration – were "really nutty."

They may have been nutty, but back then, they were also trendy.

In his book *Radical Chic & Mau-Mauing The Flak Catchers,* author Tom Wolfe pilloried the way that New York's social and cultural elite rallied to support some of the most radical elements of the militant black groups.

"The black movement itself, of course, had taken on a much more electric and romantic cast," Wolfe wrote. "What a relief it was – socially – in New York – when the leadership seemed to shift from middle class to...funky. From A. Philip Randolph and Dr. Martin Luther King, and James Farmer...to Stokely, Rap, LeRoi and Eldridge!"

There is a long, hilarious segment in Wolfe's book reporting on a party hosted by renowned conductor Leonard Bernstein at his Manhattan apartment to support the Black Panthers. Leaders of the Panthers came to the event, and while they were demonizing whites in general, they also bullied their hosts into supporting the Panther cause. By the end, the socialites were dizzily proclaiming "Power to the People!"

Wolfe called this phenomenon *nostalgie de la boue,* a French phrase literally meaning "nostalgia for the mud," or in this context, "romanticizing of primitive souls." Wolfe saw this as being a recurring phenomenon in history, where newly-rich members of the upper class adopt the causes of the more exotic elements of the lower classes.

"This meant that the tricky business of the fashionable new politics could be integrated with a tried and true social motif: *nostalgie de la boue.* The upshot was Radical Chic," Wolfe wrote.

Dwight York never hobnobbed with uptown socialites, nor did he or his followers engage in angry rhetoric or street protests. Nevertheless, Ansaru Allah Community was treated as a "sensitive site" by local police, which essentially allowed him to control all aspects of life within the community as he pleased, and to present Ansaru Allah Community as a harmonious and holy place.

York's utopian marketing concepts were not new. The first black American to shape that longing into a mass movement among urban blacks was Noble Drew Ali. Born Timothy Drew in North Carolina in 1886, he was also the first national-level leader to couple the rejection of Christianity with the embracing of Islam.

For Ali, as for the Black Muslims who followed him – and as for York, who borrowed liberally from Ali's methods and ideology – Christianity was the religion of the white oppressors. Islam was the natural religion of the black race.

In 1913, Ali opened the first of his network of Moorish Science Temples of America in Newark, New Jersey. He later made a pilgrimage to Africa and the Middle East, and when he returned, he said he had been given the title "Noble" by the King of Morocco. From then on, he was Noble Drew Ali, and he proclaimed that Morocco was the true nation of blacks in the United States, or American Asiatics, as he preferred to call them.

There was an especially violent period of race relations in America after World War I, bloodied by race riots and lynchings in both the South and the North. During that time of unrest, Moorish Science temples were erected in most major Northern cities. The movement never flourished in the South, and Ali himself visited the South and proclaimed that blacks there were not ready for the discipline and self-sufficiency he sought from his followers.

Ali was revered by his followers as a prophet, and as such, he spoke through his movement's newspaper, *The Moorish Guide*. In it, he called for blacks to seize a different identity and to reclaim the glorious heritage that had been stolen from them by the slave masters.

He wrote in *The Moorish Guide* of September 1928, "If you have race pride and love your race, join the Moorish Science Temple of America and become a part of this Divine Movement. Then you will have power to redeem your race, because you will know who you are and who your forefathers were."

Ali told his followers who they were: Moorish Americans, or Asiatic Americans. And he told them who they were not: "colored, Negroes, Ethiopians, or blacks."

All the members received nationality, or identity, cards certified by "Noble Drew Ali, the Prophet." The bearers were identified as Moslems and as citizens of the United States. However, they also claimed to be descendants of the Moors, or Moabites, the people who were dispatched by the pharaohs of ancient Egypt to settle the West African land now called Morocco.

The Moorish men typically wore red fezzes, the cylinder-shaped hats. For their holiday celebrations, particularly for the festival surrounding Ali's birthday, they wore elaborate Arabic-style costumes. An archival picture of Ali and his followers at one of these celebrations suggests a sultan and his court.

On the practical side, Ali preached that blacks should reinforce their self-proclaimed new identity with hard work, clean living, and entrepreneurship aimed at building up the black community.

Many of the newly minted Moors found their altered identity empowering and exhilarating. Some would wave their Moorish Temple identity cards at whites, shouting that they were nobody's Negroes anymore.

The taunting and the inevitable backlash grew so problematic that the Prophet had to issue a cease-and-desist order in *The Moorish Guide* in January 1929: "Stop flashing your cards at Europeans. It causes confusion. Remember, your card is your salvation."

Ali preserved his philosophy in a book entitled *The Holy Koran of the Moorish Science Temple* and subtitled *Divinely Prepared by the Noble Prophet Drew Ali.*

In his *Holy Koran,* Ali wrote that Jesus Christ was a Moor and a prophet "crucified by Rome for seeking to redeem his people from the pressure of the pale skin nations of Europe." Christianity's Ten Commandments were but a device through which "the rulers and the rich live, while the poor suffer and die."

Moors should not intermarry with the Europeans, nor should they practice the pale-skinned people's religion, Ali wrote. "The Church and Christianity were prepared by their forefathers for their earthly salvation, while we, the Moorish Americans, are returning to Islam, which was founded by our forefathers for our earthly and divine salvation," he states in the *Holy Koran.*

Despite Ali's use of "Koran" in the title of his holy book and his repeated references to "Allah" rather than God, his book bears hardly any resemblance to the Islamic Qur'an. Rather, it is written in a style that owes much to the elegant phrasing of the *King James Bible,* and many of its passages sound like basic Christian theology.

In a passage from a section entitled "Charity," Ali sounds likes he's replaying the Sermon on the Mount: "Happy is the man who hath sown in his breast the seeds of benevolence; the produce thereof shall be mercy and love.

"He forgiveth the injuries of men, he wipeth them from his remembrance; revenge and malice shall have no place in his heart. For evil he returneth not evil; he hateth not even his enemies, but requiteth their injustice with a friendly admonition."

In a section entitled "Warning For All Young Men," Ali sounds like he related deeply to the Song of Songs: "But when virtue and modesty enlighten her charms, the luster of a beautiful woman is brighter than the stars of heaven, and the influence of her power it is in vain to resist.

"The whiteness of her bosom transcendeth the lily; her smile is more delicious than a garden of roses."

Besides spreading the proclamations of the Prophet, *The Moorish Guide* was used to sell a line of products, like healing oils and hair straighteners. Disputes over the revenues generated by the sales of these products and by the general growth of the Moorish Temples led to serious internal strife.

In 1929 in Chicago, a man who led a challenge to Ali's leadership was murdered. Ali was not in Chicago at the time, but when he returned he was arrested for the crime. Shortly after his release on bond, he died under mysterious circumstances. Some say it was natural causes; others say he died from the after-effects of a police beating; others say his rivals assassinated him.

In their review of the Moorish Science Temple movement for their book *Mission To America: Five Islamic Sectarian Communities In America,* authors Yvonne Yazbeck Haddad and Jane Idelman Smith cite published accounts that listed the peak membership of the Moorish Science Temples at about 100,000 members in the mid-1930s. Other sources put the estimate closer to thirty thousand.

Although the membership has declined sharply in recent decades, a few of the Moorish Science Temples remain. Haddad and Smith state that Ali's legacy is mainly a positive one: "The Moorish Science Temple and its community have received considerable recognition for their achievements in promoting the social, economic, and moral advancement of Americans of African descent. Noble Drew Ali had a dream of uplifting the people he called Moors by reconnecting them with their African roots and encouraging them to live as devout Moslems."

Dreams and accolades notwithstanding, the scholar who authored the seminal work on black separatist groups repeatedly referred to the Moors as a cult.

"The cult members believed that the imminent destruction of the whites was signified by the appearance in the sky of a star within a crescent moon," wrote C. Eric Lincoln in *The Black Muslims in America*. Lincoln also cited the belief held by some of the remaining Moors that they have been led by men who were actually successive reincarnations of Noble Drew Ali. Lincoln's book is widely regarded as the definitive work on the subject; its original 1960 version was updated and revised in 1973 and again in 1994.

Historians' assessment of the Moorish Science Temple movement may differ, but there is agreement that it was an important predecessor of the most significant black separatist group, the Nation of Islam.

Haddad and Smith wrote that the two most important figures in the early history of the Nation of Islam – Elijah Poole, later Elijah Muhammad, and W.D. Fard, later Fard Muhammad – were both members of the Moorish Science Temple in Detroit in the early 1930s. Lincoln wrote that in the same years, many of the new members of the Nation of Islam came from the Moorish Science Temple movement.

In his biography of Elijah Muhammad, *An Original Man,* Claude A. Clegg termed the Moorish Science Temple of America "the most salient Islamic precursor of the Nation of Islam."

Both groups advocated Islam as the true religion of the black race, both had the same rigorous dietary restrictions, both shunned most forms of popular entertainment, both banned alcohol and tobacco, and at both groups' houses of worship, the men dressed in suits and the women were seated separately and were dressed in Moslem garb. Many members of the Nation of Islam took "X" as a surname, signifying the loss of their true names to slavery. Similarly, many members of the Moorish Science Temples took the surnames "El" or "Bey" to signify their new identities.

Both groups appealed most strongly to low-income blacks, those suffering most from the prevailing racism of the times.

Also, the founders of both groups were not above concocting back-stories for their belief systems, nor to adjusting their ideologies in accordance to what they thought would work best in the recruiting marketplace.

"The tales invented by Fard to explain everything from the origins of the universe to the destiny of the Western world drew from many sources, and little was too outrageous to be included, if it would attract followers," Clegg wrote. The "myth" that worked for Fard in the Depression still retained some appeal into the 1990s, he added.

Clegg wrote that he was "awed by the leader's ability to package the bizarre and the esoteric in the wrappings of rationality and logic."

For example, Fard taught that when Allah would direct his wrath toward the destruction of the white race, he would also dispatch space ships to convey the righteous black believers to Paradise.

Dwight York was anything but an original man. He would borrow heavily from Ali, Fard, and Muhammad. He would even publish suggestions that Muhammad had dubbed him the next Prophet.

The primary source for the following synopsis of the history of the Nation of Islam was Clegg's study of its leader for nearly forty years, Elijah Muhammad.

The group was founded by Fard, who was born in 1891, in either Portland, Oregon, or New Zealand. Fard was arrested in his twenties in California, and he served a prison term for drug dealing and assault. In the early 1930s, he moved to Detroit, where he peddled clothing on the streets.

Times were hard and sales were few, so Fard embellished his sales pitch with stories about how his clothes were like those worn by Africans in the homeland. Many people seemed more interested in his stories than in his merchandise, so Fard started focusing on his lectures about how blacks should reclaim their stolen heritage. He started speaking to small groups in homes, and as interest increased and his audiences grew, he moved the presentations to rented halls. His following grew into a group he named the Nation of Islam. Fard continued to sell clothing to new members.

After attending a few of Fard's lectures, Elijah Poole, born the son of a black preacher in Sandersville, Georgia, approached Fard and whispered a question into his ear.

He asked if Fard was the Messiah. Fard said yes, but he instructed Poole to keep this information a secret. Later, Fard would accept Poole, re-named Elijah Muhammad, as a teacher of Islam and then appointed Muhammad the Nation's Supreme Minister.

In late 1932, there was a ritualistic murder of a black man in Detroit. It was suspected that the killer was a member of the Nation of Islam. The murder fed into suspicions many whites held about the group, which some newspapers referred to as a "Voodoo Cult." Fard was interrogated about the murder, given a psychiatric evaluation, and released, but only after his followers staged protest rallies. Muhammad was also questioned in the investigation, and he stated that among Fard's teachings was the belief that a black Moslem had to murder four devils (whites) to obtain admission to Mecca.

Marked by police as the leader of what whites perceived as a hostile group, Fard agreed to leave Detroit. Before he vanished from the movement and from history, Fard passed the leadership of the Nation to Elijah Poole Muhammad. Because of the tensions in Detroit, Muhammad moved the group's headquarters to Chicago.

Muhammad oversaw the growth of the young movement, and he preached against America's entry into World War II. That earned him a spot on the FBI's "most wanted" list, and led to his arrest and conviction in 1942 for sedition and draft evasion. He served four years in prison, bypassing at least two opportunities for an earlier parole.

Throughout the 1940s and '50s, the Nation grew steadily. Its members worked toward self-sufficiency for their community, and business entrepreneurship was a trademark of the Nation. Blacks with higher educational and economic standing began to join the movement. Membership figures were never publicly released, but scholars, including Lincoln, estimated the ranks of the Nation to be as high as 250,000. Others put the figure closer to fifty thousand. There was general agreement, though, that Muhammad lived as a wealthy man.

During the tempestuous years of the Civil Rights movement, the public spokesman for the Nation was Muhammad's protégé, Malcolm Little, who became Malcolm X. His fiery rhetoric – like branding Dr. Martin Luther King Jr. a "traitor" for advocating integration – drew large crowds wherever he went.

While Mississippi burned, Malcolm fueled the fire that advocated achieving justice for American blacks "by any means necessary."

As Malcolm drew more of the heat, Muhammad began to be treated more like an elder statesman, even though he continued to make incendiary statements, like calling for a separate Islamic nation for blacks in America. In 1959, Muhammad toured the Middle East and returned as the nominal leader of the Black Muslim movement.

However, the Prophet did not always practice what he preached. In 1963, seven of Muhammad's female secretaries came forward claiming to have borne a total of thirteen illegitimate children fathered by Muhammad. He refused to acknowledge the children as his.

Malcom X became distraught at the revelations of Muhammad's betrayal of one of the core values of the Nation. The resulting conflict between the two men led to Malcolm X's suspension from the Nation by Muhammad in 1964. The conflict became public when Muhammad called Malcolm X "a Judas and a hypocrite" in the Nation's newspaper.

A short time later, Malcom X assisted two of Muhammad's concubines in filing paternity claims against Muhammad. Now the story was circulated nationally. There was a backlash against Malcolm X from members of the Nation loyal to Muhammad.

Adding to the air of enmity, Muhammad's son, Wallace Muhammad, openly broke with the Nation of Islam and embraced the Sunni sect of Islam, whose adherents were bitter rivals of Muhammad's.

On February 21, 1965, gunmen assassinated Malcolm X , as he spoke to a group of his followers at the Audubon Ballroom in New York. Publicly, Muhammad expressed shock at the killing; and he was never charged with having a role in the crime. However, Muhammad certainly orchestrated a propaganda campaign against Malcolm X, including making veiled threats that violence might befall him.

Factional violence raged within the Nation well into the 1970s. There was a failed assassination attempt against Muhammad in 1971, and four men believed to have been part of the plot were later murdered.

In Washington, D.C., the leader of an orthodox Moslem community was openly critical of Muhammad. In January 1973 six gunmen broke into the community's headquarters and shot and killed two men they found there. Then they drowned three young children, shot and killed another child, and shot two women, leaving them for dead. As he fled, one of the gunmen is reported to have shouted, "Don't mess with Elijah."

Muhammad died in 1975 of natural causes. There were leadership disputes after his death, but the violence has abated, and the Nation of Islam exists today as a smaller group, lower key – but still Islamic and still separatist.

It was Malcolm X who became larger in death. His life was the subject of a book by prominent author Alex Haley, *The Autobiography of Malcolm X,* which was subsequently made into a feature film. His is the face of black anger that whites have increasingly come to accept as valid and justified.

Dwight York strode onto the black separatist stage in the angry years of the late 1960s, a bit player determined to be a star.

Just who is this fellow? That turns out to be a hard question to answer, even if his name is all that's wanted.

When the federal government indicted him in 2002, they used Dwight York as his name of record. They also listed five aliases: Malachi Z. York, Isa Muhammad, Issa Al Haadi Al Mahdi, Isa Abd' Allah Muhammad, and Baba. He has used the professional names Dr. York and Dr. Love as a disco/R&B singer. His followers call him by the pet names Doc, or Pops, or Baba. He is referred to in his literature as the Master Teacher, the Reformer, and the Lamb, among other exaltations. During a couple of brief stints as a Native American, he used the name Chief Black Eagle.

There is some agreement on his date of birth, but not on the place. York claims to have been born in the Sudan on June 26, 1945. He said he was brought as an infant to the United States, and his birth was registered in New Bedford, Massachusetts. Even the most basic of his vital statistics should be viewed with skepticism, however. All through his life, York has re-invented himself as necessary, giving the distinct impression that he is making himself up as he goes along.

The most complete version of his early life that he ever revealed publicly was in his 1989 book *Rebuttal To The Slanderers.* This was an attempt to quell the damage of the first outright attack made on him, a small 1988 paperback volume of exposé entitled *The Ansaar Cult.* That book was written by an Islamic scholar named Bilal Phillips, and it was about eighty pages long. York's rebuttal book was 615 pages.

Very few of the following details of York's early life, as written in *Rebuttal,* can be confirmed. Some of it may even be true.

York wrote that his mother, Umm Fatimah Maryam, was the daughter of a merchant seaman named Salah Al Ghalat. At the age of nineteen, Maryam went to Egypt from the United States. There she began a relationship with a young man named Al Haadi, a prince of the royal family of Sudan. She did not know of her boyfriend's royal lineage. When the young man was summoned home, he left Maryam in a family way.

When she was in her ninth month, she went to Sudan to meet the family, but she was not received or accepted. Her son was born on June 26, 1945, and despite her rejection, she gave the baby the royal name Isa Al Haadi Al Mahdi.

That date and name are important to the lore that York would weave around himself. He claimed that his birth was exactly one hundred years after the man he claimed was his great-grandfather, the Mahdi. In Sudanese history, the Mahdi is the revered warrior and spiritual leader who fomented the rebellion against the British. Many Moslems believe that a Reformer, or Renewer of the Faith, comes along once in a century.

In *Mission To America,* Haddad and Smith wrote that York made the claim in his 1979 book *The Book of Lam* that he was the prophesied Reformer. They wrote York's claim "was made to try to attract Nation (of Islam) followers into the Ansar cult." The leadership of the Nation of Islam was under dispute by rival factions at the time.

According to York's version of the story of his early life, his mother returned to the United States soon after his birth. He was given the surname York in the legal documents filed in Massachusetts, because his mother had been previously married to a Portuguese man from Boston named Rafiq York.

During his first seven years, his mother used the name Dwight York for him, because his mother's family did not want to recognize his Arabic name.

Apparently though, his biological father's family had a dramatic change of heart. At the age of seven, he was taken back to Africa by a man named Shaikh Hasuwn, whom his father had designated as his Islamic guardian. During that visit to his father's family in Sudan, his grandfather looked at him and proclaimed that he had "the light." This was apparently a confirmation that York was the prophesied Reformer. In the future, York would publish many pictures and drawings of himself with his head surrounded by a glowing halo of light.

York wrote that he remained for five years in Africa, raised by Shaikh Hasuwn and an uncle on his father's side. At the age of twelve, he returned to the United States and became the protégé of Shaikh Daoud, who was then the leader of the State Street Mosque in Brooklyn.

Shaikh Daoud had York change his Arabic name from Isa Al Haadi Al Mahdi to Isa Abd' Allah ibn Abu Bakr Muhammad. In this way, York could conceal his royal connection, and thus be protected from possible reprisals from rival Moslems in America. In those years, York lived under the care of maternal aunts in Teaneck, and he went to a public junior high school there.

York wrote that he would visit Brooklyn on the weekends, and during that time he came under the influence of a man he called "Brother Love," an Islamic man who lived in the same public housing project where his mother lived with York's stepbrothers and stepsisters. He does not explain why he lived apart from his mother.

Although he does not mention graduating from high school, York claims to have studied at universities in Egypt and Sudan. But before he embarked on his higher education, he does admit to being a member of a youth gang. "Yes, as a teenager I did belong to a gang and did get into squabbles. During the '60s, I was involved in the Black 'thing' like everybody else, but I never belonged to any Black Panther nationalist or Marxist group," York wrote. "I was a youthful offender, that means as a kid, a bad boy, not a criminal."

Some of the blank spots York left on his resume were later filled in by federal investigators. According to an FBI report, York was arrested on June 25, 1964, on a charge of statutory rape, for having sex with an underage girl. His sentence was suspended and he was placed on probation.

On October 24, 1964, York was arrested for assault, possession of a deadly weapon, and resisting arrest. His probation was revoked, and he spent the next three years in prison at Elmira Reception Center.

The report also contradicts York's claim that he was never a Black Panther. In 1972, the FBI arrested a fugitive named Lawrence Townsend, identified as a former Black Panther Party member. They found literature in Townsend's apartment from York's group, named Nubian Islamic Hebrews at that time, along with other evidence that indicated York had also been a Black Panther.

York apparently supported himself as a street peddler, much like W.D. Fard. Working mostly on the streets of Harlem, York sold the black separatist pamphlets that he wrote, along with incense and oils.

In 1967, Dwight York married an American woman, Dorothy Johnson, who took the Arabic name Zubaida. They would have five children.

Then in 1973, York traveled to Sudan, where he met and married another woman, Fatimah. They had two children.

After his bigamy was attacked in *The Ansar Cult,* York wrote in his *Rebuttal* that the Qur'an allows a devout Moslem man to take four wives. York then expanded on the concept of polygamy, writing that a man can take many women, under a doctrine called "Right Hand Possession." York explained that term, writing, "It merely means a woman who is taken, when a village is conquered. Muslim men are allowed to take a woman under their wing, as the American cliché has it, and have sexual relations. Now let me make one thing clear once and for all. If a man marries virgins, he can rightfully call them his wives. If he marries women who are not virgins, or are widows or divorced, they can only become concubines, or right hand possessions, in his family. This is the law of Al Islam."

Whether or not York followed Islamic law in the realm of sexual relations and marriage, it would later become quite clear that he considered any woman he selected from his flock to be his "right hand possession." And in the process, he took the concept of polygamy to a totally new order of magnitude. The result of those liaisons was children by the dozens, and more. Documents seized when York was arrested indicated that he kept a logbook with pictures and names and birthdates for approximately ninety of his children. Former members of his cult estimate the number of his progeny is actually two hundred or more.

One former cult member recalled a parade in Brooklyn sometime during the early 1980s, staged probably in conjunction with his birthday, or Savior's Day. He was followed in the parade by a group of nineteen women, all of whom were carrying babies fathered by York and born in the past year.

York disavowed his illegitimate children, as Elijah Muhammad had done. Some of the spurned mothers of those children would ultimately participate in York's downfall, exposing him as, among many other things, a Deadbeat Dad of epic proportions.

Another thing York worked hard at was becoming a rock star. During the 1970s, he was the lead singer for a disco/R&B band called Passion. He took pains to downplay the sexual connotation in the band's name, claiming that this "passion" was akin to the passion suffered by Jesus. He claimed a religious motive for his musical endeavors. Performing with Passion was one way he said he could get the attention of young people, expose them to Islam, and recruit them for Ansaru Allah Community.

"I do not enjoy dressing up in Western-style clothes and being in the company of alcohol, cigarettes, and fornication," York wrote in *Rebuttal*. "But as a doctor, I must go wherever the sick are."

His stage name was Dr. York, and sometimes Dr. Love. Passion performed at many schools and civic functions, and York received letters of commendation and certificates of appreciation from people like Wilson Goode, then the Mayor of Philadelphia, and from the New York City public school system.

Passion also performed frequently at nightclubs. Sometimes, York would spice up the act by wearing roller skates. Some of Passion's music was clearly aimed at an adult audience. One of York's albums, cut and distributed in the form of a red plastic LP record, was entitled "12 Inch."

Just in case anyone missed the double-entendre of that title, York printed a saying of his on the album cover: "If you hold it too loose, it will fall out of your hand. If you hold it too tight, you will break it."

Part of York's musical dream was the recording studio he operated in his Bushwick village. In *Rebuttal,* York claimed that many musical stars had passed through his studio. "Amongst the many Dr. York touched and tried to save from the Devil are: (partial list) Stevie Wonder, Kool & The Gang, The O'Jays, Stylistics, Nancy Wilson (of the Supremes), and Bob Marley," he wrote. York also listed rappers he had sought to influence, including Queen Latifah, Public

Enemy, and L L Cool J. He claimed these and other rap stars had stopped their worldly indulgences and started reading the Qur'an and other holy books.

York and Passion never made it anywhere near the popular music charts. However, their lack of success was not his fault, York claimed. Instead of looking inward for any deficiencies in talent, York blamed the group's manager, a disciple of his named Abdul Kabir, or Ozzie Brown.

"He would give us to all kinds of pale lawyers, but never a Black one," York complained in *Rebuttal*. "Passion was also offered numerous deals, but because Ozzie Brown put more emphasis on making money than he did on reaching the people, which is the main purpose for the group, Passion experienced setback after setback."

Despite the musical failures, York clearly maintained control of Ansaru Allah Community. However, AAC's remarkable growth did not come entirely from the money brought in by his street peddlers. A 1993 report by a domestic terrorism unit of the FBI stated that some of the real estate expansion had been fueled by fire – in some cases, by fires that York's followers may have set. The report cited eight instances of arson that may have been linked to members of AAC. The general pattern was that when York wished to acquire a property, but the owner was reluctant to sell at York's lowball offer, there would be a suspicious fire at the property. Then, York would buy it at auction.

In May of 1976, there was an arson fire in an apartment in the building at 699 Bushwick Avenue, which York owned. Three separate pieces of furniture had been set afire. The fire marshal's report stated the fire may have been linked to York, since York had been trying to persuade the apartment's tenant to leave.

In March 1979 someone poured a flammable liquid onto the kitchen floor of the home at 9 Cedar Street, near the AAC village. The tenant reported seeing a man setting the fire. The arsonist fired gunshots at the tenant, who gathered his family and fled. The fire marshal's report stated the tenant and the landlord of the building had experienced trouble with members of AAC, who had unsuccessfully tried to buy the building.

In December 1991 a Pentecostal church at the corner of Bushwick Avenue and Hart Street was firebombed. The pastor had repeatedly refused York's attempts to buy the building. A witness who was in the church told police he had seen members of AAC running away after the firebomb explosion. York later purchased the property at auction.

An FBI informant said that an independent grocery store near AAC had been burned down by the AAC, as a way of eliminating the competition.

Another informant said that when it came to real estate expansion, York would suggest what he wanted to happen, and later, it would happen. For example, the informant said, York stated at a meeting that he wished to purchase a city-owned building on Bushwick Avenue, but its designation as an historic landmark might prevent him from using the property the way he wanted. York suggested that if something were to happen to the building, the landmark designation might no longer be an issue.

Sure enough, the building was burned down. York bought the property, cleared off the debris of the landmark building, then built a mosque for the AAC on the property. That building, painted black with gold trim, still exists. However, since York is no longer a Muslim, the building is no longer a mosque. It currently houses the "All Eyes On Egypt" bookstore, which stocks mostly tracts written by York. Also in the bookstore building is a large, wooden-floored hall, where people can still attend classes on York's latest doctrines.

Even though the fire marshal's reports on several of these arsons stated suspected links to members of AAC, no one was ever arrested in any of the cases. The 1993 FBI report contained no speculation on why the investigation of these crimes never penetrated AAC, even though there seemed to be some direct evidence leading in that direction. However, the fact that the NYPD was kept totally out of the loop of the FBI investigation of AAC indicates that the FBI must have been suspicious of the relationship between AAC and the local police.

Members of the AAC also used strong-arm tactics to extort money from businesses outside the community, according to the FBI report. In 1990, storeowners in another section of Brooklyn began receiving pressure from the AAC. The AAC told the merchants that their present security contractors were inadequate. Typically, the unarmed guards of the private security firm would deal with an offense like shoplifting by holding a suspect until police arrived.

The AAC, by contrast, demonstrated how they dealt with the same problem – beating the shoplifter and not bothering to call the police, according to the report. The pressure succeeded, in that the AAC obtained a $5,000-per-week contract for providing security for the business district.

Such terror tactics helped the AAC empire grow beyond Brooklyn. In *Rebuttal,* York claimed to have branches of AAC in twenty other U.S. cities and twenty-two foreign countries. The FBI count was somewhat lower – nine American branches and three foreign.

Whatever its actual size, the network provided staging bases and hiding places for wider-ranging criminal operations, according to the FBI. The most serious crimes alleged in the report were committed by a group that came to be called "The Shotgun Gang." Its members were also AAC members.

Approximately twenty bank robberies were attributed to the Shotgun Gang by police. The gang members used AAC properties and mosques as their contact points. The seized phone records of the six members of the gang who were arrested showed contacts with AAC operations in Philadelphia; Baltimore; Newport News, Virginia; and Washington, D.C. In some of these cities, the AAC went by the name Tents of Keddar.

On March 7, 1991, four members of the gang robbed a credit union in Baltimore. They were armed with semi-automatic handguns and sawed-off shotguns. One of the robbers got disoriented during the getaway and returned to the credit union, where he held twenty-one people hostage for about an hour and a half, before he surrendered.

A week later, four members of the gang hit a bank in Wilmington, Delaware. Afterwards, they were chased by police, and a gun battle began. One of the robbers was killed, and police later discovered that his beeper contained the phone number of the Philadelphia affiliate of AAC. Another man arrested for that robbery had used the address of that same affiliate to obtain a pager.

The gun used by the hostage-taker in the Baltimore robbery was purchased by the wife of a man with AAC connections. That man told an FBI informant that he told his wife to buy the gun for two other men – the head and assistant Imam of the AAC mosque in Newport News.

The FBI was unable to trace any of the proceeds of the Shotgun Gang bank robberies back to York or the AAC. An attorney for one of the defendants in this case said he was unaware of any outside direction of the men's crimes. What was more likely, he said, was that the men met through their membership in AAC, and then they decided to go out and start robbing banks.

Less violent means were used for other AAC endeavors, but bringing in the cash was everyone's job. In Brooklyn, many of the men went out and sold books and incense, but mostly incense, on the streets. According to several former members, they were expected to come back with a daily sales quota, usually $100; and anyone who didn't make the quota was liable to receive a beating from members of the Mujahad.

The women of AAC worked within the community, in the shops or offices, or tending the children. They also generated money for York through welfare fraud, according to the FBI report. Some of the women were told to apply for welfare, using their American names and addresses other than the AAC buildings where they actually lived. Another scheme was having a pregnant woman share samples of her urine with women who were not pregnant but who used the samples to qualify for public assistance benefits.

Perhaps the main ongoing business operation of the AAC was to print, distribute, and sell York's books. Besides revenues, the books generated interest in the AAC and in York. Customers who wanted to learn more were invited to attend classes held in the different AAC properties. Those who wanted to become even closer to "The Reformer" were asked to fill out applications to become members of AAC.

By the late 1980s, York claimed to have authored more than two hundred religious and ideological books. Some of the space in many of the books was given to advertisements touting the body of work as "the most dynamic books ever published."

Hyperbole aside, the titles were definitely provocative and attention-grabbing: *Is God A Wimp?, The Fallacy of Easter, Santa Or Satan?, Was Christ Really Crucified?, Who, What, And Where Is The Devil?, Islamic Marriage Ceremony And Polygamy, Christianity: The Political Religion, The Sex Life Of A Muslim, Slave Trade, Holy War (Jihad),* and *Did The Hog Come For Mankind?* (The last book was a polemic arguing in support of the Moslem prohibition against eating pork.)

The books were nearly all printed on inexpensive paper stock, in black and white. One of York's female workers once questioned York about why the books were so flimsy. She said he answered that if they fell apart, the customers would buy new ones faster. As the years passed, the covers began to be printed on heavier paper, with color art work.

In general, the content was often highly strident in tone and difficult to follow, with typefaces that frequently reverted to all-capitals boldface to emphasize a point. York would often seek to reinforce his argument by printing a supportive quote from the Bible, alternating with a quote from the Qur'an often printed in Arabic script. Sometimes, there seemed to be a connection between the quotes and the argument; most often, though, the relevance was hard for a non-believer to discern. Many times, the search for any coherency at all was futile.

Nevertheless, there are some nuggets in the books worth a closer examination. At the least, they offer some explanations for why York's come-ons worked so well for so many years.

People who worked in York's bookstores say that his consistently best-selling book was a forty-four-page tract called *Leviathan 666*. It basically argues that the white race is, as a whole, an embodiment of the devil. It attacks Western culture in general and the materialism York associates with it in particular. The plight of the African-American is primarily the result of a white conspiracy, he argues.

"You were not born with the spell over you, but it is something you inherited from your foreparents," York writes in *Leviathan 666*. "You see, the physical agents of Leviathan (Paleman) led the ruling class of slaves into believing there was a chance for freedom, with enough money.

"Through miseducation, the European attempts to program and institute a sophisticated system of control."

By pursuing the Paleman's notion of material success, York argues, "the Blackman began to think of himself as an American citizen, when in reality he was more of a slave than ever."

This argument seems to have found a receptive audience among those who had good reason to believe they'd been shut out economically from access to the American Dream. What York did not tell his readers, though, was that while he was castigating the materialism of white society, he himself was free to indulge himself in a wide range of materialistic addictions – clothes, land, cars, pop music, and most of all, sex.

York even wrote a sort of sex manual, a 1980 book entitled *The Sex Life Of A Muslim*. It is mostly a glossary of sexual terms and practices. Some of the definitions and explanations give some insights into how York could rationalize his own highly promiscuous behavior, while at the same time he was laying down some very rigid sexual prohibitions for his followers.

Adultery, for example, is defined as an act that violates marriage, but not always in a bad way. There is an "out clause" in the definition: "When any male or female set out to disrupt a happy marriage by seeking sex with another mate – the key word is 'happy.'"

Homosexuality is defined as "male sexuality – any male who thinks of himself as female and tries to act the part, in or out of sex."

Birth control is termed "blasphemous."

York seems to betray a fixation with female genitalia. In the book, he lists 24 names for different shapes and appearances of a woman's private parts. Some of the less raw names on the list include "Voluptuous, Vast One, Glutton, and Biter."

There is an eight-page section of *The Sex Life Of A Muslim* that defends the practice of anal sex. Passages from the Qur'an are cited to refute the prohibitions many Moslems have against this practice. "The Sunni Muslim sect is under the false impression that anal sex is unlawful," York wrote.

York also wrote a strange section on the crime that ultimately brought him down. In defining pedophilia, York presents this form of aberrant behavior as part of the white race's plot against blacks, particularly black children. In real life, all of York's victims were black children.

"Just to show you how sick the Devil (Paleman) is," York wrote, "he has made pedophilia organizations which attempt to change the law regarding sexually abusing minors. They wish to legalize sex between mature adults and your children, i.e., those under thirteen."

In his 1977 book *Islamic Marriage Ceremony and Polygamy,* York presents a lengthy defense of this practice. "Polygamy can serve as a remedy to many social problems of modern civilization (prostitution, illegitimacy, venereal disease)," York wrote. "Women who would wander around in moral depravity received a home in a religion which is based in morality."

York makes it clear who should dominate a polygamous relationship: "Man, created by Allah superior to the female."

In order to make polygamy work, he wrote, "the women must respect each other." And from the polygamous husband's point of view, "the best type of wife to have is a young, intelligent woman."

He lists ten virtues of a Muslim woman, some of which include "Always, she be Clean; Always She Be Smelling Good; That She Obey Her Husband; Always Be Beautiful In Front Of Her Husband."

Polygamy was OK; interracial relationships were not. "Nubians are not to mix their seed with the cursed Paleman."

Perhaps because many of York's potential recruits were at least nominally Christian, York consistently attacked the basic tenets of Christianity.

In *Santa Or Satan? The Fallacy Of Christmas,* York wrote, "Like all of Satan's (The Paleman's) delusions, Christmas appears as an Angel of light and good, when in reality it is a Devil of darkness and evil."

The celebration of Christmas is just another part of the Christian plot. "Christianity is merely a tool used by the Devil (Paleman) to keep you, the Nubian (Black) man, woman, and child blind to your true heritage and perfect way of life (Islam). It is another means of slavery," York wrote.

Christmas is nothing but a "Ho Ho Hoax," he wrote, and anyone who believes in it is "a victim of two hundred years of lies."

The lies he refers to relate to the Christian concept of the divinity of Christ. In this book, as well as in several others, York wrote that Jesus was a mortal black prophet, whose mother was a Nubian woman named Maryam, and whose father was the Angel Michael.

Similarly, in a book called *The Fallacy Of Easter,* York attacked the central doctrine of Christianity. "While you have been solemnly observing what you think is a feast commemorating the Resurrection of the Messiah Jesus, the Devil has been laughing right in your face. The Devil knows that the Messiah Jesus was never crucified. He knows there was no such thing as a Resurrection, and he definitely knows that Easter, just like Christmas, is nothing but a false pagan holiday," he wrote.

Seeing on the printed page York's repeated characterizations of whites as the Devil does not fully transmit the virulence of his racist views. That comes across much more forcefully in his taped sermons.

In one such tape, from a series he called "New Covenant," York is shown preaching in the countryside to a group of followers. He castigates any in the group who might retain any belief in Christianity, saying, "That's sad, that you can worship the same god as your slave masters."

York claims on the tape that whites are "cursed with leprosy." Also, whites are trying to commit genocide against blacks, through AIDS, drugs, and birth control. Plus, they are trying to turn black men into homosexuals.

"They are a diseased people," York states. "They belong back in the caves, not here on the surface of the earth with us."

When York delivers his ugly punch lines, laughter comes from the audience on the tape. That may sound odd, or even vicious, but this white author has to admit, York can be quite funny. He delivers his messages of hate with a comic flair and timing reminiscent of an early Richard Pryor, or a Dick Gregory.

Both of those comedians were able to poke fun at white folks with a great deal of finesse, and York seems to have that same skill. His words don't seem quite so harsh, when he plays the line for a laugh. He doesn't have to preach violence. All he wanted from the people who bought his books and tapes was their unquestioned loyalty, their free labor, sexual submission, and all their money.

Academia barely took notice of York and his chameleon-like cult, and the few pertinent academic discourses that could be found were superficial at best. In their monograph "The Ansaru Allah Community: Postmodernist Narration and the Black Jeremiad," included in the book *New Trends and Developments In The World of Islam,* authors Susan J. Palmer and Steve Luxton explored what they called "the enigma of charisma." They termed Dwight York "a striking example of a maker of narrator-controlled fictional worlds." They compared York's shifting identities and costume changes to a "holy madness." They were also struck by the contrast between the insulting portrayals of whites in York's literature and the generally cordial way they were treated by York's street peddlers they interviewed. In their conclusions, however, the authors seem to legitimize the group, writing, "If one chooses to take their religious perspective seriously, one begins to see them not as ignorant dupes of a fanatical charlatan, but rather as a sophisticated audience engaged in the creation process."

Dr. Ali B. Ali-Dinar, then the outreach director of the African Studies Center at the University of Pennsylvania, wrote a 1994 monograph entitled "Claiming a Nubian Identity: Ansarullah Sect in the USA." Al-Dinar notes, but does not question, York's claim to be the new Mahdi, writing, "Thus, for Iman Isa, the quest for identity was settled by forging his own pedigree which associates him with the Mahdi and consequently legitimizing his movement in relation to the Ansar creed."

The most thorough academic analysis of York's writings was the one Haddad and Smith did for a 32-page chapter on York and AAC, in *Mission To America.* The writers characterize AAC as "a black religious sect that has undergone profound changes in its teachings."

They make no judgment on the validity of York's writings or on his ideologies. They accept his claim to be a Muslim religious leader at face value. They note that a Moslem scholar wrote a book shortly before theirs was published, in which he concluded that the AAC was a cult and York was a heretic to Islamic law; but they take no position on that issue.

In a 2004 interview, Haddad, now on the faculty of Georgetown University, said the methodology for their analysis consisted primarily of a review of the approximately seventy of York's books they had collected. After that process, she said she was left with the impression that York was something of a "crackpot."

Just before her book's publication, she said, she had a disturbing phone conversation with a man she believed to be York. The man objected to some things in the proof pages she had sent to AAC. She said she refused to make the changes the man demanded, since she was satisfied that the material was accurate. Then, she said, the man warned her that if she published the book with the disputed passages, "someone might kill you."

Coming from York, or from someone associated with him, such threats should not have been taken lightly.

On the morning of April 19, 1979, Horace Green drove away from his single-family brick home on Bushwick Avenue, just down the block and across the street from the AAC mosque. He was the founder and head of the Bushwick Improvement Society, and in general, the go-to guy for area residents who had complaints about the Muslims, as most people in the neighborhood referred to York and his followers. Green made the three-block trip to the community and day-care center he operated on Hart Street. It was about 7 a.m; people were already on the streets.

Green pulled up inside the chain-link fence topped with concertina wire that divided the center's parking lot from the street. As soon as he emerged from the car and turned to go into the building, a man jumped from his hiding place behind a trash dumpster and shot Green four times in the back.

The killer brushed past eyewitnesses as he ran away. They described him as a bearded black man wearing a knee-length black coat, black cap and pants and a silver earring in his left ear. That could have described just about any man in AAC, since they all wore beards and black robes at that time.

During the initial investigation, police questioned a neighborhood woman, who told them that the Muslims, as they were called by most others in the area, had given her a lowball offer for her home. She refused to sell, adding that she intended to complain to Horace Green about the Muslims' heavy-handed tactics. The AAC man warned her against doing that, saying of Green, "We've had some bad experiences with him."

Cora Green, Horace Green's widow, said in a 1998 interview with this author that she at first thought it was too obvious that the killer was an AAC man. It must have been someone dressed up like the Muslims, in order to throw suspicion on them, she said.

Even twenty years after the murder, she said she could think of no reason why her husband was gunned downed in the streets where he lived, worked and was widely loved. He had been a member of the district planning board, a vice president of the Community School Board, a board member of the governing council of the area's Boy Scout troops, and active in AFL-CIO affairs. He had recently made an unsuccessful run for a seat in the state legislature.

She had always been highly confident that the killing was not about money or sex. "This was not an ordinary shooting," she said. "This was in broad daylight. It was so brutal, so merciless."

Her husband did not talk much to her about his relationship with the Muslims. However, she knew he had been troubled by their plans, safe streets or not, she said.

"They wanted their own schools, their own city," she said. "The streets were crime free, but the police didn't seem to want any confrontation with them. The school officials didn't want a confrontation."

She did recall that her husband had used his position on the planning board to oppose the Muslims' plan to buy an abandoned hospital building and convert it into living spaces for more of its members.

Also, she said, he would not have shied away from a confrontation. "My husband was very outspoken," she said.

He was also, according to statements in the police investigative file, highly respected and warmly regarded by most people who knew him. His political associates generally liked him, and the daycare center he ran had a reputation for delivering a high level of services.

The murder case quickly went cold, even though Mayor Koch's office had posted a $10,000 reward for information leading to a conviction in the case. There were no takers. Officials in Koch's office regularly called the 83rd Precinct to check on the progress in the investigation. There was nothing to report.

A few months after the killing, NYPD homicide detective Bill Clark was assigned to the case. The idea was that a fresh set of eyes might see something that others had missed.

Clark saw the obvious – a big red, flashing arrow pointing to someone inside AAC. "There was never any doubt," Clark said in a 2005 interview, that the prime suspect was a man who at the very least dressed just like the Muslims.

Ordinarily, Clark would have gone into the AAC and selected possible

POLICE DEPARTMENT
CITY OF NEW YORK

SKETCH No. 161
CASE No. 4514/83
DATE 4-19-79

The above is a sketch resembling a suspect who is sought
for Homicide-GUN, in the 83rd Precinct at 0650hrs, on April
19, 1979

This sketch is based on a description supplied by a
witness. Description as follows;

Male, Black, 35 to 45yrs of age, 6'2", slim build, 180lbs,
dark skinned.

A police sketch of the suspect in the April 1979 assassination of Horace Green.

Roy Savage, known as Hashim the Warrior, in a New Jersey Courtroom in 1991, awaiting trial on a double
murder charge, unrelated to the Green murder.

candidates for a lineup, so that the witnesses might make an identification. He had a fairly detailed composite sketch of the suspect drawn with the help of the witnesses. But he was never able to take that first step.

Though he never believed York was the actual killer, Clark was convinced that it was someone from inside AAC. But when he decided to question York about the case, the department's "sensitive site" policy required that he not only make an appointment in advance to meet with York but also that the meeting should take place on York's turf. Further, Clark had to arrange to be accompanied by a community relations officer from the local precinct, where the prevailing view was that York was A-OK.

"Unlike many of the shows on television, if you can't interrogate suspects, your hands are tied," Clark said. He speaks with expertise on the difference between television crime shows and real life. After his retirement from the police force, Clark became a story consultant and then an executive producer of the long-running series *NYPD Blue*.

In the investigation of the Green homicide, the requirement that he go to York violated a basic tenet of police work. "Normally, you don't expect to interview a possible suspect in their own environment," Clark said.

The case quickly went cold again, this time for twenty years. Clark, who still keeps a framed newspaper article about the Horace Green case on his office wall, said it still grates on him that he had been required to tread softly around York, when he believed York should have been treated like any other potential murder suspect.

"He was given a license to do what he did," Clark said.

It angered Clark even more to learn in 1998 – nearly twenty years after he was forced to close his investigation – that an FBI intelligence report on York and Ansaru Allah community had identified the person they believed to be the murderer. The suspect's was one of York's trusted aides in 1979; Clark had been right from the start.

How could it happen that a homicide detective found himself unable to use basic police powers in a high-profile investigation of an assassination of a highly-regarded political figure – a man who was every bit as black as Dwight York?

"There was a double whammy – race and religion," Clark said.

York never needed to resort to violence himself. He had people around him who had amply demonstrated that capacity.

Shortly after the murder of Horace Green, Roy Savage, or Hashim the Warrior, moved out of AAC in Brooklyn. In the FBI report, Savage was described as being close to York and a leader of York's security force, the Mujahad. He was also the person named in the report as Horace Green's killer.

The following story of what later happened to Savage is taken from interviews with former Newark Police Department Detective Jack Eutsey and from his files on the case.

Savage moved to Newark, New Jersey, and he took three women from AAC with him. What happened after that became the subject of a police investigation, and the following summary of those events is taken from case files and from interviews with the lead detective on the case.

Though the women were nominally his "wives," Savage forced them to work selling incense and oils on the streets of Newark. Their sales allowed the group to live in a luxury apartment in Newark.

Savage lived as the women's lord and master. Frequently, the woman who made the most street sales was accorded the privilege of sleeping with him that night. When he was confronted by one of the women's relatives and asked to release her, Savage demonstrated his dominance by debasing the woman, making her lick the sidewalk in front of her parents.

Another woman who lived with him had three children. One day, Savage delivered the children to her relatives. All he would say is that their mother "went away." The woman was never seen again.

One night in September 1983, one of the women, Carolyn Hubbard, did something that Savage thought was disobedient. A fight started, Savage went into a rage and stabbed the woman in the neck. When another of his women, Jackie Cobb, tried to intervene, he stabbed her as well.

An eight-year-old girl named Hausakimah, the daughter of Carolyn Hubbard's sister, Cheryl Hubbard, was present in the apartment at the time of the killings. Savage yelled at her to go to the bedroom, while he dragged the bodies into the bathroom, where he butchered the corpses. Cheryl Hubbard came back to the apartment in time to help with the cleanup.

Savage hacked the corpses into pieces, and packed the body parts into five suitcases. As a way of terrorizing the two remaining women into silence, he cooked some of the body parts in his oven and made them eat bits of the flesh.

Disposal of the body parts turned out to be a big problem. After a couple of days of indecision, he loaded up the suitcases and took them down to his car. The security guard in the lobby noted something amiss and wrote in his logbook, "Stink! Stink! Stink!" Beyond that, however, he did nothing.

Savage took the suitcases to an apartment in Harlem that he sometimes used. While he pondered his next move, he lit more than a hundred scented candles in the apartment, to help mask the smell. He then proceeded to party. He apparently tried to score some drugs, but the deal went bad, and Savage was roughed up and thrown through a second-story window. He received a concussion and some serious lacerations and was hospitalized.

Meanwhile, smoke from all the candles was billowing out of Savage's apartment window, and the fire department was called. Firefighters put out the candles and left; one firefighter later acknowledged that he opened a closet door and saw the suitcases, noted the foul odor and fluids seeping from the bags; but he did nothing about it and did not mention it in his incident report.

However, someone went to the hospital to tell Savage that the fire department had been at his apartment. He pulled the intravenous needles from his arm and rushed back home, wearing nothing but his hospital gown. Later, a neighbor became suspicious, after seeing a large man dressed in Muslim women's robes leaving the apartment and carrying heavy suitcases. This time, the police were summoned. They found bloodstains in the empty apartment, but no bodies.

Savage had taken at least one of the suitcases back to Newark. He took it to a public housing project that was being decommissioned, so that some of the upper floors were already empty. Three people were on the elevator with him as he rode up; all of them would later say that they noted the horrible smell, but they did nothing and reported it to no one.

Two or three days later, residents in the apartment house complained about the smell. A maintenance man found the suitcase, took it downstairs and tossed it into a dumpster. The suitcase popped open.

"That's when I got called," said Eutsey. He started with no crime scene and two unknown victims. The suitcase had contained the limbless, headless torso of one woman and the finger of another.

Eutsey put out a bulletin throughout the New York area, stating what he had found and asking for help from other departments. Soon, he got a call from an NYPD detective who had a crime scene at a Harlem apartment, but no bodies. That detective met with Eutsey and brought along some photographs he had taken from the apartment.

Eutsey knew some of the people in the pictures. One of them was the daughter of a friend from his youth, when he grew up in the Newark housing projects. He went to see the friend. The daughter, Jasmine, was called in. At first, she was reluctant to say anything, but after Eutsey had explained the gruesome details, the young woman, Jasmine, started to cooperate.

Jasmine said she had been one of Savage's women for a time, but she managed to leave. She identified the other women in the pictures and she told Eutsey where the group lived.

This was enough to make Savage a suspect and to obtain a search warrant for his Newark apartment. When he was first questioned, Savage offered the explanation that he had been mugged on the streets of Harlem and then hospitalized. In the hospital, he claimed that a woman he didn't know came to his bedside, pointed a gun at him, and ordered him to move a suitcase from Harlem to New Jersey.

Cheryl Hubbard was similarly uncooperative, claiming she didn't know where her sister and Jackie Cobb had gone. However, the little girl, though frightened and reluctant at first, told the truth. Savage was arrested for the two murders.

When she continued to refuse to cooperate with investigators, Cheryl Hubbard was also arrested and charged with obstruction of justice. But as soon as she made bail, she took her daughter and fled.

Eutsey soon got a lead on where she might have gone. There is a section of Manhattan's Morningside Heights district that people call "Little Newark," because of the number of men from Newark who go there to fade into the cityscape, because they have unsettled criminal matters back in Newark. Eutsey went to Little Newark and found some sources who were willing to trade information on the murder case for some help with their lesser problems back home.

They told him that Cheryl Hubbard had probably gone back to where she came from, the AAC in Bushwick. They also said the word on the streets was that the women of AAC were held in subjugation, and Dwight York was known as "the pimp imam."

But when Eutsey tried to follow his witnesses inside AAC, he encountered the same resistance that had stymied Bill Clark's investigation of the Horace Green murder. York refused to allow Eutsey permission to enter AAC.

"The NYPD tried to be helpful, but they couldn't go in themselves," Eutsey said. Eutsey was out of his jurisdiction, and AAC was still a "sensitive site."

So, Eutsey simply got himself a robe like the Muslim men wore, put it on and went inside. It turned out to be an easy game of charades.

There was a steady stream of in-and-out traffic for Eutsey to merge with; and once inside, the men and women were not as rigidly segregated as he had feared.

When he found Cheryl Hubbard, he didn't need to trick her or coerce her. He simply explained her legal situation. She'd already committed a crime by ignoring a summons to appear before the grand jury in New Jersey, and if she continued to refuse to cooperate, she'd be in even worse trouble.

By the time he convinced the woman to take her daughter and leave with him, Eutsey had become convinced that Savage had arranged for flight to Brooklyn and into the AAC. Also, he said, York was almost certainly complicit in the plan.

As it turned out, the girl became the key witness for the prosecution. Savage was convicted and sentenced to life in prison, but he won a second trial on appeal. He was convicted again and given a sentence of eighty-eight years, which he is now serving in a New Jersey prison.

Eutsey's assessment of Savage: "He was an animal." Yet, he found the women who lived with Savage were all intelligent and articulate. "Savage had total dedication from the women surrounding him," Eutsey said. And Savage's hold on the women continues, he said. Even now, more than twenty years after the crimes, Cheryl Hubbard continues to make prison visits to Savage, the man who slaughtered her sister. That's something Eutsey said he's never been able to understand.

York has tried to minimize his association with Savage. In 1998, York told this author that he considered Savage "a nut." He said he knew nothing about Savage's suspected involvement in the Horace Green murder, or about the killings of the women who'd left AAC with Savage. That was the only time York has publicly discussed Savage or the other allegations in the FBI report.

However, three former members of York's cult have told this author that Savage has frequently written letters to York from prison. Most of those letters were barely coherent expressions of undying loyalty to York, according to one of the former cult members who read the letters. When this person asked York what to do about Savage's letters, York responded, "Send him some books."

York also denied any involvement in the violent crimes attributed to members of Ansaru Allah Community in the 1993 FBI report. York pointed out, correctly, that he was never formally accused of any of those crimes.

"They're making me out to be a monster. I'm not a monster," York said, making another claim that would turn out to be diametrically opposed to the truth.

Just as he believed he could make criminal accusations against him disappear, York was also an accomplished magician in the theatrical sense. In fact, he published a series of photographs purporting to document his powers. In a book from his early years entitled *The Man Of Miracles In This Day And Time,* the cover consists of a sequence of four photographs, going from York holding out his empty hand to York pouring a stream of "Sacred Ashes" from one hand to the other.

"We have a man with us in the U.S.A. who can make things appear from nothing, heal the sick, levitate," proclaimed the promotional advertisement printed alongside the photographs. "And he knows the answers to all questions."

York's son Malik knew better. Raised as a child prince of Ansaru Allah Community, Malik remembers the way that York would perform the feat of the Sacred Ashes.

Sometimes, Malik recalled, York would stroll amongst a group of believers at prayer, extending his hands over some of their heads as he walked. Every so often – Poof! – a puff of golden powder would spurt from York's hands. The man or woman on whom the dust settled would pray in delight and thanksgiving, for the gesture had signaled that he or she had exhibited an especially high level of devotion to Imam Isa, or Dwight York.

However, Malik had seen his father secrete tiny capsules in his hand. The Sacred Ashes – like so much else about York's early years as a cult leader – was nothing but a cheap magic trick. Nevertheless, the magic worked for a long time.

Dwight York in different guises during the New York years.

CHAPTER 3
Bushwick Babylon (mid-1980s – 1993)

Sixty years ago, Thorstein Veblen wrote that at the very bottom of the class system, there was a "spurious aristocracy," a leisure class of bottom dogs devoted to luxury and aristocratic poses. And there you have him, the pimp.
– Tom Wolfe, *Radical Chic & Mau-Mauing The Flak Catchers*.

The bride was made to blush long before the wedding night.

Nevertheless, even a brokered and doomed union can be made to appear holy, when the deal is sealed with a heavy dose of kitsch and kismet. The fact that this particular bride and groom had only met twice did not deter the father of the bride from making their wedding as lavish as his version of Islamic law would allow.

Of course, none of the ugly pre-marital goings-on between the bride, Afifah, and her father, Dwight York, were divulged.

Neither was any explanation of the father's absence offered.

In the slick-surfaced, heavy-stock, full-color program for the wedding was a 10-by-6 keepsake. Its cover was bordered in exquisitely detailed Arabic-style patterns, done mostly in reds and greens. Highlighting the central area of the cover was a photograph of a single red rose.

The English-language script in the central area of the cover made it quite clear that this event was nothing less than the marriage of a princess:

"The Ansaru Allah Community cordially invites you to the 2nd Wedding of the Century," it began. The guests either already knew, or were left to guess, what had been the 1st.

"The East: As Sayyid Kamal Ahmad Hassib will be united in marriage to the West: Afifah bint Sayyidat Dhudaida."

Date: September 17, 1989

Time: 2:00 p.m., after Dhur, sharp

Address: 719 Bushwick Avenue
             Brooklyn, New York 11221

On its inside pages, the program laid out the details of a splendid ceremony. Once the guests were seated in the masjid, or mosque, the plan for the ceremony was explained to them, in both English and Arabic.

Incense bearers, including the bride's older brother, then filled the auditorium-sized room with scent. Another brother walked the aisles, playing the "ceremonial wedding call" on an Arabic stringed instrument. Then, the bride and groom entered the mosque, using separate doorways and each carrying a lighted candle.

The groom's "right-hand man" then read quotations about marriage written by an Islamic cleric. The actual wedding ceremony was officiated by another brother of the bride. After the exchange of vows, the couple was given a new candle, which they lit simultaneously from their individual candles.

The groom then proceeded to the wedding canopy, accompanied by the musicians and incense bearers. There they were joined by male friends and relatives, and they walked under the canopy as it moved outside the mosque and onto the sidewalk of Bushwick Avenue. The women of the wedding party then joined the men under the canopy, and they all walked across the street, where the men and women lined up on either side of the sidewalk.

The whole neighborhood was crowded with well-wishers, many of whom had come for this event from the far reaches of Dwight York's empire. Prayers of thanksgiving were offered by the officiating cleric, who raised a glass of kosher wine to toast the couple. Then the bride walked around the groom seven times, as a symbol of protecting him from evil.

The couple publicly offered their mutual consent to the marriage and exchanged wedding bands. Final prayers were offered, the wine glasses were ceremoniously smashed, and then a large gong was sounded, signaling the end of the ceremony.

The crowd showered the couple with raisins, almonds and rice, as they proceeded into the banquet hall inside the mosque building. The invited guests were given glasses of juice and dates as they entered the hall.

Then the wedding feast began, with hors d'oeuvres and Islamic music, then a sit-down dinner with more music. The finale was a traditional cake cutting.

Even though he was Imam, the spiritual and temporal leader of the community, York was a no-show. He was under arrest for passport fraud at the time; but he had already made his play for his daughter.

A few weeks earlier, one of York's concubines came to Afifah.

"Your father wants for me to care for you and prepare you," the woman said to Afifah, who was eighteen at the time.

"Prepare me for what?" Afifah wondered.

"Your father wants you," the woman said.

"Wants me for what?" the young woman wondered again.

At this point, the older woman realized that she needed to be more blunt.

"He's the first for all of them, for all the girls," she said to Afifah.

Finally, Afifah got the picture – her father intended to be the one to initiate her sexually. To put it mildly, she was shocked. At that point in her life, Afifah was a virgin, who had been raised according to the strict religious dictates of AAC.

She didn't know much about the world. In fact, as she put it, "I didn't even know how to cross the street."

She also barely knew the man who was trying to have her prepped for an incestuous liaison with him. York was the Imam, the unquestioned ruler of her world, but he was not really involved in her life, or in the lives of his numerous other children. "I didn't really know him as a father," she said.

Years after that moment of realizing what her father wanted of her, Afifah said she should have seen it coming. He had given signals, some of them overt.

There were times, she recalled, as she was passing through puberty, when York would have her stand before people of the community. He would make admiring comments on her physical beauty.

"Look at my daughter. Her body is so perfect," York would say.

At those times, Afifah felt highly uncomfortable, but she said nothing.

She found her voice, though, when her father's concubine transmitted his desire to have sex with his daughter. She adamantly refused. York responded with a decree that Afifah would marry the man who taught Arabic in the community. Afifah barely knew who the teacher was.

During the weeks before the ceremony, Afifah said, she was kept in virtual seclusion. Her mother Dorothy (Zubaida) was restricted from seeing her and given only a minimal role in the ceremony. All the typical bridal preparations were handled by York's concubines.

She went through the ceremony, though she viewed the whole affair as a sham. Her betrothal had been an act of retribution by the father she'd spurned.

So, why did she do it? Why would she marry a virtual stranger at the insistence of a father who had tried to command her to commit incest?

Afifah may have been strong enough to refuse her father's advances, but she was not yet strong enough to break away from his cult. Ansaru Allah Community had been her whole life. Her father ruled the community and provided for all her spiritual, social, and material needs. She'd been told all her life that the outside world was full of enemies. And even if she had entertained any thoughts of going to the police, what would she tell them? Her father had not actually violated her; and besides, the local police seemed to let him do whatever he wished.

Soon after the wedding, she started to make a plan for independence. She started sneaking out at nights, so that she could attend a nearby beauty school, and thus acquire a trade to support herself. About a year after the wedding, she left.

"I walked out with what I had in my pocketbook, and I never looked back," she said.

York responded by cutting her off from the source of income that he had set up for her. He had placed some buildings in Philadelphia in her name, but after she left, he ordered that the buildings be gutted, thus making them worthless to her.

After Afifah's departure, her mother started spending more time with her at her apartment. One day, York sent his security guards to inform Afifah's mother, who was York's only legitimate wife, that she had been expelled from AAC.

During those same years, more of York's family ties became severely frayed. And while his family was unraveling, York also started to disengage himself from the Islamic strictures of AAC.

In 1983, York paid $145,000 for an eighty-acre tract of woodlands in the Catskill Mountains, near the small town of Parksville, in Sullivan County, New York. At first, the property was mostly a summer retreat York called Camp Jazzir.

Malik York said his mother told him that York used about $5 million to build himself a mansion, complete with indoor swimming pool and recording studio, at Camp Jazzir.

York didn't bother to get the required permits for some of the construction at the country property. In a pattern he would repeat in Georgia, York engaged in a running battle with county inspectors. Local officials took him to court and forced him to stop using run-down buildings on the property as living spaces for some of his followers.

Unlike the confrontations that would flare down South, however, York never played the race card publicly in the Catskills. He never tried to characterize the orders of the building inspector as racial discrimination. Instead, he simply made the required changes and applied for the proper permits.

Camp Jazzir was miles from the nearest paved road, and there were virtually no full-time neighbors. However, across the lake bordering the property was a hunting and fishing lodge owned by Phil Mullins, who was then the Sullivan County building inspector. Mullins recalled that the Camp Jazzir property was previously a summer camp for a Jewish group, but it had not been used for years when York purchased it.

A couple of times, Mullins had to put stop-work orders on the expansion project at the main lodge. Each time, though, a leader of the group, usually Karim, would go to the county courthouse and obtain the necessary permits. Members of the group erected barricades on the roads leading to their construction sites. They placed a speaker device in the trees near the barricade, he said, so that people who wanted to come in could announce themselves.

There were no signs of any sort of religious affiliation of the group, certainly nothing to suggest they were Muslims. They did erect some Native American-style totem poles, Mullins recalled.

The men of the group appeared to have an obsession with guns. They made large purchases from a sporting goods store owner who happened to be a relative of Mullins.

"They bought just about every rifle that could be bought up here, and every round of ammunition," Mullins said. Frequently, there were sustained bursts of gunfire in the woods of Camp Jazzir. Mullins thought it was probably target practice. Mullins recalls once being confronted by a man with an automatic rifle, and soon more than a dozen other armed men joined the discussion, which was ended without conflict.

The FBI report stated that York and some of his male followers had come under investigation by New York state police for excessive purchases of guns and ammunition – dozens of AK47s, rifles, handguns, and thousands of rounds of ammunition.

Besides the guns, York also started playing more openly with girls.

Mullins recalled that local residents became suspicious about the number of girls and young women that could be seen around the camp. "There were a lot of young girls, but you never saw those kids in town," he said.

The local police were watching York's activities at Camp Jazzir, but their investigation never proceeded to the point of attempting to obtain a search warrant. Once, though, Mullins entered the camp on his authority as a building inspector and brought an undercover state police officer with him. Mullins recalled being impressed by a large room in the main lodge, an area perhaps the size of half a basketball court. The floor was entirely covered with a deep plush white rug. The main décor was artificial palm trees, and mounted on the walls were several big-game trophy heads, including a rhinocerous.

Even though York never faced any criminal charges in Sullivan County, he must have been aware of the suspicions directed against him, Mullins said. "Pressure was being brought to bear, and I think he knew it," Mullins said.

Malik, a teenager by this time, was assigned to oversee some of the construction projects at the camp. His father's construction plans were strange and costly. In particular, York ordered that his main house be built with a wing encompassing two trailers, where the women and children would be housed. There was a secret passageway built between them. Malik also noticed that when his father was at Camp Jazzir, a van loaded with teenaged and adolescent girls from AAC in Brooklyn usually came up, too.

These were the Backstreet Girls, the ones York had allowed to spend extra time and have extra privileges at his recording studio in Bushwick, the one he called Backstreet.

A few people in the community knew, or suspected, that York was taking sexual liberties with the Backstreet Girls. Nuha, a woman who'd left a nursing career to join the community, said she recalled a time when a fifiteen-year-old girl told a small group of women that York had had sex with her.

The women found it hard to believe the girl. "Why would he sacrifice all of this to do something like that?" Nuha said she asked. It was more or less common knowledge that York enjoyed his pick of the women of the community, whenever he wanted. One of the other women, who turned out to be one of those who prepared the girls for sex with York, had a simple explanation: York was "bored sexually."

Once the girls were accepted into the Backstreet group, they were given an elevated status in the community. "They were special girls. They didn't have to listen to their parents," Malik said. Some of them would openly flirt with his father.

At Camp Jazzir, his father would sometimes use an intercom to summon one or more of the girls to his private quarters, he said.

A combination of curiosity and suspicion led Malik to search his father's rooms at the camp. Among the things he found was a videotape marked with the name of one of the Backstreet Girls. That particular girl was one whom Malik was attracted to. He considered her to be his girlfriend.

As he watched the video, the bubble of puppy love was quickly burst. Malik saw his girlfriend disrobe and make a series of suggestive moves for the camera. He soon confronted the girl, demanding an explanation for what he had seen in his father's room.

The girl was blunt and unashamed in her response. "I gave your father a blow job last night," she told him.

Malik said his father's growing pre-occupation with the girls was part of a broader drift away from the strictures of Islam, and partly a search for sexual variety. After years of having his pick of the women of AAC, York started gravitating toward underage companions. "He got bored," Malik said.

Unlike the earlier years in Brooklyn, his father was not as visible in the community's religious ceremonies. For example, he often failed to participate in the Islamic naming ceremonies as he used to do. People started asking, "Where's the Imam?" Malik said.

Never fluent in Arabic, York started using the language less and dressing in blue jeans rather than the uniform robes of the community, Malik said.

There were also signs in York's books that he was pulling away from the community he founded. Advertisements in some of the issues of York's books printed in the late 1980s solicited contributions "to support The Lamb in his retirement."

Some of the disengagement may have been a practical matter of finances, Malik said. Some of the young men of the community, who had been told as they grew that they were to become the leaders of a black elite, had reached the age where it was time to begin their higher education. They started asking, "Where's my college?" he said.

Dwight York wasn't about to pay for anybody's college education, no matter if they had been raised in AAC, no matter if they were his own sons. "He was never going to keep his promises," Malik said. "He never thought it would last that long."

Nevertheless, the show went on. Afifah got a full-scale religious ceremony for her wedding, but after that, York's legitimate family and the community he had built rapidly fell apart.

Karim said it was like watching Mr. Hyde win out over Dr. Jekyll.

"When Dr. York came in, that spiritual person, Imam Isa, was no more," Karim said.

Karim said he could sometimes see York struggling with his conflicting personalities. One night while York's band Passion was setting up for a performance, York simply shut things down, saying "I can't do this. This isn't right," Karim said.

York's personality swings were obvious to those who were close to him, Karim said. "Imam Isa was not fearful of anything, but Dr. York was paranoid about everything," he said.

Once, he recalled, a man of the community brought a female psychologist friend into the community. The woman met York and offered a diagnosis: he was a paranoid schizophrenic with delusions of grandeur. Karim said the man gave the woman a beating for speaking negatively about the Imam.

There was also an obvious shift in the basic aims of the community, Karim said. "Under Imam Isa, we were raising leaders, but Dr. York was just raising followers," he said.

Psychology aside, Karim said, the devolution of York was also a confirmation of an old adage about dictatorial rulers: "Absolute power corrupts absolutely."

Malik said he started to speak out against his father to others in the community. Some of the younger members urged him to assume the leadership of the community, but his mother Zubaida counseled him to respect his father, even though she herself was engaging in frequent and fierce arguments with York. York berated her. She criticized him for keeping his stable of girls, charging that while he may have been able to distort Islamic law enough to justify his harem of women, there was no sanction in any religion for what he was doing with the girls.

Malik described those times as a "kind of civil war" within the community. He recalled several furious arguments with his father. During one such fight – over York's dalliance with the woman of one of his other sons – York threatened the other son with an ice pick. Malik then brandished a gun at his father. His mother Zubaida intervened, saying, "This has gone too far," he said.

Malik said he knew then it was time for him to go. "I walked, and then my mother walked," he said. Those in sympathy with his mother also left, but there were plenty of loyalists who stayed.

Zubaida's departure also meant that there was hardly anyone left who could restrain York or say no to him. Karim said that through most of the early years, York's personal spending was limited to the allowance that Zubaida provided him from the community funds. He recalled a time when York stormed into the office area, furious that he was out of money. Unlike the others, Zubaida spoke back to him, argued with him; and in the end, York stopped demanding more money.

Zubaida York lived only about five years after she left AAC.Malik York said his mother was sorrowful for most of that time. It made her sad to realize what had become of the Utiopian dream she had helped to build, and what had happened to many who had believed in that dream.

"We set them up like lambs to be slaughtered by the wolf," she told her son.

It was more than familial dysfunction that was making retirement look more and more attractive to York.

First, York was becoming a target of the FBI. The 1993 FBI report cites fifteen confidential informants. Also, the report stated that current and former members of AAC were being interviewed. Surely, alarms were ringing in the AAC security apparatus.

However, there was an even more immediate and serious threat, which came in the form of a highly public challenge to York's core claim of being a devout Muslim religious leader. It came in the form of a small book published in 1988 and written by an Islamic scholar named Bilal Philips.

The title itself –*The Ansaar Cult* – was a charge that no one had dared make. For the more than two decades that York had been the sole ruler of AAC, no one had openly called it a cult.

But now, Philips had used "the C-word," and in the title of his exposé of York. Moreover, he documented his accusation by citing numerous passages from York's own books that Philips claimed were far outside the bounds of Islamic law, and by providing statements from former members that clearly described AAC as a cult. Philips did not have any investigative or police powers; he simply asked the obvious questions. Which raises another question: What took so long?

Philips called York's cult a combination of Black Power and Islam. "Isa's (York was called Imam Isa at the time) version had an appeal to those seeking Islam, but who could not divorce themselves from the strong nationalist sentiments of that era," Philips wrote.

In the main, the book was a religious attack on York's credentials as a Muslim cleric, spiritual leader, and prophet. The frontispiece of the book is a letter from a leading Islamic cleric of Saudi Arabia at the time. Basically, the letter called York a heretic and a charlatan.

"It is therefore better to comment on their doctrines in a way sufficient to clarify their falsehood, shamefulness and remoteness from the correct path," wrote Abdullah Al-Bidaah, supervisor of publications for the Islamic research agency of the Kingdom of Saudi Arabia.

That letter served as Philips's charge to write his book and expose York. From the beginning, York used Islam as a recruiting gimmick, Philips wrote. "Dwight York changed his name to Isa Abdullah and began inviting black youths to a black nationalist version of Islam which he had begun to concoct," Philips stated.

Practically from the beginning of his run, York ran his community as a cult, Philips charged. York demanded that all new members turn over all their money and sign over all their possessions to the community. He also required members whom he assigned to sell and beg outside the community to turn over all their earnings to him.

Philips criticized York's 1973 trip to Egypt and Sudan, during which York got himself photographed in front of religious monuments and with descendants of the Mahdi, whom York claimed as his great-grandfather. After he returned to the U.S., York began publicly claiming that he was a direct descendant of the Mahdi and that he had somehow obtained a doctorate during his four-month excursion. Philips stated that York "invented" both claims.

Philips noted that York was successful in the short run in countering objections to his claim to be the new Mahdi. He invited a real member of the Sudanese royal line, Sayyid Ya'quob al-Mahdi, to visit York's mosque in Brooklyn. The Sudanese man came, prayed with York, and praised the group. The following year, another prominent Sudanese, Saddiq Al-Mahdi, visited the community and promised to send Arabic teachers.

These visits were propaganda bonanzas for York. He published numerous photographs of the distinguished guests during their Brooklyn visits in a special edition of the AAC newspaper, called *The Final Link*. These expressions of approval did not silence York's critics in other Muslim communities in the U.S., Philips stated, but they did help him solidify his support within the ranks of his own followers.

Phillips wrote that around 1980, York started escalating his claims of divinity. "The cult printed countless posters and pamphlets with pictures of Isa with the caption, 'The Saviour Has Returned'," Philips stated.

More claims to divine status were included in York's *The Book of Lam,* Philips stated. He quoted from the book: "He will not return as a prophet, but as the Mujaddid, the Reformer. Isa al Masih (York) will be the head of Christ and we, the pure ones, are the Body of Christ. Many men have claimed their appointment by the creator, but they have no proof from the scriptures to back them up, neither do they have the understanding of the scriptures to explain them and make them clear, as does Isa al Masih."

In 1981, York added another title to his movement, *United Muslims in Exile*. Philips said this was York's attempt to establish himself as a worldwide Islamic leader.

In 1985, York made what Philips called his "most heretical pronouncement," calling himself "the incarnation of God for this age." In his book *I Am The Shadow Of The Father (You Are The Sons Of The Green Light),* York wrote, "I, the Avatar of the West, have been chosen to be a temple of the incarnated divinity. It is my soul, thus I come forth."

In Philips's view, York flaunted Islamic law in his manual *The Sex Life*

Of A Muslim, by promoting such practices as anal sex and oral sex. "In the case of making permissible that which Allah prohibited, Isa reveals the more seamy side of his teachings, in which he promotes immoral and perverted sex practices, ranging from the despicable to the prohibited," Philips wrote.

York's convoluted attempts to justify his positions by using his translations of passages from the Qu'ran are called "incomprehensible" by Philips. Regarding one such passage, Philips stated, "Hence, this translation of Isa clearly illustrates his ignorance of some of the most basic rules of Arabic."

Most of *The Ansaar Cult* consists of similar attacks on York's credentials as a Muslim. However, in an appendix that included statements from fourteen former members of AAC, Philips's book became the first public exposure of life within York's cult. They painted a very ugly picture.

A man named Siddiq stated that he was one of York's earliest followers, joining the group in June 1968. At that time, he was a member of the Darul-Islam movement in Brooklyn. That Sunni Muslim group later splintered, with one part re-emerging under the leadership of high-profile activist H. Rap Brown, who gained lasting notoriety for his statement, "Violence is as American as cherry pie." Brown changed his name to Jamil Abdullah Al-Amin, and he was convicted in 2002 of killing a black sheriff's deputy in a shootout in Atlanta. He is serving a life sentence.

Siddiq said he first met York when York and a few of his male followers came to a religious festival at Darul-Islam headquarters. The visitors wore the fez, nose rings, and bones in their ears.

Though he was warned that York and his people were "crazies," Siddiq stated he was attracted to York, who seemed to have answers to questions that had troubled him. "As I found out later, the answers were all either fabricated or distorted, but nonetheless, he answered all my questions," Siddiq stated.

He stayed with York for about fourteen years, serving as York's driver for much of that time, and for a period, the spokesman for AAC, and later as the enforcer who collected the quotas, up to one hundred dollars per day, from the men York sent out into the streets.

"I had an opportunity to see him the way very few people could see him," Siddiq said. "He is surely not a Muslim. When I have seen him praying, it is for show, when it is politically astute for him to pray...This 'nigger' is just gaudy, gold everywhere."

For most of the first five years he was with York, there were only five-to-fifteen male followers in the group, he stated. Around 1973, the men on the street shifted from selling York's books to begging, and that's when the money started rolling in, he stated.

"Once during that period, I took a half million dollars to the bank," he stated. The heavy influx of cash allowed York to start acquiring the Bushwick properties that became the base of his holdings.

Within the Bushwick compound, York established the rules and living patterns for everyone who lived there, Siddiq stated. There were separate quarters for the men, women, and children, no matter if they had entered the group as a family.

Married or mated couples were only allowed to have private time as allowed by York's rules, he stated. If the man brought in his quota of money, and if the woman had performed her work satisfactorily, they might be allowed time in "The Green Room" to have marital relations. Typically, a couple was lucky to get to the Green Room more than once every other week, and many of the women in particular, found it embarrassing that others knew who had been allowed to use the Green Room, he stated.

Meanwhile, York placed no limits on his own sexual appetites, Siddiq stated. He literally had sex with any woman in the community, anytime he desired.

"Sisters would come in, brothers' wives, and he would take them to the back and have sex with them, and then go out and Salaam (greet) the brother. I mean, like everything was all right," Siddiq stated.

By a conservative estimate, York committed adultery daily, often more than that, Siddiq stated. York also encouraged female homosexual acts among his concubines and condoned homosexual acts among some of the men. At times, York would invite Siddiq to participate in group sex. "I did not come to Islam for that," Siddiq stated.

When he traveled with York to Trinidad in the early 1970s to help establish a satellite community there, York had sex with some local women, and Siddiq said he questioned York about the religious propriety of those acts.

York replied, "Siddiq, there are many things about Islam that you do not understand," Siddiq stated.

However, Siddiq did understand—because he was there to witness it—that York lived lavishly, while his followers subsisted on next to nothing. "They are eating beans, while this 'Negro' flaunts and spends ten thousand dollars on shoes. I was his driver. I took him to buy them," Siddiq stated.

As soon as new members joined AAC, they had to empty their bank accounts and give the money to York, as well as signing over any cars or property they owned, Siddiq stated.

Just as York took his followers possessions, he used their children to help keep up the façade of a devout religious community, Siddiq stated. "The thing that keeps him in power – besides Shaytaan (Satan) – is the children," he stated. The children were trained to be visible signs of Islamic purity, reciting the Qu'ran from memory and parading in their robes down the streets of Bushwick, he said.

"It is a beautiful sight, if you don't know it is a mirage," Siddiq stated.

York frequently exempted himself from the prayer routines followed by devout Muslims. And if AAC men were doing work that York wanted done, he would exempt them from the Islamic prohibitions against working on the Sabbath, Siddiq stated.

When asked why he stayed so long with York, he responded, "He was like a father to me." Even after he became disillusioned with life in AAC and left, he still believed in York and was loyal to him. Once, he stated, his brother started talking negatively about York, and Siddiq said he became so angry that he seriously considered making a violent attack on his brother.

He admitted that he was transfixed by York's power to control others. "It's so fascinating, because here is this black man who waves the nationalist flag, pushing the black thing and downing the white man. The white man is the devil, the blue-eyed are condemned to be despised as apes. He's the only one who has all the answers. He is in absolute control and the people worship him," Siddiq stated.

The Ansaar Cult never reached anyone's best-seller list. It was sold mostly at Islamic bookshops in the New York area and distributed at some mosques.

Nevertheless, it sent York into a frenzy. He cranked out a shrill response, in the form of a 615-page paperback book entitled *Rebuttal To The Slanderers,* and subtitled, *The Ansaar Cult, The Truth About the Ansaarullah Community in America, Truth is Truth.*

York dedicated the book to "those who have tried to slander me, and especially to Abu Ameenah Bilial(cq) Philips." York deliberately misspelled Philips's first name in the dedication and throughout the rest of the book. His explanation for the distortion: "The 42nd name of the Devil is Bilial! THIS IS NOT A COINCIDENCE."

Devil or angel, Philips's book provoked a nearly line-by-line rebuttal from York. Often, York would take one sentence from Philips's book and use pages of argument in his own book, bolstered by long quotations from holy books in English and Arabic, to attempt to rebut what Philips had written.

For example, Philips mentioned in a personal aside in his book that he was somewhat amused by York's practice of wearing a nose ring, because in most Islamic countries, only a stud bull would be fitted with such an apparatus.

York's response came in all-capital letters, underlined for emphasis and punctuated with multiple exclamation points: "WHEN I WAS TOLD THAT IT WASN'T A LAW FOR MEN TO WEAR A NOSE RING (AND WE WERE WEARING THEM) THE MEN TOOK IT OUT!!!"

Much of York's book is a rambling, overheated diatribe. But the section where he responds to the statement of Siddiq is a prime illustration of York's pattern of response to a serious allegation. He virtually ignores the allegation, while attempting to smear the person making it.

In *Rebuttal To The Slanderers,* York begins the section by presenting background data on Siddiq, in the form of what appears to be internal member evaluation forms of AAC. York claims that Siddiq had a history of drug use and a minor criminal record, as well as five wives and fifteen children.

Siddiq was then described as "disrespectful to those in authority" and as having a "negative attitude." He was said to have an "I am somebody attitude. Refuses to come down off his high horse."

Apparently, these criticisms were meant to undermine Siddiq's general credibility; but when it came to responding to specific allegations, York uses some verbal sleight of hand – he doesn't quite deny the accusation, but he pulls some countercharges out of his sleeve.

In response to Siddiq's allegation that he witnessed York promoting and participating in sexual acts prohibited by Islamic law, York responds with a statement on his own sexual orientation and an innuendo about Siddiq's.

"Well, let me make it clear that I am not a homosexual in any way, form or fashion; and I've never indulged in any homosexual act whatsoever!" he wrote. Then he tries to turn the issue back onto accuser. "As far as I am concerned, Siddiq is confessing to you all that he is a homosexual." It didn't seem to matter that Siddiq had not accused York of being a homosexual, nor that York failed to respond to the accusation of promoting forbidden sexual practices.

Regarding the allegation of York's promiscuity with the women of AAC, York's response was again to turn the question back on his accuser. "Siddiq definitely has a psychological problem," York wrote. "His jealousy was blinding him and making him see things that didn't exist." York does not deny his alleged profligacy; instead he chides his accuser for "insulting" the women of the community. "You're lucky, Siddiq, that they don't stone you to death."

York admits that he did commit adultery during the 1973 Trinidad trip and that he did impregnate a woman there. He called the liaison a "marriage in the name of Allah." He then stated the affair was justified, in that everyone was happy in the end. His concubine in Trinidad married a man who raised the child York left her with, the family later moved to Brooklyn, and the stepfather became "a very close friend of mine."

That claim would later be vehemently disputed by a man named Asad, the stepfather York mentioned. Years later, he charged that York ruined his family, called York an agent of the devil, and had to rescue another of his daughters from York's cult.

York made no direct response to Siddiq's charge that York orchestrated orgies and bade his concubines to have sex with each other.

But York did have a comeback for Siddiq's contention that the members of AAC worshipped York as a deity. "As far as people worshipping me, Siddiq is just jealous of the admiration that my followers feel for me and the love that they express," York wrote.

The underlying theme of *The Ansaar Cult* was that York was posing as a Muslim cleric, while he was operating a cult for his own sexual pleasure and monetary gain. In response to that, York plays word games. He wrote that he takes the cult characterization as a compliment. In his analysis, the word "cult" is the root of "culture" and "cultivate"; so, in the sense that he was cultivating a culture, yes, they were a cult.

Philips supported his cult allegation with statements from fourteen former AAC members, most of whom stated that they gave all they had to York when they joined – one of the basic trademarks of a cult.

In *Rebuttal*, York includes countering statements from eighteen then-current members of AAC. Those statements take up twenty-four pages of the book. Each of the AAC members offer responses to the same set of questions, about why they joined the group, why they stayed, the miracles they have witnessed York perform, and the advice they would give to those who attack York. They all gave testimonials to their love for York and to his greatness.

Yet, in these statements, the AAC insiders confirm some of Philips's basic allegations. The members were all asked what became of their personal belongings when they joined AAC. Five of the members said they had little or nothing when they joined, one made no response, and four said they were able to keep what they had.

However, eight of York's followers admitted in York's own book that they gave whatever they had to York. These eight members added that they did so willingly, seemingly believing that such a free-will proviso would get York off the hook for running a cult.

York, too, seems to think he could just wash his hands of any accountability. "I am not even the Imam anymore," he wrote in his rebuttal book. "I have retired since 1988 A.D."

While York fended off his critics by means of his self-published book, there were real people living real lives in York's cult, struggling to find the Utopia that York had promised them. It was only in recent years, after his arrest in 2002, that some of these people have felt free enough to tell their stories.

A woman who would come to be called Nasira thought she had bought salvation from the New York street peddler – and it had only cost a few dollars.

It was the street-corner purchase of a Dwight York booklet called *The Fallacy Of Easter* that radically changed her life.

At that time, early 1981, Nasira was twenty-seven years old, raising a six-year-old daughter by herself. She was living on medical disability payments, unable to continue her work as a bookkeeper. She was on the outs with her parents, and on the lookout for some alternative to the Christian faith in which she'd been raised.

"I was disillusioned with religion, with society in general," she said. "But I also wanted to be more spiritual."

The answers, she thought at the time, were in that little book. When she first read it, she became angry.

"They had lied to us," she said. All that Christian stuff about a white Jesus who got crucified and then rose from the dead was a hoax. White people used that story as the basis for their Christianity, and Christianity was nothing but a tool the whites used to keep blacks in their place. And while they were lying about that, the whites stole the glorious history away from the black Nubian people.

"We were all descended from those great people – the Queen of Sheba, Cleopatra," she said. It was all there in the book.

Nasira remembers how much *The Fallacy Of Easter* influenced her, because it was on Easter Sunday that she had her Islamic epiphany. She and her daughter, who would come to be called Aludra, were on a bus, heading for their old church and a traditional start to their Easter Sunday.

"I just stayed on the bus, passed by my old church, and went to Ansaru Allah Community," she said.

She joined, but she was not allowed to move in. It would take five more years of studying and of working twelve-to-sixteen-hour days without pay—not to mention taking a mate assigned by York, having two more children with that man and then breaking up with him—before she was allowed to live on the inside. And then it would be fifteen more years of slave labor—during which she bore two more children, these fathered by York—before she found the courage to leave. What precipitated her departure was her discovery that while she was one of his concubines, York was molesting all three of her older children.

But in those early years, Nasira thought being a woman of AAC was "a beautiful situation." From the outside, the community looked so secure and stable. The tiny front yards of the AAC buildings were planted with flowers. The children were so well behaved. "It was so clean and orderly," she said.

She did whatever York wanted her to do. She read as many of his books as she could. She prayed at all the proper times. She accepted the mate York assigned to her, partly because she knew York was displeased when his followers rejected the matches he made – even though, in theory, they had that right. She even started wearing a small nose ring in her right nostril.

She was happy to receive an assignment to tend the children, a job she later learned was considered undesirable, and even a punishment, by many of the women in the community. And she was proud that the other women were impressed with the good manners and poise of her oldest daughter, Aludra.

Aludra, however, was not particularly proud of her mother, nor of their new life.

"I grew up in America, but in a foreign country," said Aludra, who was six years old when her mother first joined AAC.

Her own life had to be radically altered, while her mother sought acceptance within the community. Having to learn a new language wasn't even the worst part.

For one thing, she chafed at her mother's insistence that she wear a Muslim-style head covering. Especially in the time while she was still in public school, she wanted to wear her hair like the other girls. "Oh no," her mother would tell her, "You're a princess."

In those years before they moved into AAC, they stood out within their family. She remembered going to a family barbecue at her grandmother's house. Her mother wouldn't let her eat what everyone else ate; they had to follow the Muslim prohibitions against eating pork. Instead, she had to eat the tofu and wheat bread that her mother had brought.

Aludra also was not fond of the man whom York had mated with her mother. He was an accomplished street peddler. He would often make his quota and then spend the rest of the day laying around their apartment. Worse, she thought the boyfriend was just leading her mother on. She believed her mother had accepted the match, thinking it would be a ticket to faster acceptance into AAC. What Aludra saw was a man who gave her mother two more babies, but who would not break away from his other wife and children.

"Parents don't understand what they put their children through," she said.

In 1986, Aludra, her mother, and her stepsister and stepbrother were finally allowed to move into AAC. For both her and her mother, life on the inside did not quite match what they had expected from a religious community.

Nasira wasn't satisfied with how the children were being cared for. Once, her son, a baby at the time, was ill, and she took him to the woman who served as a nurse for the community. The nurse simply refused to treat the baby, and there was nothing Nasira could do about it.

She also saw that as some women rose in their position in the community, that is, in their ability to get close to York, they gained the freedom to dispense with some of the stricter dictates of Islamic law. "It took me a while to realize that we could actually turn on the TV and watch it," she said.

Nevertheless, she remained devoutly faithful to whatever York preached. She believed him when he said he was the Messiah, the Reformer. She believed him when he said he was the descendant of the Mahdi. She believed him when he said his birth had been accompanied by the passage of a comet and that his heart had been removed, washed clean and then returned to his body.

Meanwhile, Aludra was miserable.

At the age of eleven, she was inserted into a community where almost all the children were required to learn and speak Arabic. Once, when she was caught speaking English, the woman in charge of her group of girls beat Aludra with a belt across the back of her legs.

Such punishments came with a strict surtax. "The house rule was, don't tell your mother," Aludra said. If any of twenty to thirty girls she lived with complained to their parents, both the girl and the parents would be punished further.

The girls would try to make light of the beatings, joking with each other about which of their wardens wielded the meanest belt. Aludra said she was determined not to show her pain. "I told myself, don't cry, no matter how much it hurts," she said.

It embarrassed her to be inspected periodically by the women in charge. She was an adolescent, and it felt awkward to have an adult checking her breath, her hair, the hemline of her robes. Even worse, the women performing these duties appeared to resent having to do them.

"It's ironic that they say kids are the future, but some of the people looked at it as a punishment to work with the kids," she said.

Aludra was kept out of the public school system for an entire year, during which her only formal education was the Arabic classes at AAC. But when she did return to the public schools, she excelled. Her gift was artistic ability. In junior high, she won an art contest. Her teachers told her that she might be a strong candidate for acceptance into a magnet school for the arts.

When "Doc," the name many in the community used for York, heard about her accomplishments, he ordered her to stop entering the art contests. Nor would she be allowed to proceed to high school in Brooklyn.

Instead, when she was twelve or thirteen, she was admitted to the small clique of adolescent and teenage girls at Backstreet, the building within the community that York used as his recording studio.

"Getting to go to Backstreet was a big thing for the girls," Aludra said.

In Doc's private domain, the girls did not have to follow the rigid rules set down for the rest of the community. They no longer had to listen either to their parents or to the bitter women who served as babysitters.

York set up a basement room at Backstreet especially for the girls. There, they could wear regular clothes, even short skirts. They were free to enjoy the pizza, ice cream, and soda Doc provided. They could watch videos, and sometimes, have boys join them. Aludra became fond of York's son, Malik.

The early days at Backstreet were a revelation to Aludra. For the first time, she saw the man whom she'd been told was a god behaving just like any other man. "The first time I saw Doc drinking something, I thought, like, you eat and drink? I thought you were like Jesus."

After a time, one of York's concubines started the process of educating Aludra about what was expected of her, in return for all her new privileges. The woman told her she needed to be prepared for relations with her eventual husband. In their spiritual homeland, Sudan, such practical lessons about sex were given first to a maiden by a male relative, maybe an uncle, or a father.

It would soon be made clear to Aludra just who would handle those duties of initiation in her case. But first, the concubine gave Aludra some preparatory lessons. The woman used a plastic penis to demonstrate the proper way to perform oral sex on a man. For reinforcement, pornographic videos started to be included in the video fare made available to the girls at Backstreet.

One day, the concubine instructed Aludra to dance nude and she videotaped the performance. Later, the woman told her that York was quite impressed with her.

He must have been, because he added the tape to his private collection, where it was later discovered by his son Malik – who had thought that he was Aludra's boyfriend.

York also relayed his desire to see more of Aludra's younger stepsister, Jokara, who was then about six. She's cute, York told her, bring her around to Backstreet.

In the early 1990s, York started spending most of his time at his Catskills retreat, and the Backstreet Girls were set up in special quarters close to him. The girls were told to expand the junior harem, and so the group grew to about a dozen at times.

In the country, York dropped any subtleties about what he wanted from the girls. He demanded that they perform a whole range of sexual variations with him. Aludra said she was about fifteen when York initiated her. First, he had her perform oral sex on him, and then, he performed anal sex on her. Sometimes, York set up a camera on a tripod to videotape their sexual encounters, and sometimes he had one of the concubines do the taping.

York manipulated the girls to make them continue to comply with his sexual demands, Aludra said. The ones who gave him sex without complaining got better food and sometimes, little presents. Those who refused got cut off. Additionally, York would disparage the non-compliant girls in front of the others, thus stoking the rivalries among the girls for his affections.

York also segregated his special girls from the rest of the community. They were no longer allowed to have boys in their midst. "Those boys just want to get in your pants," York once told Aludra.

He rewarded his girls with little bits of authority that elevated them in the community. For example, he would give the girls notes with his handwritten orders, which the girls would then deliver to the proper adult in the community. Sometimes, these notes would be eviction orders.

York also encouraged the girls to think ill of their parents. "Your parents don't care about you," Aludra heard him say. What he did not say was that the girls were cut off from their parents primarily by the rules York had established. Adults worked at least twelve hours a day. The children lived separate from their parents.

Nevertheless, he played on the children's ambivalence toward their parents, who were so close, yet so far away. "How could parents in their right minds let you girls go off upstate?" he once told Aludra. He also told her that the only reason he did not kick her mother out of the community was his affection for her (Aludra).

"He said his own mother had deserted him, so we couldn't have friends," Aludra said. It was around this time that York ordered Aludra to bring to him her stepsister Jokara, then eight, and another girl, then six, to him. He later told Aludra that the younger children were accomplished in performing oral sex on him.

At first, Nasira was honored that York had selected her oldest daughter to be part of his special group of children. "It was a privilege to be close to Baba," she said, using another of the community's pet names for York. She herself was moving up in the organization, getting assigned to office jobs in the important real estate section.

It didn't concern her that Aludra and the other girls spent so much time with Baba. Once, when she asked what the girls did to pass all that time, Aludra hung her head and answered, "Watch TV." Later, Nasira regretted not pressing her daughter for more information, but at that time, she suspected nothing.

Perhaps that was partly because Nasira's personal relationship with York was heading into deeper waters.

After she first moved into AAC, she wasn't interested in taking on another man. Her previous relationships had failed, and she was left with three fatherless children to raise. York sought to mate her with three different AAC men, but she refused them all. There was always a possibility that if she accepted a mate, and that man was transferred to a community in another city, she would have to follow. She didn't want to move; life was complicated enough. Besides, some of the AAC men were clearly unstable.

She thought she would be able to remain unattached and free to pursue spiritual growth within York's brand of Islam.

"I think I put the 'N' in naïve," Nasira said, looking back at those times.

Things became even more complicated when York made his move on her. First, he sent a message that he found her attractive. She remained coy. So, he dropped the romance and gave her an ultimatum – unless she became one of his concubines, she could forget about keeping her relatively privileged job.

So, she joined the harem. Mostly, it was a liaison of practicality for her. "At no point could I say I was in love with Dr. York," she said.

York also had a practical motive for elevating her from office worker to "wife." "Who better to run things than your wives," he told her.

She became one of the women who maneuvered against each other and waited anxiously for the summons from York. "The competition was horrible," she said.

At that time, she never guessed that while he was having sex on his demand with her, he was doing the same to her children.

Asad, the man from Trinidad who raised one of York's daughters and whom York had called his "close friend," didn't remain friendly, after he discovered that his wife had become one of York's concubines. Years later, he would lose all traces of friendliness, when he discovered that York was also preying on his children.

York's entanglements with Asad's family started in 1973, when York made a community-planting visit to Trinidad. There was a division between Muslim groups on the island then, reflecting differences between Muslims who'd immigrated from Asia and black Muslims descended from people brought to the island as slaves. York had a strong appeal to the latter group.

"He appeared righteous," Asad said of York. "He claimed he was from a perfect family. He told us to read his books on Islam and black history. He quoted from the Qu'ran and the Bible."

He joined the group in Trinidad. He also married a young woman who was pregnant with York's child. Over the next ten years or so, they had six children of their own. They ran a small boutique, and he thought they had a stable life.

Then, his wife expressed a desire for her oldest daughter to meet York, the girl's biological father and the spiritual leader of their community. She took the girl and left for Brooklyn; after awhile, she sent back word that she intended to stay. She said the rest of the family should join them.

Asad took his children and followed his wife. He soon discovered that Brooklyn was no island in the sun.

"People actually lived in filth," Asad said. "The apartments had rats, and some had no lights." In spite of their conditions, the people of AAC worked to better York's life, not their own.

"The brothers would bring in all their money, and he wouldn't give them a cup of coffee. He treated them with so much scorn," Asad said. Anyone of the men who returned to AAC without making their quotas were liable to be beaten by York's thugs.

Also, the practice of an Islamic lifestyle wasn't as important to York as it had seemed back in Trinidad. Instead, religion just seemed to be another of York's tricks. "He used Islam as the bait, and then he put his claws into people when they joined," Asad said.

The major revelation for him, though, was the change in his wife.

"He made her one of his wives," Asad said. He found himself powerless to fight the decision by the mother of his children to become one of York's concubines. "I couldn't even talk to her," he said.

After only a few weeks in the community, Asad left, but he stayed close. He got a job in the New York area, and brought most of the children to live with him. He visited his wife and oldest daughter in Brooklyn and at one point convinced her to move back with him and try to reconcile. It didn't work, and she moved back to York.

In the late 1980s – about the same time as York publicly called him a friend – York sent Asad a message stating that he was no longer welcome to visit AAC. At that point, Asad divorced his wife.

Their two youngest daughters stayed with their mother. One of the little girls caught York's eye.

Alima, pregnant and sick, was sleeping one night in a trailer at Camp Jazzir. A woman shook her awake, saying she had a message for her from York: Get out. Now.

Alima begged for a chance to talk to York. She had borne him two children, and she was carrying their third. Surely, there must be some mistake.

Her other two pregnancies had been hard, but this one had been a nightmare. She was frequently sick. She couldn't get enough to eat. She was afraid something might be wrong with her baby, but she'd never been allowed to go to a doctor. In her condition, she couldn't work the twelve-to-sixteen-hour shifts York demanded of his women. In the cutthroat world of York's harem, this only gave her rivals ammunition to use against her.

She was accused of being lazy, of feigning illness to get out of work. These were sins punishable by banishment.

Her appeals were futile. York refused to meet with her. She asked if she could leave her other children in the community until she got better, because she couldn't care for them in her present state. That too was refused. She left that same night with her son and daughter for the Brooklyn AAC, but she was considered an outcast there as well.

Alima wound up calling her parents in New Jersey and going back to the home she'd run away from about twelve years earlier, at the age of sixteen. They sheltered her, and she went to a hospital to deliver the baby.

At the hospital, she followed York's orders by not naming him as the child's father. Instead, she filled the blank with the name "Rafiq Cone." She wasn't even a baseball fan, but the name of the star pitcher popped into her head.

Alima knew that York would never acknowledge this child, whom she named Abraham. The baby could not breathe properly, he was afflicted with dwarfism, and he had a severely malformed spine. Doctors told her the child would spend his life in a hospital bed and never be able to speak or to learn. Alima turned back to York for help.

York didn't have much to do with his healthy children. This profoundly disabled baby could never be acknowledged as the progeny of the god incarnate. York made arrangements for Alima to move to Florida to an AAC community there. She went on welfare, and Abraham was made a ward of the state.

Despite everything, Alima wanted to go back. "I was still in love with him," she said.

She tried calling York, but he would not come to the phone. "It literally tore my heart apart," Alima said.

Her heart had been York's since she was a teenager.

There was a strong emphasis on the Bible in the home where she was raised, but there was also alcoholism and a lot of anger. She wanted to run away, but she didn't have much in the way of survival skills. "I was a Mama's girl, not street-wise at all," she said.

She got as far as Philadelphia, across the river from her home in Camden. There she found the local branch of York's cult. Though she was interested in the content of York's books, she was more deeply influenced by the authoritative manner in which they were presented.

"They seemed to have the answer to all my questions, so I assumed they were telling me the truth," she said. "I was in awe."

There was also a strong appeal to belonging to a self-contained, peace-loving community. "I didn't want to be out in the world, the world was going to destruction," Alima said. "I wanted to be where there was love and unity."

She told her parents that she was moving into the community. She told them about learning Arabic, wearing the veil, and working long hours in the laundry and the kitchen. Her father told her it sounded a lot like slavery. Her mother signed a permission form so that she could join.

About a year later, she visited the Brooklyn base of AAC and had her first encounter with York. He gave her a quick glance and commented, "She's got long eyelashes."

A few months later, she was summoned to come to live in the Brooklyn community, where she was first assigned to do research for York's books. She found material for him in every source from supermarket tabloids to religious tracts.

After a few months, York sent an emissary to tell her that he was attracted to her. The woman also told her that she would be given the honor of being called to clean York's private quarters.

Alima was eighteen years old and a virgin, but she knew what that sort of summons meant. She went to York willingly. "He's so smart. He knows all those languages. He's so rich," she recalled thinking at the time.

Being a concubine didn't exempt her from observing the community rules, particularly when she was in public. Whenever she needed to go outside AAC, she had to apply to the AAC Census Department for a pass. To obtain the pass, she had to fill out a form stating where she was going, what she planned to do, whom she was going to see, and how long she intended to be away.

When she did leave, it was almost always as part of a group of women, all of whom had been instructed to avoid contact with men and to look down if they happened to pass a man on the streets.

Her diet was the same as most others in AAC – beans, rice, soup, lentils, macaroni and cheese, and some vegetables. York liked his women slim, and he wanted them to stay that way.

She became pregnant with her first child by York, believing that bearing the Master's child would bring her honor. "All the women wanted to bear his child," Alima said. "They wanted to be part of his holiness." Perhaps that was why they competed so intently for his affections. "They were scratching at each other to get a night with him," she said. "He was the god."

Her birthing experience turned out to be less than honorable. When she went to the hospital to deliver, she was accompanied by a small group of AAC men and women, who answered all the hospital's questions for her. She obeyed the order to put a false name on the space for "father" on the birth certificate.

York took no particular interest in the baby boy, which was par for the course. When her son was born, York had at least thirty other children under the age of ten around the community. Within the next month after Alima gave birth, she estimated that three or four other concubines gave birth to children fathered by York. Throughout the years he reigned over the cult, he probably fathered somewhere between one hundred and two hundred children, she estimated.

York cared as little for the mothers of his children as he did for his offspring. Once, he told Alima, "Women are like automobiles. When you get tired of one, just get a new one."

Samarra became a member of Ansaru Allah Community not by her choice, but by her mother's. In 1986, her mother moved into AAC, bringing Samarra and her older sister with her. They stayed in Brooklyn for a short time, and were then assigned to move to the community in Philadelphia.

In 1990, they were summoned to move into Camp Jazzir. By this time the sister was old enough to gain access to a settlement from a car accident that had been placed into trust for her and Samarra, so she left to live on her own. Samarra's share would later play an important role in the development of York's new religious schtick.

At the country retreat, one of York's concubines started talking to Samarra about sex, in particular, the prospect of her having sex with York. He followed up these discussions with personal conversations with the girl on the same topic, usually touching her as they talked. She was about fourteen. For a while, she held out, saying she wished to remain a virgin.

But she also wished to be part of the Backstreet Girls, the growing gaggle of teenagers and adolescents that York mostly kept sequestered within the camp. The other girls told her that in order to belong to the club, she had to pay the same dues as all the others, that is, she would have to have sex with York whenever he demanded.

When she made her first payment, she was fifteen. She was old enough to have reservations about what was happening, and sometimes she was strong enough to turn him down. When that happened, York would criticize her in front of the other girls. When she was "good," York would buy her little trinkets, as he did for all the others.

"The Love Man Is Back!" proclaimed the promotional article meant to help re-launch York's musical career. The wavy-haired, goateed man depicted in an accompanying photograph was none other than Dwight York.

Being a semi-retired Muslim cleric apparently started to be a bit of a bore for York. By the late 1980s, when he was in his mid-forties, he had, for most practical purposes, moved to the mountains. It seemed a good time to make another musical move as well.

He opened a record store in the Sullivan County seat, Liberty. He also started passing out fliers, both upstate and around Brooklyn, promoting his music-related ventures, which included a new recording studio and a talent and modeling agency. He also set up a management agency, and among his clients he listed the "hot" female R&B group called "SHE."

Another of York's groups was called "Petite," who York described in a promotional article as "four young ladies who sing their hearts out." In another self-promotional article, Petite was referred to as "an all-female group that York considers as his children."

In a personal bio released by York in 1986, he claimed he was "pondering a rap-reggae group consisting of three girls called "Undercover Lovers."

York stated in a 1985 article that his interest in developing young talent was primarily to help improve society. "When I started 'Passion,' it was with one thought in mind – to help the children. Our children today are surrounded by so many negative examples that we wanted to promote a positive image through something which the youth could identify with closely – music."

He was not shy about promoting himself as well as his clients. "Passion Records' Dr. York certainly looks like one hell of a romantic dude," stated a 1985 promotional article. "The white dinner jacket, gold medallions, silk handkerchief and wet-look hair must surely be enough to turn any woman wild."

He described himself as "a lover of classical art who speaks seven languages." He boasted that his studios would become "the Motown of the East Coast." When he released an album called "New" in the late 1980s, he claimed that it received "rave reviews from the young and old."

He was, however, a prophet without a hit in his own land. His explanation for that was to claim he was more popular abroad than in the U.S. He was, by his account, taking the world by storm. He stated he would soon launch a worldwide concert tour, but that never happened. One of his promotional articles stated, "His influence is spreading everywhere, enabling him to acquire the favor of music lovers all over the world."

Like the phantom world tour, his career never took off. But he had an explanation for that, too.

In the late 1980s, he produced a music video called "Let's Talk." It was a showcase for his singing talents, featuring five solo performances, a couple of dance numbers, and a couple of songs by his musical protégés. In between the songs, the video depicted York making commentaries on his music and his life. Those commentaries were also York's opportunity to blame a conspiracy in the music industry for his overall lack of success.

"The majors would never make a deal with Dr. York, they can't control Dr. York," he said in one of the video's commentaries. The major record labels wouldn't sign him, because they were afraid of his power, he claimed.

"They're afraid of another Barry Gordy Jr., afraid of another Motown," York stated. "They won't give a black man a shot, unless he comes from them. If black entertainers ever came together, we could make it. But as long as we're divided, we're conquered."

In a segment of the video headed "Dr. York, the man behind the empire," York gives a tour of his recording studio facilities and puts in a plug for his talent agency. Despite the decidedly non-Islamic trappings, York claimed that his Muslim faith "motivates me to do everything I do."

However, the message in York's music was strictly secular. As he sings, with his slick hair and pastel tuxedos, he projects a sort of Barry White-wannabee image. The camera lingers on him affectionately, as he moves through a castle setting and charms beautiful black women with his ballads.

Despite all the money, time, and energy he clearly invested in his music, York never charmed the music industry or the record-buying public. He never got a contract and never made a hit record. Anyone who views one of York's music videos would likely agree with the judgment of the music industry; in terms of musical talent, York simply wasn't very good.

He did, however, use the lure of the music industry to reel in another "wife."

One day in 1991, a young woman who would come to be called Badra had some time to kill while she waited for a bus in Liberty, New York. The bus stop happened to be near York Records, a new music store. She went in to browse. She saw the "Love Doctor" poster on the wall, and there, in the back part of the store, was the man from the poster.

She had no idea who "The Love Doctor" was, but she could see that he was leering at her quite openly. It kind of creeped her out, she recalled.

The Love Doctor in the flesh had a brief conversation with the store manager, then he left. Then, the manager came to her and told her that the man he was talking to was Dr. York, the owner of the store and a big deal in the music business. He had a big place out in the country near Parksville, the manager told her, and he wanted her phone number.

At the time, Badra was too distracted to be impressed. Her life was crumbling beneath her. She was a twenty-year-old mother of two daughters, four-year-old Azizah and two-year-old Farah. Her parents had broken up; her mother moved away and her father stayed on in Liberty, but she and her father did not get along well. Plus, her relationship with the father of her youngest daughter was falling apart.

She turned down that first approach, but a couple of weeks later, she was in an entirely different place in her life. She had broken up with her boyfriend and feeling very much alone. So, she gave her phone number to the record store manager.

Soon, Dr. York called to ask her out. The man was more than twice her age, but he did have some appealing qualities, and he had come along at the right time. She was open to something different, ready to hop aboard a nicely-decorated bus that had stopped for her, no matter where it was heading.

"I was depressed. I wanted to get on with my life," Badra said. "Here's this guy driving around in a Cadillac, and he's interested in me."

She quickly entered into a romantic relationship with York and accepted a job working at a new record store he was opening in a nearby city. It seemed like a great deal. York told her that the women of his community would babysit her children while she worked.

Things didn't work out quite as smoothly as planned. She had moved back in with her father, and they argued over issues like how much of the utility bill she should pay. When she cashed in some bonds that her father had bought for her daughters, tensions in the household escalated even more.

At the record shop, business was falling off the charts. York had stocked the shelves partly with his books. She had no interest in the books, and people weren't buying them or the records. York told her he could no longer afford to pay her a salary for her work.

He had a better idea, though. "You love Doc. Why don't you move in with me?" he told her.

The deal was, she would become what York called "Wife No. 19." However, he also promised Badra that she would really be Number One in his heart.

That didn't work out either. After Badra and her daughters moved into Camp Jazzir, she discovered that life as a concubine was not all that York had cracked it up to be.

Not only was she clearly not Number One, she had a hard time seeing how she was Number 19. She was just one of the harem, women who slept in rooms where nearly all the space was taken up by stacks of bunk beds. They didn't spend much time in the crowded sleeping quarters, however. She worked long hours without pay as a seamstress, and she and the other concubines were always on call for York's pleasure. And this was supposed to be the privileged group within the community.

York would frequently send his summons via speakerphone, summoning the woman he wanted at that moment. All the women seemed to be so anxious to hear their names called. "They all wanted to be close to him," she said, adding that she answered dutifully whenever her name was called.

However, she was viewed as something of an outsider, since she had not made a religious conversion, as had most of the other women. She wore the robes, but she never bought the religion stuff – and she wasn't as careful as she was supposed to be about following the rules.

Once, York became furious with her, after he caught her talking with a man of the community. She told him that she just wanted to go for a morning walk, and there was nothing personal about the conversation. Nevertheless, York roared at her, "You just want to show your ass in front of the brothers!"

Her punishment was to be moved from the concubines' quarters into the dormitory where the rest of the women lived. York told her that her daughters could stay with the other concubines, and she allowed it, believing her girls would be treated better there.

During this time, her father died. Her ties to her old world, however strained they might have been, were gone now. Her new world was turning out to be a disappointment, but she didn't see any alternative. She stayed and obeyed.

The question of why she remained still causes her to pause. Her best answer: "I was a zombie."

The country life wasn't agreeing all that well with York either. The Sullivan County authorities were not as pliant as some in Brooklyn had been. He couldn't build whatever he wanted on his land, and once, the county took him to court to stop some un-permitted construction. York lost. Also, he was facing a tax bill in the neighborhood of $200,000, and he didn't particularly want to pay it.

Returning to his base in Bushwick, with all the ongoing conflicts there, didn't seem like a very attractive option.

Then there was the matter of the FBI. York had long warned his people to be vigilant for FBI infiltrators. In the early 1990s, that concern was more prudent than paranoid. He was the target of a domestic terrorism investigation, one that was being made with as many as fifteen confidential informants. Clearly, the heat was on.

In late 1992, Nasira, who was then working in the real estate department, was told by York to start looking for properties in Atlanta, Georgia. She found an apartment complex in the city that might work as a new home for their community. The seller wanted to negotiate directly with York, but York refused. "He didn't know business details," she said.

Nasira kept bargaining with the owner and was able to get the price reduced considerably, even though York did not take part in the negotiations. He seemed to like the prospect of moving to Atlanta, though. He even made plans for his private quarters, applying to buy a condominium in the exclusive Buckhead district of the city.

Just before the deal was to be closed, Kathy Johnson, York's favorite concubine at the time, returned from a separate property-scouting mission to Georgia. She had located a four hundred-acre tract of pasture and woodlands for sale in the central part of the state. The asking price was slightly less than $1 million.

York nixed Nasira's deal and went with Kathy Johnson's property. "Guess who got fired for that – moi," Nasira said.

In February 1993, York announced that in two days, he and a select group of his followers would be leaving for Georgia. The others were told to wait until they were called.

York also left about $100,000 in unpaid bills behind. He told his department heads, "Y'all figure it out."

Nasira said they were able to pay off most of the bills by re-printing one of York's strongest-selling books, *Leviathan 666*. As for York, he "snatched up the girls and left," she said.

Those left behind recall that period as especially miserable. York shut down his main house on the Camp Jazzir property. That left about sixty people, most of them women and children, living in the double-wide trailers that had been the concubines' quarters. The power in the main lodge had been shut off, and most of the windows had been pulled out and shipped south.

"Everyone piled into 102 (the number designation for the trailer)," Nasira said. "There was absolutely nothing to do. There was a line for the bathroom twenty-four hours a day."

It was the middle of winter. The group of urban blacks was confined to trailer in a snow-covered woods, miles from the nearest town.

"It was just horrible," Badra said. People tried to wash their clothes, but they never fully dried out in the cramped quarters. She kept thinking this must be some kind of loyalty test.

Actually, it was more of a weeding-out process. Only the followers deemed most loyal by York would be called to come to the new land. Those calls came spaced a few weeks apart, and those selected were driven down to Georgia in small groups. Those who were not called were told to go back to Brooklyn.

No one in those trailers had ever lived in the South. They knew little or nothing about where they were going. Yet, they were relieved and joyful when they received their calls.

They were going to rejoin their master, Dwight York, in the Promised Land of Putnam County, Georgia.

CHAPTER 4
The Artificial Nuwaubian (1993-1997)

It was not possible to tell if the artificial Negro were meant to be young or old; he looked too miserable to be either. He was meant to look happy, because his mouth was stretched up at the corners but the chipped eye and the angle he was cocked at gave him a wild look of misery instead. – Flannery O'Connor, *The Artificial Nigger*

It was as if Dwight York tossed himself, with B'rer Rabbit's pluck but B'rer Bear's brains, into the thorniest of literary briar patches.

Almost certainly, York was unaware that his new Promised Land in Georgia was home to some of the primary architects of the traditions of Southern literature. He thought he was starting a new, racially pure nation. Instead, he was making himself the latest in a long line of strange characters who have populated racial dramas of fact and fiction, set in the small slice of Middle Georgia consisting of Putnam County and its near neighbors.

This is where Joel Harris Harris first heard the plantation slave tales that would become the Uncle Remus stories. About a century later, just down the road from that same plantation, Alice Walker, the daughter of black sharecroppers, started scribbling lines of poems in the red dirt and in the margins of Sears,

Roebuck catalogues. Less than twenty miles south of that area, a frail white woman named Flannery O'Connor retreated to her family farm, Andalusia, where she wrote some of the most powerful prose of her time.

The authors never knew each other, yet they are connected through their themes and their settings. All three were, at stages of their lives, painfully shy people; yet they wrote forcefully about race.

None of them, however, ever conjured up a character quite as bizarre as Dwight York. Much of what they wrote, however, helps the reader understand how York and his seemingly alien band seem to fit quite comfortably into the racial spectrum of their South. Their work also seems to presage the themes of the Nuwaubian saga and to provide at least a partial explanation for York's appeal.

The land of their fiction seems eerily perfect for this real-life drama. It was almost as if Putnam County selected York, not the other way around.

Joel Harris Harris grew up as a fatherless child in antebellum Eatonton. His father, a young itinerant laborer, deserted his mother, who worked in taverns and took in sewing to support herself and her son.

The small, redheaded, freckle-faced boy was essentially free to roam the town and the surrounding woods. He did odd jobs for tradesmen, both black and white. He ran down rabbits and raccoons in the woods and raided peach orchards and melon patches.

In 1862, when he was about fourteen, Harris came across a want ad in *The Countryman,* a regionally-circulated newspaper chronicling current events, business, politics, and literature, and news of the ongoing Civil War. The paper was written, edited, and printed at a plantation outside of Eatonton called Turnwold. The ad read: "An active, intelligent white boy, fourteen or fifteen years of age, is wanted at this office, to learn the printing business."

Harris got himself to Turnwold, met the plantation master Joseph Turner, and got the job. He moved to the plantation. As he worked as a printer's devil, he also had time to explore Mr. Turner's library, one of the best private collections in the South.

He also had plenty of time to spend with the plantation slaves. He listened to old slaves tell stories in which the heroes were wily rabbits and the villains, predatory foxes. What the boy heard were stories that were more humorous in tone than angry. If, in the unlikely event that the slaves shared any of their rage at their condition, those elements never made it into the stories Harris would re-tell as a man.

Rather, Harris saw the gentle yet slyly intelligent themes of the stories as a way of portraying a side of the black character that contradicted the lazy, stupid image that prevailed in those times. He saw there was more to blacks than was being depicted in minstrel shows.

In his introduction to his first published collection of plantation tales, *Uncle Remus, His Songs And Sayings,* Harris sought to explain the underlying racial truths he saw in the stories: "At least it is a fable thoroughly characteristic of the Negro; and it needs no scientific investigation to show why he selects as his hero the weakest and most harmless of the animals, and brings him out victorious in contests with the bear, the wolf, and the fox. It is not virtue that triumphs, but helplessness; it is not malice but mischievousness."

Harris was a teenager when Sherman marched to the sea through Putnam County, and he became an adult in the conquered South of the Reconstruction era. He worked at newspapers in Macon, New Orleans, and Forsyth, Georgia, before coming to the *Atlanta Constitution* in 1876 to write a daily column of what he called "pithy and philosophical sayings."

One day in 1877, Harris apparently ran low on pith. So, for his column, he re-told one of the stories he'd heard as a boy from the plantation slaves. It was the tale of how B'rer Bear invited B'rer Rabbit for dinner, intending to make the rabbit his main course; but the rabbit outwits the bear.

The column brought a strong response. Readers wanted more, and for the next fifteen years, Harris obliged. His columns became nationally syndicated and collected into more than a dozen books. By the turn of the century, his devoted fans included President Theodore Roosevelt. Once, the President had a short layover at the Atlanta train depot, and he insisted that Harris be fetched, so that the two could meet.

In his youth, Harris had been a staunch Confederate, one who admired men of letters, though he refused to put himself in their ranks. He thought of Southern literature as something apart from, and perhaps more noble than, the general run of writing. In a letter to the editor of a Southern literary magazine, *The Mercury,* Harris wrote, "I believe it *(The Mercury)* is the only publication in the state, with the exception of *The Countryman,* which does not model itself on the vile publications of the North...Hoping that you succeed in all your endeavors to establish an undefiled Southern literature, and that *The Mercury* may prove a blessing to the Confederacy, I remain..."

Despite his Rebel sympathies, Harris grew to admire President Abraham Lincoln. He often told people that, after the war itself, Lincoln's assassination was the second worst tragedy to befall the South.

Perhaps it was that sense of loss that led Harris to romanticize the relationships between blacks and whites in the Old South. In *A Story Of The War,* Harris recounts how his real-life model for Uncle Remus tells a woman visiting Atlanta some years after the war how he took over the job of supervising

From a Nuwaubian poster.

the plantation slaves. "Miss Sally," the wife of the plantation owner "Marse Jeems," asks him to take charge while her husband was off fighting for the *Confederacy.*

"Mistiss, you can des'pen on de ole nigger," Remus tells Sally.

Later, Marse Jeems rides back to the plantation, but Remus spots a Union sniper getting ready to shoot him from a hiding place in the trees.

"I know'd dat man wuz gwinter shoot Marse Jeems if he could, en dat wuz mo'n I could stan'. Manys en manys de time dat I nuss dat boy, and hilt'im in dese arms, and toted 'im on dis back, and w'en I see dat Yankee lay dat gun 'cross a lim' en take aim at Mars Jeems, I up wid my ole rifle, en shet my eyes en let de man have all she had."

The Northen woman in the story seems perplexed. "Do you mean to say that you shot the Union soldier, when you knew he was fighting for your freedom?"

"Co'se, I know all about dat," Remus answers, "en it sorter made cole chills run up my back; but w'en I see dat man take aim, en Marse Jeems gwine home to Ole Miss and Miss Sally, I disremembered all 'bout freedom en lammed aloose."

Harris notes in his introduction to the book that this particular Uncle Remus story is true.

Harris loved Eatonton till he died, and Eatonton still loves him a century after his death. Even today, B'rer Rabbit is sort of an unofficial mascot for Eatonton. His likeness can be seen on banners around the downtown. There is a mural on the wall of a downtown building depicting the animal characters of the Uncle Remus tales, as they were brought to life in the Disney animated movie

"*Song Of The South.*" A few blocks from the county courthouse, there is a small "Uncle Remus Museum" dedicated to Harris and his characters; but here too, it is the idealized version of the rabbit, the bear, and the fox that are displayed most prominently.

Not everybody loves Remus.

Alice Walker, another literary giant born and raised in Putnam County, thought the old slave was a compliant hostage in a nefarious cultural hijacking.

In her first novel, *The Third Life Of Grange Copeland,* Walker "lammed aloose" on Uncle Remus, much as he had done on the Yankee sniper. Speaking through her title character, she wrote, "Grange thought Uncle Remus was a fool, because if he was so smart that he could make the animals smart too, then why the hell, asked Grange, didn't he dump the little white boy (or tie him up and hold him for ransom) and go to Congress and see what he could do about smartening up the country, which, in Grange's view, was passing dumb."

Grange went on to state that Remus should have been "making the white folks let go of the stuff that's rightfully ours," rather than doing things like starring in cartoon movies and television commercials. "We needs us a goddam statesman and all he can do is act like some shag-assed minstrel," Grange stated.

Eatonton in the 1950s was a good place for an intelligent black girl like Alice Walker, the youngest of a sharecropping couple's eight children, to develop a sense of outrage.

"I was an exile in my hometown," Walker wrote in the essay collection *In Search Of Our Mothers' Gardens,* "and grew to despise its white citizens almost as much as I loved the Georgia countryside, where I fished and swam and walked through fields of Black-eyed Susans, or sat in contemplation beside the giant pine tree my father 'owned,' because when he was a boy and walking five miles to school during the winter he and his schoolmates had built a fire each morning in the base of the tree, and the tree still lived – although there was a blackened triangular hole in it large enough for me to fit inside."

The following background material on Walker was taken from *Living By Grace,* a biography of Walker by Chris Danielle.

When she was eight, Walker was playing cowboys and Indians with her siblings, when one of them discharged a BB gun, and the pellet hit her in the eye, wounding her severely. Later, a brother would tell her that her father flagged down a passing car to obtain a ride to the hospital, but when the white driver heard the request to transport a bleeding black girl, he drove off.

The accident left Walker with physical and emotional scars. For a long time, she tried not to look directly at people, in order to conceal her disfigurement. She became solitary and shy. But at the age of fourteen, she went to visit her older brother, Bill, in Boston; he arranged for an operation that repaired her damaged eye. After that, she was voted Most Popular at her segregated high school and was named Queen of the Senior Prom.

After high school, Walker was at a crossroads. She loved her home place, but she was outraged by its prevailing racist attitudes. "On hot Saturday afternoons of my childhood, I gazed longingly through the window of the corner drugstore where white youngsters sat in air-conditioned comfort and drank Cokes and nibbled ice-cream cones. Black people could come in and buy, but what they bought they couldn't eat inside," she wrote.

Her ambivalence about leaving home was reinforced by her inspiration over Dr. Martin Luther King Jr.'s vision of a Georgia rid of the stain of racism. She was in the audience in Washington, D.C., when King delivered his "I Have A Dream" speech, and she wrote of how it affected her: "I saw again what he was uniquely able to make me see: that I had a claim to the land of my birth. Those red hills of Georgia were mine, and nobody was going to force me away from there until I myself was good and ready to go."

But she did leave, first for Spelman College in Atlanta, and after two years there, for Sarah Lawrence College in New York. She would say that for her to continue to love her birthplace, she had to leave it.

However, she carried with her the impression that her hometown was a sometimes brutal place.

"'Eatonton is a violent little town,' is what is said by locals when all other attempts to explain some recent disaster have proved useless," she wrote in an afterword to *The Third Life Of Grange Copeland*. "The black people there, as in so many parts of the world, are an oppressed colony, and in their frustration and rage, they of course kill each other."

Even as a girl, Walker saw the results of violence committed by blacks against blacks. Her sister worked as a beautician for both the living and the dead, running a beauty parlor in the same building that housed a funeral home. Once, her sister brought Alice to the undertaker's side of the building, where she showed her the corpse of a woman beaten to death by her man. The memory of the dead woman's horribly battered face would fade from Walker's memory, even though she used it for a description of a killing in one of her books. What stayed with her, she wrote, was the sight of the woman's calloused foot, which could be seen through the hole in her newspaper-lined shoe.

After college, Walker married a white man, with whom she worked in the Civil Rights movement in southeast Georgia and in Mississippi. They divorced and she moved to Northern California, where she took a sabbatical to write her best-known novel, *The Color Purple*, about Celie, a black woman of the small-town South who ultimately survives poverty and domestic abuse.

In 1986, the movie version of *The Color Purple* was given its world premiere in Eatonton, but that event is little remembered. There is no operating movie theater in Eatonton today.

Walker also set up a scholarship fund for students from the Putnam County area, but over the years, she was practically the only contributor, and its works have essentially ceased.

Unlike the more visible monuments to Harris, it's a little more difficult to pick up traces of Walker's life in Eatonton. At the local tourism office, a visitor can get a flyer that outlines a self-driving tour of Alice Walker sites, including the farm her family sharecropped and the church where her parents took her to worship.

She later rejected her parents' Christianity, which she termed "a white man's palliative in the form of religion" – not so much different from the observations Dwight York would use to persuade people to disavow Christianity and follow him.

However, Walker saw nobility in the way her parents lived out their faith. "Their lives testify to a greater comprehension of the teachings of Jesus than the lives of people who sincerely believe a God must have a color and that there can be such a phenomenon as a 'white' church," she wrote in her essay "The Black Writer And The Southern Experience."

Despite her sometimes harsh memories of Eatonton, Walker still visits the area irregularly. Her sister, Ruth Walker Hood, who lives in the Atlanta area, said Walker likes to spend time with friends and relatives and doing things like shopping at the Piggly Wiggly supermarket.

Walker has also returned to an admiration for Flannery O'Connor. As a college student, Walker was enthralled by the unstintingly realistic view of race in O'Connor's works. Later, Walker temporarily crossed O'Connor off her list of favorites, mostly because black writers were most often excluded in those times from discussions of important Southern writers.

In her essay "Beyond The Peacock," Walker writes of a 1974 visit she made with her mother to Andalusia, O'Connor's farm near Milledgeville. The Walker family had sharecropped a farm just up the road from Andalusia for about a year, when Walker was a girl.

The two Walker women first went to the place where they had lived. Minnie "Lou" Walker remembered it as the home where she had her first washing machine. Alice Walker was a bit dismayed that the house had been allowed to crumble, while O'Connor's modest farmhouse at Andalusia had been maintained and cared for, even though it was also abandoned.

But when they got to Andalusia, the scene struck a pleasant chord in Alice

Walker's memory. As a girl, she had passed that field many times on her way to town, and she remembered the setting as "the only pleasant thing I recall from that year...it represented beauty and unchanging peace." She had never met the frail woman who lived and wrote there.

For Walker, O'Connor succeeded, perhaps more than any writer, in realistically portraying the lives of whites and blacks in the South. In *Beyond The Peacock,* Walker wrote of O'Connor, "She was for me the first great modern writer from the South...And yes, I could say yes, these white folks without the magnolia (who are indifferent to the tree's existence), and these black folks without melons and superior racial patience, these are like the Southerners I know."

Walker proclaimed herself "shocked and delighted" at O'Connor's characters, "whose humanity if not their sanity is taken for granted, and who are miserable, ugly, narrow-minded, atheistic, and of intense racial smugness and arrogance, with not a graceful, pretty one anywhere in sight who is not, at the same time, a joke."

As Walker and her mother were preparing to drive away from Andalusia, O'Connor's peacocks fanned their tails for them, to the point of blocking their exit for a short time. The birds were O'Connor's trademark pets; she loved them and wrote eloquently about them. O'Connor welcomed all sorts of visitors to Andalusia, and had she lived long enough, Walker would likely have been among them. Perhaps the peacocks were just passing along O'Connor's regrets.

In some ways, it would be hard to imagine a woman more different from Alice Walker than Flannery O'Connor. Born in 1925, O'Connor's early life was cushioned by affluence, her emergence as a writer was assisted by important literary patrons, and her physical condition made her more of a recluse than an activist. And all her life, she was a devout, thoughtful Catholic – not to mention the fact that she happened to be white.

However, what these two women shared made their differences seem insignificant. They each had a deep, abiding passion for literature, and they both saw the field of Southern literature as distinct and important. They both wrote honestly about matters of race, yet neither of them cared a fig for the genteel, stock characters of the stereotypical South. One can easily imagine their going to a screening of *Gone With The Wind* and howling together in laughter throughout.

It should be noted, however, that O'Connor seemed to identify with the much-abused Tar Baby character from the famous Uncle Remus tale. Especially in the final stages of her life, she signed some of her letters with variations on Tar Baby, such as "Tarbutter," "Tarbug," "Tarpot," and "Tarfunk."

O'Connor was born in Savannah and went to the Catholic girls' school near the cathedral. In summers, she would visit her mother's family's white-columned home near the center of Milledgeville, the pre-Civil War capital city of Georgia. Her maternal grandfather was a successful businessman who served for a time as mayor.

In 1938, the family moved to Atlanta, when her father Edward O'Connor took a job there with a federal agency. After a few months, she decided Atlanta did not suit her. She and her mother moved to Milledgeville, where Flannery finished high school and then enrolled in the local Georgia State College for Women, which is now Georgia College and State University, the school in the state university system designated for emphasis on liberal arts.

Her father typically spent the weekends with his family. But about the same time that Flannery started college, he died from lupus – a disease she would soon discover that she had inherited.

After college, she decided, as had Alice Walker, that it was time for her to leave home. She was accepted for graduate work at the writing program at the State University of Iowa. Later, she lived at Yaddo, an artists' colony near Saratoga Springs, New York. In 1949, she moved into poet Robert Fitzgerald's home in Connecticut to work on her first novel, *Wise Blood*.

Months after signing a contract with a New York publisher, she became ill. The first diagnosis was rheumatoid arthritis; the second, lupus. She moved back to Milledgeville, to live at Andalusia with her mother.

O'Connor firmly believed she was leaving Georgia forever after her undergraduate days. "I stayed away from the time I was 20 until I was 25, with the notion that the life of my writing depended on my staying away," she wrote in a 1957 letter to a friend. "I would certainly have persisted in that delusion had I not got very ill and had to come home. The best of my writing has been done here."

O'Connor left her farm only rarely during the fourteen years that remained of her life. Yet from that physically limited perspective, she saw what the South was becoming – and she presaged some of the themes of the Nuwaubian saga, such as black rage, the shame of child abuse, and the dangerous side of religious zealotry.

In her story *A View Of The Woods,* change and progress become linked with violence and tragedy: "Progress had suddenly set all this in motion. The electric power company had built a dam on the river and flooded great areas of the surrounding country and the lake that resulted touched his land along a half-mile stretch. Every Tom, Dick, and Harry, every dog and his brother, wanted a lot on the lake."

The lake in the story is actually Lake Sinclair. In O'Connor's time, the creation of the lake transformed parts of the region from remote, backward

Indian and Egyptian themes intermingled at Tama-Re.

places into areas where city folks wanted to build their vacation retreats.

On the shores of nearby Lake Oconee, there is now a Ritz Carlton Lodge. Instead of lakes lined with second homes, there are exclusive, gated communities all over the vast lakeshore. That movement is transforming the region's demographics, economy, and politics. For example, the population of Putnam County is now approximately 30 percent black; in Joel Chandler Harris' time, the ratio was reversed – 30 percent white and 70 percent black. It was only after Alice Walker left and Flannery O'Connor died that the total population passed the numbers of the antebellum times. In recent years, the Republican Party has assumed control of areas that were solidly Democratic not so many years ago. The project was developed by a personal friend and major fundraiser for President George W. Bush. That man comes from a family in Greene County, which adjoins Putnam, whose family's land holdings increased stratospherically in value after the creation of the lake. On the grounds of the Ritz Carlton Lodge, there is a separate guest house, called the Presidential House, that can be rented by anyone willing to pay $16,000 a night. It is booked fairly regularly.

What in the world would Flannery make of that?

For a white woman – or for any person, white or black – O'Connor was not afraid to write realistically about black rage. She saw the same thing that Dwight York was able to appeal to so successfully, namely that a significant number of blacks were simply tired of taking anything handed to them by whites, whether it was a set of religious beliefs or the gift of a penny.

In *Everything That Rises Must Converge,* a middle-aged white woman of the Old South, white gloves, ugly hat and all, takes a bus ride to her weight-reduction class, accompanied by her grown son, Julian. Along the way, they uncomfortably share their seats with a large black woman and her young son. The black woman wears the same ugly hat as the white woman, who passes the bus ride spouting racial platitudes.

As they all get off at the same stop, Julian's mother condescendingly offers the black youth a penny. O'Connor suffers the mother to experience the New

South: "The huge woman turned and for a moment stood, her shoulders lifted and her face frozen with frustrated rage, and stared at Julian's mother. Then all at once she seemed to explode, like a piece of machinery that had been given one ounce of pressure too much. Julian saw the black fist swing out with the red pocketbook. He shut his eyes and cringed as he heard the woman shout, 'He don't take nobody's pennies!' When he opened his eyes, the woman was disappearing down the street with the little boy staring wide-eyed over her shoulder. Julian's mother was sitting on the sidewalk."

O'Connor's fiction also is prescient about other themes that played out in the reality of the Nuwaubian saga, such as the black experience of Christianity.

In *Wise Blood*, Hazel Motes, the tortured, self-proclaimed preacher of the "Church Without Christ," stops his truck in the middle of a narrow road to contemplate a "Jesus Saves" sign. When confronted by an irate trucker he is blocking, Motes delivers a line of racial theology that Dwight York might have made good use of: "Jesus is a trick on niggers."

O'Connor could also have been writing about the emotional conflicts within York's special girls, in her rendering of Mary Fortune, the physically abused ten-year-old in *A View Of The Woods*.

Mary and her grandfather, Mr. Fortune, go on an outing that turns into the sale of the land in front of Mary's family's home. Mary is distressed that the store planned for that land will ruin their view of the woods. As the deal is sealed, Mary starts hurling bottles at her grandfather and the buyer.

Mr. Fortune takes Mary, a child he has doted on since her birth, to the place where he has seen her endure repeated beatings by her father, a man he despises. With "a look that went slowly past determination and reached certainty," Mary denies what she and the old man both know is true.

"Nobody has ever beat me, and if anybody tries it, I'll kill him," the girl says. Neither character backs down, and a death is the result.

None of Dwight York's victims were as combative as Mary Fortune. Most of the Nuwaubian girls submitted quietly, if reluctantly, to his predations. But several of the children identified by other witnesses as victims steadfastly denied that they had been molested. Perhaps, like Mary, they feared the pain of admitting the truth might be worse than what they had already endured. Perhaps so many of the victims complied without protest, because they had been conditioned to submit to whatever their god and father figure wanted of them.

In this context, York's abuse might have been rationalized by the children as acceptable or tolerable; while contact with, or protest to, the outside world was evil and forbidden. Like Mary Fortune, who couldn't admit that her father abused her, York's special girls and boys dutifully answered his summonses, day after day, night after night, year after year.

It's natural to wonder why the children didn't tell someone. But whom would they tell? In most cases, the children had at least one parent in the vicinity; but that parent was also conditioned to serve York's every whim. Some of them thought it was an honor for their child to be selected to be so close to York; others later conceded they were so brainwashed into being devoted to York, they failed to be responsible for their children. Perhaps they should have seen, but they couldn't, or wouldn't. Besides, the children were warned that their parents would be punished if they told the truth.

There was certainly nowhere for the children to run. Most of the victims were adolescents or younger while they were being abused. Where could such a child go? They had been moved from big cities in the North to an isolated, rural part of the Deep South; and they had been taught that the outside world was full of demons.

Would the writers' eyes of Harris or Walker or O'Connor have seen York for what he was? Maybe so. Harris wrote about the authentic black life, for his time. Surely, he would have seen through York's artifice.

Walker had a special place at the sharpest point of her pen for black men who abused black women and children.

O'Connor made a literary specialty out of strange characters like York. Literary people even coined a term for such creations of hers: "grotesques." She sometimes rankled over that label, but she took on the topic in an essay, "The Grotesque In Southern Fiction," explaining why portraying reality meant exploring the bizarre.

"I am always having it pointed out to me," she wrote in that essay, "that life in Georgia is not all the way I picture it, that escaped criminals do not roam the road exterminating families, nor Bible salesmen prowl about looking for girls with wooden legs. Every time I heard about the School of Southern Degeneracy, I felt like B'rer Rabbit stuck on the tar baby.

"Of course, I have found that anything that comes out of the South is going to be called grotesque by the Northern reader, unless it is grotesque, in which case it is going to be called realistic."

Unfortunately, O'Connor was not available to offer her observations as a consultant to the agencies struggling with the issue of how to deal with York. She certainly would have called it as she saw it. "Whenever I'm asked why Southern writers particularly have a penchant for writing about freaks," she wrote in the "Grotesque" essay, "I say it is because we are still able to recognize one."

Dwight York was the embodiment of one of O'Connor's grotesques.

However sordid the reality of York's utopian dreamland may have been, he was peddling a dream with demonstrated, longstanding power. He certainly wasn't the first black man to come to Georgia with the vision of establishing a community where blacks could live together and establish their own rules.

In the late 1960s, a Civil Rights activist named John McCown picked Hancock County, Georgia – which lies just to the east of Putnam County – as an obvious target for a black political and economic takeover. Hancock's population was about 80 percent black, the highest of any of the 159 counties in the state. It also had one of the highest poverty rates.

McCown's voter registration drives quickly led to Hancock becoming the first county in the nation since Reconstruction to have a government dominated by blacks. He succeeded in obtaining massive grants from federal agencies and the Ford Foundation. His accomplishments were cited as a "national model" by an official of the Nixon administration.

With the money, McCown helped start up black-run enterprises, including a huge catfish farm, a concrete block factory, a small airline, a sheet metal plant, a pallet plant, and a nightclub called the Academy Club. McCown came to be known as the "Black Boss," which is also the title of a book about him by John Rozier. The following material is taken mostly from that book.

In response to those early successes, McCown's white opponents sought to entrench themselves by retaining control of the county seat, Sparta. At one point in the early 1970s, there was a literal arms race between the hostile camps. Sparta's white police chief purchased machine guns for his officers, and McCown responded in kind. During this tense time, a woman who worked for McCown was stopped by Sparta police and given three traffic tickets.

McCown thought the incident was simple racial harassment, so he ordered the woman to refuse to pay the fine. Then he led his supporters in a blockade of the main street of Sparta; the protesters parked their cars in the street and walked away. McCown was arrested. Soon after that, an historic white-columned mansion in Sparta was burned down; no one was ever charged in the arson.

Then-Governor Jimmy Carter came to Sparta to mediate a truce. As the open hostility waned, however, so did most of the business ventures started through McCown's efforts. Federal investigators started looking into McCown's handling of the government funds, and the big foundations pulled out their support. All the businesses quickly died, though the nightclub lasted for a few more years.

Knowing that he was a target of the federal investigators and fully expecting to be indicted, McCown went to the Academy Club for drinks one night in January 1976. Though he was not a qualified pilot, McCown led three of his friends to a small plane parked at the airport. Witnesses said the plane took off, then abruptly went nose down and plunged back to earth. All aboard were killed.

To this day, Hancock remains the Georgia county with the highest percentage of black residents, and poverty is as intractable a problem as it was when John McCown hit town. His birthday, however, is still remembered with a holiday for the county's public school system.

The utopian dream goes back even further, to the times just after the hostilities ceased in the Civil War.

Tunis Campbell, a black man from New Jersey, was made the head agent for the Coastal Georgia region of the Freedman's Bureau, the federal agency established to regulate matters dealing with freed slaves. In that region, Savannah was the largest city, and at the time, perhaps the healthiest city economically in the state.

Campbell was able to organize and fund a cooperative of black farmers and fishermen on St. Catherine's Island, just off the coast of McIntosh County, about fifty miles south of Savannah. Later, the base of his operations was moved to the mainland, in a marshy part of the county called Harris Neck.

However, his success at mobilizing former slaves into an economic and political force created enemies who were determined to bring Campbell down and to besmirch his legacy.

"Campbell was written off by Georgia historians as a mountebank and a scoundrel, but he was one of the first men of his time to understand the strength of black unity and power," historian Dorothy Sterling wrote in her history of newly-empowered blacks in the Reconstruction Era, *The Trouble They Seen*.

Sterling saw much to applaud in Campbell's accomplishments: "The times transformed him into a teacher, preacher, state senator, justice of the peace, and capable political boss in a Georgia county where blacks outnumbered whites four to one."

In 1875, Campbell was arrested and charged with false imprisonment of a white man, in an incident involving the detention of the captain and crew of a merchant ship docked at the port of the county seat, Darien. With his white enemies pushing the prosecution, Campbell was convicted and imprisoned. Without his leadership, his movement disintegrated and whites regained political control of the county.

However, Harris Neck survived as a largely self-sufficient, though isolated and poor, black community. Blacks retained ownership of most of the land, and there was a black-owned oyster packing plant supplying employment to those who didn't fish or farm for a living. The folks in Darien pretty much left Harris Neck alone.

"We lived off the land and the sea," said Evelyn Greer, a black resident of McIntosh County who grew up in Harris Neck. "What we had, we had plenty of."

In 1942, however, the local détente ended, due to the home-front activities of World War II. The federal government decided to build a military base on the coast of McIntosh County, and most of the land seized for the project was the property owned by the blacks of Harris Neck.

The landowners were paid a small sum for their property, and then they were brutally evicted. When a little-publicized deadline passed, the approximately seventy families who were to be relocated were given a matter of hours to take their belongings and get out.

Greer can still remember that day. A girl at the time, she went back with her mother to retrieve a gramophone they had left a few hours earlier.

They arrived just in time to see their house being burned down. What wasn't being burnt was being bulldozed.

"It was awful, like Judgment Day," Greer said. "It was the first and last time I ever saw my mother shed tears."

The only structure the people of Harris Neck were allowed to save was their church. Before the forced eviction, the men of the community had taken it down and reassembled it a few miles away.

The oyster plant was gone, and with it, the market and livelihood of most of the fishermen of Harris Neck. Blacks saw it as a conspiracy.

"The plan from Jump One was to have all the blacks removed," said Rev. Edgar Timmons, a grandson of the man who owned the oyster plant.

The only reason the people of Harris agreed to leave their land without contesting its seizure was that they believed they'd been promised that the land would be returned to them after the war, their descendants claim.

It wasn't. The barely-used military base was shut down in 1946, and the land was deeded to McIntosh County, ostensibly for use as an airport. In the years that followed, McIntosh officials, including Sheriff Tom Poppell, used the land as their own, grazing their cattle on areas that included the black cemetery at Harris Neck, and trying and failing to start business ventures, including a drag strip and a nightclub.

In that era, McIntosh County was wide open for crime. Clip joints and gambling houses fleeced the tourists traveling along U.S. 17, a main north-south highway at the time. The county was known for its "truck stops" that didn't sell gas. It was also notorious for the number of trucks that mysteriously lost their cargoes somewhere in McIntosh.

Sometimes, those cargoes were distributed among the poor blacks of the county, who gave the sheriff their loyalty in return. An incident where a woman was delivered of some much-needed construction material supplied the inspiration for the title of Melissa Fay Green's book on the county in that era, *Praying For Sheetrock.*

Poppell was eventually toppled during a Civil Rights-era equality drive led by Thurnell Alson, who eventually became the county's first black county commissioner since Reconstruction, the first black with any real power since Tunis Campbell. He was later deposed as well, after being arrested for drug dealing.

There was no relief, however, for the blacks of Harris Neck. In 1962, the federal government reclaimed the land from the county, because it had never been used for an airport. Instead of giving it back to the people from whom the land had been seized, the land was turned into a federal wildlife refuge.

Descendants of the landowners protested and litigated, to no avail. In the early 1980s, a federal suit by the descendants was dismissed, the judge ruling that the statute of limitations had passed and that the dispute was a matter for state courts, not federal. At the same time, however, the judge found that the people of Harris Neck probably did get flim-flammed.

"It appears likely that an attempt was made to mislead the United States into conveying the property to McIntosh County instead of to the other priority holders," the ruling stated. "It may be that there is some legal basis to attack by legal process the government's acquisition of the plaintiff's tracts two generations ago."

The land remains a wildlife preserve. According to federal environmental officials, it is an important habitat for migratory birds, especially a rare variety of wood stork.

Since development of the wildlife refuge is prohibited, it has had the effect of raising the value of much of the adjacent land, most of which happens to have been owned by whites. Concurrently, those adjacent lands have become desirable, as more wealthy people seek residences with proximity to pristine natural beauty.

Some recently-developed residential projects offer homesites that start in the $200,000 range. One such development has its own landing strip for private planes, and some of its houses have small hangars attached, rather than garages.

Things have changed politically in McIntosh County. The county has a black sheriff, Charles "Chunk" Jones, who has been re-elected three times. "The old days are gone," Jones said. "Before, they used politics to divide blacks and whites. Now, the people are better off when we can keep that line erased. We're not having that anymore."

Nevertheless, the fate of the utopian dreams of blacks in McIntosh County and Hancock County illustrates the type of racial dynamic that Dwight York was able to play upon so successfully. A charismatic black leader doesn't need to invent the specter of white hostility to an effort by blacks to build their own community and control their own fate. There is ample evidence in history to convince blacks that such efforts will engender harassment and discrimination by whites.

In Putnam County, by contrast, the charges of harassment and discrimination by county officials were dark fantasies conjured up by Dwight York and used by him to fuel bitterness among his followers. Just as he had done in Brooklyn, he used legitimate areas of racial grievances as a cloak to hide his thriving criminal enterprises. He was never oppressed by local racists, as he repeatedly claimed – though he was able to fool a lot of people, some of them in high places, into thinking he was.

If York was going to keep his international empire propped up and continue to sell his brand of utopia from his new base in Georgia, one of the first things he had to do was to find a new way to dress it up. No matter what you're selling, trinkets or books or religion, packaging is everything.

Islam was out. The disguise that had served him so well for a quarter century in New York definitely had to be discarded. One of the reasons York pulled out of Brooklyn, he claimed, was that rival Muslims were trying to kill him. There had been seven attempts on his life, York claimed, and the assassin who killed Jewish radical activist Meyer Kahane had York next on his hit list.

So, York did much the same thing as W.D. Fard had done in the formative days of the Moorish Science Temple movement – he sharpened his sense of fashion design. Fard, a fabric salesman, had tailored his movement's ideology to what people would buy, intellectually and commercially. Fard merged his separatist philosophy with what he could sell. His line of cloth for African-style garments coordinated nicely with his preachings and teachings about the virtues of the African homelands. Noble Drew Ali, who followed Fard, chose to place the African emphasis on Morocco, where he claimed he had been given a title of nobility by the Moroccan king.

Still, York had to decide what costumes he could persuade his followers to buy and how to shape a matching ideology. Like any successful businessman launching a new venture, York test-marketed.

In his first few years in Georgia, York tried on for size a few religious-sartorial combinations. First, there were the cowboy-and-Indian ensembles. York proclaimed himself Chief Black Eagle, leader of a modern-day re-assemblage of the Lost Tribe of the Yamassee, a group of Native Americans who resisted the early waves of European colonization and then disappeared from history.

York also claimed that his tribe had a spiritual and historical connection to Putnam County. There was a mystical link, he claimed, between his tribe and a site in northern Putnam County called Rock Eagle, about ten miles away from

York's property, a place where mounds built by prehistoric Native Americans of the region have been preserved.

The cowboy motif turned out not to be a big hit. York wanted his followers to dress in uniform when they left their land. He initially told them they'd blend in better as cowboys. He didn't stop to think, apparently, that there are precious few cowboys, white or black, in Putnam County. There are plenty of cattle, but they are almost all dairy cattle. Those animals need to be milked, not cow-punched, herded, or trail-bossed. Given that, the small groups of black men moseying around Eatonton with their ten-gallon hats and new boots were anything but inconspicuous.

Besides, the stuff was expensive. Some of York's followers said they had to borrow boots from someone else any time they went to town. Sometimes, the boots didn't quite fit.

York would later insist that the cowboy phase had primarily been a loyalty test for his followers. In *The Holy Tablets* he wrote, "The dress then changed to western attire to get everybody away from doing their own thing. Those that truly followed the Lamb wherever he may lead them trusted in him and wore western clothes and even listened to country western music, simply because he asked them to."

Nevertheless, the Stetsons were traded for red fezes after a year or so in Georgia. Concurrently, the settlement on Shadydale Road began to be referred to as a fraternal community called the Ancient Mystical Order of Melchizedek. That one didn't have a whole lot of traction, either. Some of the trappings of AMOM were retained and dusted off for later use, but in the years 1994 to 1996, York was still groping for his definitive philosophical fashion statement.

He needed something big, something different, something attention grabbing, something suitable for simultaneous development with a thematically consistent line of clothing that he could sell.

What he came up with was called the United Nation of Nuwaubian Moors, a concept composed of an extra-large dose of Egyptian schlock, served with a side dish of intergalactic mumbo-jumbo.

The Egyptian angle provided more than ample historical material to allow him to turn the front part of his property, the part bordering Shadydale Road, into a small-scale re-creation of ancient Egypt. He would set his slaves to work building pyramids, much as the ancient pharaohs had done; only, his pyramids would be thirty-foot-high wooden-framed affairs, with plywood surfaces painted black and gold.

For a philosophical backdrop, he would use more or less the same fundamental argument that had served him well in his Muslim days. The old canards still had mileage on them. People would still listen, when he preached

Dwight York speaking at Tama-Re on Savior's day 1998.
Photo by W.A. Bridges, *Atlanta Journal-Constitution*

that whites had stolen the heritage of the black, or Nubian people. American blacks were not descended from slaves, as the whites would have them believe; they were descended from the divinely-favored race that gave the world such things as geometry and architecture.

This time around, however, he decided to add a new twist. Instead of casting himself as an only slightly mystical Muslim prophet, York placed himself on the furthest tip of a thin branch of the tree of believability. He would now claim that he was a supernatural being sent from the Planet Rizq to save a chosen few—well a chosen 144,000, earthlings—preferably black.

Salvation would come via spaceship, and only York could issue the tickets.

For this grandiose concept to look like a religion, a holy book was needed. York decided on something fancy, leather-bound, and somewhat Bible-like in appearance. Printing such a tome would take money, which York acquired from one of his teenaged concubines.

Samarra, who'd been one of the Back Street girls in Brooklyn, turned eighteen a year or so after the group moved to Putnam County. On her birthday, she came into a large sum of money, a settlement of more than $100,000 from an automobile accident. Her parents had put the money into a trust fund.

She had also recently come into the state of motherhood, having borne a son fathered by York.

As soon as she was of legal age, York dispatched her back to New York to get the money, which she dutifully gave to him. She told police that she did it willingly; having grown up in the cult, she had no concept of money nor did the money mean anything to her at the time. It was also beyond her ability at that time to challenge York's will, though that would change.

York used Samarra's money for the printing costs for his 1,700-page tome, *The Holy Tablets*. He even acknowledged Samarra's funding in the book. On a page labeled "Gratitude" near the front of the book, York first gave thanks to "The Most High." (Allah had fallen out of favor in York's pantheon.) York went on to bestow a false title of "Dr." on her and then to thank her "for her financial help in getting this work out."

According to several people who helped compile the book, however, York failed to acknowledge the many sources he tapped into – and in at least a few significant portions, clearly plagiarized.

Aludra, who was thanked by York for her artistic contributions to *The Holy Tablets*, said she and other young women were assigned to compile material for that and other books by scanning pages of other books by computer for direct placement into York's books. There was never any effort made at attributing the source materials, she said.

"There was a lot of plagiarized text," Aludra said. "Many times, Doc would bring home books or be given books or tapes, and he would play it, ask some people to take notes and put it together, and change around some words, and Voila! a book was 'created.' Pictures were done the same way."

Another former Nuwaubian who witnessed how the books were assembled said York frequently did not even bother to read the material that was being printed into books he purported to have authored. "He told the women what he wanted a book to be about, and they'd put it together," she said. "He'd have some brothers proofread it for typos and errors of information. Sometimes, York would flip through them; some parts that sounded like him in the books were from recorded classes, or he'd dictate. Pathetic."

York took material from dozens of other books to assemble *The Holy Tablets*, according to another former Nuwaubian. This person said he was instructed to go out and buy about thirty books, many of them popular New Age tracts or books positing prehistoric visits to Earth by extraterrestrials. Those books would become the core of *The Holy Tablets*.

Some of the assemblers of York's new bible made an effort at least to re-write their source material. Others didn't even bother to do that much.

Much of the material in a section in *The Holy Tablets* called "Chapter Three, Karama, The Scientist" was directly lifted from a section of *The Sirius Mystery,* by Robert Temple.

For example, on page 303 of *The Holy Tablets*, there is a section about a mythical race of beings called the Dogons and their astronomical theories about the star Sirius B. That section begins: "The Dogons believe that the most important star in the sky is Sirius B, which cannot be seen. They call this tiny star Po Tolo, Tolo meaning 'star' and Po is a cereal grain commonly called Fonio in West Africa.

"Digitaria also revolves upon itself over the period of one year and this revolution is honored during the celebration of the Bado Rite, that occurs every sixty years called a Sigui, which happens when Sirius B completes its rotation around Sirius A and rotates on its own axis around itself.

"Sirius B is composed of a special kind of material which is called Sagala, from a root meaning 'strong.' And this material does not exist on the Earth. This material is heavier than all the iron on Earth. Sirius B is made of super dense matter of a kind which exits nowhere on Earth."

Startlingly similar material – in some cases the same stuff, word for word – appears on pages 63 through 76 of *The Sirius Mystery*. Whoever stole the material did so on a selective basis, picking a paragraph or two to copy into *The Holy Tablets*, and then skipping a few paragraphs before plagiarizing another paragraph or two.

That pattern is repeated in several other sections of *The Sirius Mystery*, where whole paragraphs of that book turn up verbatim and unattributed in *The Holy Tablets*.

Besides the plagiarized text, there are twenty illustrations and diagrams from *The Sirius Mystery* that appear in *The Holy Tablets*, scattered throughout pages 304 to 325, copied exactly but totally unattributed.

Pages 291 and 292 of *The Holy Tablets* consist of photographs of ancient Egyptian tombs. The first shows an unidentifed man standing beside a "shaft in the East Wall of the Queen's Chamber." The second shows "an empty sarcophagus in the King's Chamber."

Those same two photographs appear as plates in *The Orion Mystery,* by Robert Bauval and Adrian Gilbert. In that book, the man standing beside the opening in the tomb wall is identified as one of the authors.

In another example of blatant plagiarism, on page 593 of *The Holy Tablets*, in a section called "The Human Beast," it states:

"A new source of light is now reaching our solar system and interpenetrating Earth's magnetic field, altering the biological rhythms...This is forcing the species to leave behind its old time-cell of perception on the physical, emotional, mental, and spiritual levels. This must take place before the species can go into a new time cell of consciousness.

"As the arcs of light begin to change, a different light force is beginning to work with the electromagnetic forces. This is causing the magnetic fields of the brain cavity to be sufficiently raised to a higher mental frequency, allowing Enosites (one of York's book's terms for humans) to receive 'whole light beings' upon the reinsertion of the barathary gland and the reactivation of the supreme melanin."

That and some following passages appear to have been lifted nearly verbatim from *The Keys Of Enoch,* by futurist J.J. Hurtak. On page 379 of the fifth edition of Hurtak's book it states as follows:

"A new source of Light is now reaching our solar system and interpenetrating Earth's magnetic field, altering the biological rhythms. This is forcing the specie to leave behind its old time-cell of perception on the physical, emotional, mental, and spiritual levels."

Throughout *The Holy Tablets*, there are recurring characters with the same names and descriptions of characters in the books of Zecharia Sitchin's bestselling series *The Earth Chronicles*.

Without the slightest nod to Sitchin, York fills out his supposedly holy book with references to the Anunnaki, the same enlightened beings who populate many of Sitchin's books; though York did take the trouble to change the spelling to "Anunnaqi."

York transferred many of the names of characters and places from Sitchin's book into his own. Nibiru, Tiamat, Enki, Enlil, Marduk(called Murdoq in *The Holy Tablets*), Sud, and Gilgamesh are among those who made the leap from Sitchin's works to York's.

However, York does appear to rely strictly on his own imagination when he writes of his origins and of his personal nature in *The Holy Tablets*.

He states that he comes from a planet called Rizq in the "Great Galaxy" Illyuwn. He describes a war on Rizq that happened when Humbaba (a warior [sic] being) "attacked Rizq with a shield depleter. The bomb caused the natural atmosphere of Rizq to deplete."

So, the inhabitants of Rizq, the "Rizqiyians," had to leave their planet in search of gold dust, with which they intended to build a dome over their planet to thwart future depleter attacks.

York claims that he "incarnates from time to time for those who are in need of my presence in the flesh. I am an angelic being, an Eloheem." He claims that he exists in "the plane of divine truth, spiritual perfection and attainment, a plane exempt from all carnal desires, supreme spiritual bliss. It is the level of consciousness which is the daily expression of those you call the ranks of angelic beings."

In his discussion of the correct sex life in this elevated plane, York writes, "If a man or woman can't control their sex, get away from them. They will self-destruct and destroy others with them. Controlling sex means having sexual intercourse without selfish desires, and that unnatural acts are against the laws of nature."

York states that he has visited Earth in three separate incarnations, the latest of which was his birth in human form on June 26, 1945. While he was in his mother's womb, he was implanted with three candles which glowed with a green light, a sign of his surpassing mental and spiritual abilities. He calls himself the Nubians' "long-awaited savior."

In charting his effort to provide salvation for his followers, he states that he began with Islam, because that was what his people wanted at the time. "Now, you have everything you need to go on to the next level," he states, referring to the new doctrines of his Nuwaubian phase.

He tells of his journey on earth, how he started various fashion and racial trends. He credits himself for starting the practices of blacks wearing nose rings, braided hair, and beads in their braids.

He also claims that he's the one who first got racial name-calling right. Blacks were not blacks, or African-Americans or Negroes; those who were not "dead blacks" were Nubians, or Nuwaubians. And whites were no longer whites, he added. "I said stop calling them white people. They're not white, they are lepers," he states.

He claims to have left Brooklyn for Camp Jazzir, because of the doctrinal errors of the "so-called Arabs" who opposed him. It was also the right time for the "Prepared Savior" to submit his followers to nineteen weeks of loyalty tests in the form of blizzards.

"The next move," York wrote, "was to the Mecca of Nubians, Georgia."

York never said how far it was in distance from Rizq to Putnam County. It was probably as immeasurable and as difficult to travel as the cultural gap between his farm and the county courthouse in Eatonton.

Putnam County Sheriff Howard Sills in front of county courthouse in Eatonton.

CHAPTER 5
The Little Town That Wouldn't (1993 - 1998)

It was a great blessing for a young fellow in the clutches of poverty to be raised up among such people as those who lived in Eatonton, and whose descendants still live there. – Joel Harris Harris

Eatonton is a violent little town – Alice Walker

She came in for a set and style. She got a shock.

There must have been some mistake on the poster on the beauty parlor wall. This was Eatonton. There certainly weren't any fancy Egyptian-style nightclubs around here; certainly none that catered to black folks. Or were there?

Sandra Adams was a Putnam County Commissioner, a black, and the first woman elected to that post. She wasn't alarmed that she had come into her regular beauty salon in Eatonton and seen a four-color poster advertising a nightclub in her county. It did rankle somewhat, however, that she didn't know a thing about this place, this Club Rameses.

The poster was full of pictures of black folks dancing, dining, and generally having a grand time in a place with colorful Egyptian décor. It also promised entertainment by top-flight bands and singers, excellent food, and a one-night trip to an ancient land. The club's address was listed as 404 Shadydale Road, about eight miles east of town. Wasn't that where the Pyramid People had their farm?

"What was going on out there, who were these people, and why didn't we know about it?" Adams asked herself.

Under other circumstances, Adams might have been delighted to have a new business come to her county. In late 1997, there weren't many places to spend your dining and entertainment dollars in Putnam County. There was one nice restaurant out towards Lake Oconee, but that one catered to the wealthy white folks who were starting to buy places in the gated communities, one of which even included "plantation" in its name. There was Rusty's, a meat-and-three place with perpetually tired waitresses across from the Uncle Remus Museum in downtown Eatonton, and, aside from a few fast-food restaurants, that was about it.

Geographically, Eatonton was somewhat integrated. There were mostly-white neighborhoods and mostly-black neighborhoods, but they were only a short walk from each other, and they were not separated by walls and gates.

The center of town was dominated by the county courthouse, a graceful brick structure set in the center of a block-square green. Its white cupola has a clock set in each of the four sides. It had remained basically unchanged since it was built in Eatonton's Victorian heyday, until the county decided in 2005 to fill much of the space on the green with two, architecturally compatible new wings added to the courthouse building.

South of downtown, Main Street is lined with nondescript businesses, some shacks, and a couple of good produce stands.

On the north side, there is Madison Avenue, a street so charming that people literally make the ninety-minute drive from Atlanta, just to stroll its uneven sidewalks. It is the old homes that draw them. One, a Victorian with acres of porch outside and more acres of hardwood paneling inside, is operated as a bed-and-breakfast inn. A Greek Revival just down the other side of the street is such an outstanding example of the type that a gay couple sold their place in San Francisco, moved in, and restored it spectacularly. There is an antebellum mansion that is supposed to come with its own ghost, that of a murdered mistress from the antebellum times. At the end of the street, there is a mansion with acreage for which the state's historical preservation groups are seeking a buyer.

But on that day in the beauty parlor, Sandra Adams was not thinking about her hometown's charm. Nor was it a bad perm that was making her hair stand on end.

Adams is an imposing woman, large in stature and sometimes strident in her vocal presence. She had been born in Putnam County but was raised in Newark,

New Jersey. Her mother was a neighborhood activist there, often confronting the police and city officials with the grievances of the black community. Adams returned to Putnam County in the early 1990s, took a job with the school system, and made her historic run for the county commission in the November 1996 election.

Upon taking office, she wanted to soften her image, show folks that she could be one of the guys. At one of her first commission meetings, she told her fellow commissioners – all men – she wasn't looking to stir things up. "If y'all just remember to put the toilet seat down, we'll get along just fine," she told them.

Adams repeated her questions about the nightclub to the county's lone building inspector at the time, Dean "Dizzy" Adams (no relation). He knew right where it was, and he knew that this was going to be trouble.

Just a few weeks earlier, Dizzy Adams had slapped a stop-work order on the building that he thought housed the nightclub advertised on the poster. He'd gone out to the Nuwaubians' property and seen that a concrete foundation had been poured for a 100x50-foot building. Problem was, no one had bothered to obtain a permit for the building.

The manager of the Nuwaubian property, a man named Victor Grieg, had complained that the stop-work order violated his group's constitutional rights, but he came into town, paid a fine, and got a permit. The permit, however, stipulated that the building under construction was to be used as a storage facility, not an Egyptian-themed nightclub.

Dizzy Adams had had trouble out there before; and shortly after the group moved in, some federal agents asked him if he'd ever seen stockpiles of weapons on the place. He hadn't, but he never looked for such things, either. So before going out to Shadydale Road, he stopped by Sheriff Howard Sills's office.

As the new sheriff in town, Sills looked and talked like a prototypical rural Georgia lawman. His thinning blond hair was augmented by a neat brush of a mustache, and he spoke in an often-salty drawl. After that, though, the analogy falls apart. Sills has a degree in criminology and a background in courtroom practice that effectively makes him a prosecutor with a badge.

He is impatient with delays, waffling politicians, federal bureaucrats, unprofessional cops, and just about anyone who doesn't see a case his way. Yet, he does a lot of his grandmother's yard work, and when he travels to a new city, he often checks out the big bookstore in town. He often buys the latest James Lee Burke crime novel in hardcover, keeping up with Burke's troubled hero Dave Robichaux, a cop who fights the system as fervently as he fights the bad guys and his own demons.

Sills can trace his family roots in Putnam County back to the first decade of the nineteenth century. He was adopted by his paternal grandparents when he was too young to know why. His mother was an alcoholic, and he never lived with his father.

He was about twelve when his grandfather died, and after that his surrogate father was George Lawrence, the district attorney for Putnam County and the Oconee Circuit. They called Lawrence "Big George," even though he was a physically small man. Lawrence had a big reputation and record as a prosecutor, and he was appointed by the state's attorney general to try some of the highest-profile cases of his time.

Sills would sometimes travel with Lawrence on such assignments, thus learning how to try a case before he learned how to investigate one. Lawrence urged his young protégé to pursue a career in the practice of law, but Sills had developed a distaste for the corruption he'd seen too often in his legal apprenticeship. Besides, he preferred the action end of the law.

Sills worked as a sheriff's deputy and as a security director for banks for twenty-two years, before he was elected sheriff of his home county in 1996.

On the day that Dizzy Adams came to him and said he was having trouble with that strange group living out on Shadydale Road, Sills had never had any direct dealings with the newcomers.

But this wasn't the first time Dizzy Adams had had some trouble with the Nuwaubians. There had been a series of low-level squabbles relating to reluctance to abide by the county's zoning ordinance, and a few months earlier, Adams had been refused entry to the property.

Sills wanted to make a first assessment of the situation without flashing his badge. So, dressed in street clothes, he went out to the property with Adams, riding as a passenger in Adams's car. Again, they were stopped by the armed guard at the gate and refused admittance to the property. Adams protested that he had the legal authority to come onto the property to inspect buildings. The guard made a phone call.

After a twenty-to-thirty-minute wait, Sills saw a six-man entourage heading toward their car. At the center of the group was a short, thin man wearing a loose, black pajama-style outfit, with gold braids on the sleeves. He wore enough jewelry to stock a small shop. He was protected from the sun by the parasol held over his head by the man behind him.

The man, who Sills would soon learn was Dwight York, came up to the car and launched into a curse-laden, name-calling tirade directed at Dizzy Adams. The sanitized version of what he screeched at them was: This is my land and I can do whatever I please on it. The two visitors drove off.

When he got back to town, Sills did some legal research. Then, in what would be a regular, almost daily practice for the next six years, he sought Big

George's advice. At that time, Lawrence was retired and his lung cancer was in remission. From the beginning of his counsel, Lawrence warned Sills to be careful.

Then Sills went before the county commission, asking for a resolution granting him the authority to enforce the county zoning ordinance, at which the Nuwaubians were clearly thumbing their noses.

In Georgia, the office of sheriff is created by the state, to enforce state laws. Sills told the commissioners he needed specific additional authority to enforce their ordinance. The resolution passed unanimously.

Then, Sills returned, in uniform and wearing a gun, to the Shadydale Road property. He informed the Nuwaubians of the authority he'd been granted and told them he expected no more obstruction of county employees seeking to perform their legitimate duties on the Nuwaubians' property. He was assured that there would be no more similar problems.

The Nuwaubians didn't bar Adams from the property, but they did ignore his efforts to make them comply with the zoning laws. Victor Grieg's payment of his fine after Adams placed a stop-work order on the new building turned out to be just a ruse.

The building was completed and soon after that, hundreds of cars, many of them from metro Atlanta, started coming to the Nuwaubians' land on Friday and Saturday nights. This was not investigated further at the time; the Club Rameses was not visible from the highway, and as far as the county officials knew, it was only a storage building anyway.

Not long after Sandra Adams saw the poster in the beauty parlor, and for the first time that anyone in Eatonton could remember, Putnam County made the big-city news.

The same posters were being plastered around Atlanta, and they caught the attention of a local television producer. A film crew was dispatched to Putnam County, and a report aired, with footage of a happening place called Club Rameses, packed with people who were drinking, dancing, and partying. The report included the information that county officials in Eatonton had no records of any permits or liquor licenses issued for the club.

When he saw the television news report, Sills knew that the nightclub had to be the same building that had been permitted only as a storage facility. He also got some angry calls from people who complained, "Why do I have to get a liquor license to sell beer and they don't?"

The sheriff also made some angry calls of his own, in particular to Victor Grieg, the manager of the Nuwaubians' property. Grieg tried to tell him that it wasn't really a full-scale nightclub, saying, "We only sell wine coolers." Grieg had no answer when Sills told him that the lack of a liquor license was only part of the problem; there were also the matter of a building being used without a certificate of occupancy. The worst problem, however, was that the Nuwaubians had clearly deceived county authorities about what their supposed storage building was really being used for.

Before making his next move, Sills asked for an inspection of Club Rameses by state fire marshals. The nightclub was shown to be a deathtrap. The inspection revealed hazardous wiring, overcrowding, lack of a sprinkler system, and about a dozen other serious safety violations.

It would soon be last call at Club Rameses. Sills knew what he had to do next, but he also knew he would have to proceed cautiously. He had recently received an alarming piece of news from police investigators in Clayton County, a suburban county just south of Atlanta.

Deputies from Clayton had flown in their helicopter to Eatonton to brief Sills on something they'd found in the investigation of a burglary ring in their jurisdiction. Several of the suspects arrested had given their address as 404 Shadydale Road, Eatonton. When the Clayton deputies searched the suspects' apartment, they found videotapes that had apparently been used in training classes conducted by the Nuwaubians.

One of the tapes was of a speech being made by Dwight York. In it, York repeatedly stated that his cult was a sovereign nation, and his farm in Putnam County was their homeland. York made what seemed to be a clear call to arms when he stated on the video, "When they come, and they will come, we have to be ready."

On May 8, 1998, Sills made ready to shut down the nightclub. The action came at a time when the number of people living at Tama-Re was probably at its zenith, around 350 to 400 people. As a precaution, Sills stationed a reserve force of about forty riot-ready deputies, some borrowed from nearby counties, at a black church in the countryside, not far from the property. Then, he led a force of seventeen deputies onto Tama-Re. This time, they had an injunction and they didn't pause to ask permission at the guard gate.

It took only about thirty minutes for the sheriff to post closure notices on the walls of the nightclub and padlock the doors. York did not appear and the reserves were not needed, but other Nuwaubians videotaped the proceedings, getting as close as they could to the deputies and making complaints about violation of their sovereignty.

Club Rameses was more than a big money maker for York. It was an important lure for bringing potential recruits to him. "Beer, wine, limousines – it was like an ice cream truck and kids," Sills said. The nightclub was certainly a bigger draw than the speeches and lectures York would often give on Sunday nights. Its closure would severely constrict York's dreams for what he could become as the master of this pasture.

More importantly, Sills delivered a message: The law in Putnam County would not look the other way for York. There would be no "hands-off policy," as there had been in Brooklyn. There would be no "safe-streets" commendations from politicians, though York would later prove adept at gaining some high-level political support. The lights in Club Rameses would never go on again.

"It was the first time ever that York had a public official stand up and tell him he couldn't effectively do whatever he wanted to do," Sills said. "Up until then, he'd had nothing but acquiescence.

"York knew then he was going to have trouble here. The game was on."

It was a game that York never really wanted to play by the rules. He didn't need stamped and signed building permits; if he had wanted them, he could have sent someone down to the courthouse to get the paperwork straight. He never did that, because what he needed in Putnam County was a bogeyman. Perferably of the white persuasion.

But this was not the '60s. It was the 1990s, and by and large, the white folks in this small, mostly rural county in Middle Georgia, were not playing the roles York had cast for them. Of course, York and his cult members would continue to sling the mud of racist allegations frequently and heavily throughout the next three years; but the people of Putnam County refused to oblige by behaving in a racist manner.

None of the Nuwaubians' claims of racial discrimination were ever upheld by any state or federal court. The Nuwaubians' bullying and intimidation tactics never succeeded in provoking violence against them. By and large, the clerks and elected officials simply did their jobs, despite the repeated confrontations with hostile, accusatory cultists.

Even though York never offered any evidence or documents to support his ugly claims, the mud he slung did have considerable sticking power. Thirty years after the height of the Civil Rights battles and 130 years after the Civil War, the outside world was still quite ready to accept that Putnam County was a racist backwater. Plantations had thrived there and segregation had been the rule, so, to many, it was still a place where it was easy to believe a black man crying discrimination. Stereotypes were stronger than truth.

Less than two months after the shutdown of the nightclub, York opened his 1998 Savior's Day festival to the media, the first and only time that ever happened. The television crews and newspaper reporters who came to the farm, now called Tama-Re, saw the land and the community at their best. The crowds were mellow and large. Estimates ran as high as five thousand visitors from dozens of states and a few foreign countries. The ceremonies were elaborate and the costumes colorful.

York's followers responded pleasantly to questions from the media. Mostly,

The Little Egypt train transported people around the grounds at Tama-Re.

they claimed that their belief system adopted the best from all the holy books of the major religions. Yet, they would also claim that anything in those holy books that contradicted their "Right Knowledge" was simply wrong.

On Saturday, the peak day of the festival, York appeared and held court for the media. He openly proclaimed his desire to set up his own government, operate his own public services and schools. His people needed their own, separate society, he claimed, because of the racism and crime in the society that surrounded them. At its core, York's message was harsh and confrontational; but it was such a lovely summer day, and he was so charming as he spoke, that none of it sounded too threatening at the time.

Soon after the festival, though, York's tone changed dramatically. Flyers and newspapers started circulating around Eatonton, and they printed vicious personal attacks on virtually anyone and everyone who opposed York. The diatribes were anonymously produced by groups calling themselves Concerned Citizens of Eatonton and People Against Violence in Eatonton. They were clearly front groups for York, though the individuals making the accusations never stepped forward to identify themselves.

Looking back, some people in Putnam County who became caught up in the turmoil said they should have seen it coming. York's first three or four years in Putnam County were quiet and free of openly hostile conflicts. Yet, there were also signs of the troubles to come.

Marianne Tanner was then the county registrar and head of the two-person staff of the county planning and zoning department. She also had a relative who lived out near the Nuwaubians. After one of the early Savior's Day festivals on York's farm, Tanner's relative brought her a copy of a book that had apparently been dropped by the roadside near the property. It was called *The Holy Tablets*. A brief scan of the book left Tanner deeply frightened.

"It was the most horrifying thing I'd ever seen," she said. The parts about reptilian creatures fighting wars and spaceships coming to save the chosen people were especially scary to her. She gave the book to Sheriff Sills. "I was scared to tell anyone else," she said.

In the time shortly after York bought the property, the first representatives of the group who came to her office seemed to want to establish a normal working relationship. The first Nuwaubian that Tanner met was a young man, dressed in new-looking cowboy garb, who identified himself as Dwight York Jr. "He was clean cut, talking about the music business, saying they wanted to be friends with everyone," Tanner said.

At first, the issues the Nuwaubians' brought to her office seemed minor, like a request to set up a stand to sell hamburgers and lemonade at their annual festival celebrating their leader's birthday. The property wasn't zoned commercial, but the request for a temporary variance was approved.

The first significant project the Nuwaubians sought approval for was the construction of a recording studio on their property. Their application for a building permit was approved. Then there was the matter of a request to move fifteen or so double-wide mobile homes onto the property for living quarters. There was a problem in getting the Nuwaubians to place the trailers on the part of their property that had been re-zoned residential, and the platting documents were never filed properly; nevertheless, Tanner and the department inspector, Dizzy Adams, decided not to make a big issue of it. The Nuwaubians were not the only rural residents of Putnam County who had out-of-compliance trailers on their property.

Tanner became seriously disturbed, however, by something she discovered at a self-storage facility near her house that she managed. A Nuwaubian woman had been seen apparently using an un-rented storage unit, stopping by in the mornings and late at night. When Tanner lifted the door, she found a small piece of foam bedding, a pillow, a coloring book, and some food and eating utensils. It was obvious to her that a child had been left to spend the days in the storage space.

Police found papers with the woman's name and an address in Athens,

Georgia, about sixty miles away. Social service workers in that county contacted the woman, who satisfied them that her child was not being abused. The matter ended there, but it chilled Tanner to think about what kind of person could leave a child in a hot, dark, aluminum cubicle all day.

One day, Tanner became even more unnerved by a phone call she received from one of the Nuwaubians. The caller wanted to know if it was all right for them to bury someone on their property.

Sheila Layson, the Putnam County Clerk of Circuit Courts, saw what she called "a sad situation" played out in the courthouse many mornings during that early period. A Nuwaubian woman would often bring five or six young children into the courthouse with her, take them into the public restroom, and later emerge with all the children scrubbed and dressed.

"They made a mess, " Layson said, "but if she wanted to give them a bath in the sink, I couldn't do anything about it."

When Frank Ford came to his downtown Eatonton office one morning and found a newspaper printed by the Nuwaubians on his doorstep, it made him wonder what kind of folks were living out on the Shadydale Road property. In those early days, the newspaper carried long stories purporting to prove that the first President of the United States was a black man, or making the case that their leader, Dwight York, was descended from Ben York, a member of the Lewis and Clark expedition.

In 1997, Ford sent a notice of intent to sue to a member of the Nuwaubians, on behalf of a printer who claimed the group owed him $10,000. Soon after that, a Nuwaubian woman came to his office and paid the claim in cash. The woman refused to accept a receipt that Ford made up, and then became quite argumentative. Finally, she accepted a written statement that the claim had been settled, and she left.

Ford took those early encounters in stride. "They were strange, but a lot of us are strange. So what," he said.

Ford's wife and law partner, Dorothy Adams (no relation to Dizzy Adams or Sandra Adams), was also the Putnam County Attorney. In that capacity, she saw how the county commission of the mid-1990s bent the zoning rules in the Nuwaubians' favor.

In 1997, the county's planning and zoning board turned down the Nuwaubians' request to build a second large pyramid on their property. Their application stated they planned to operate a restaurant and gift shop inside the pyramid, but the board ruled that such commercial uses were not permitted under the existing residential zoning of that part of the property.

Still, the county's zoning law was fairly new – it was first passed in 1991 – and it wasn't always vigorously enforced. Adams was at a commission meeting when the pyramid issue was brought up. Bill Moore, the commission chairman at the time, told her that the commission had decided to override the planning board's recommendation and approve the permit. Adams told Moore that the commission would be in violation of its own zoning laws. Moore responded, "The buck stops with me." The second pyramid was built, and Moore died the next year of natural causes.

Large red flags went up for Arne Lassen, during the 1993 negotiations that led to the sale of his property to Dwight York. They had reached agreement on the selling price, slightly less than $1 million. York agreed to pay about half the purchase price in cash, and Lassen would finance the remainder.

A sticking point came over the issue of whether Lassen could come onto the property after the sale. Since he was financing the deal, Lassen wanted that right. York offered an extra $200,000 in cash, if Lassen would drop that demand and stay away.

Lassen was uneasy about the deal and about the buyer. He contacted a friend in the FBI and asked him to make some inquiries about York. He told his friend that he was inclined to back out of the deal.

His friend told him his concerns were well-founded. Without mentioning details of the investigation of York by an FBI anti-terrorism unit, Lassen's federal contact told him that some federal agents in New York had been quite interested in York. Those same agents were also rather embarrassed that York had dropped off their radar screen, so they were glad to know where he had gone.

However, Lassen was also advised to be careful. It might not be a great idea to back out of a deal with these people. Some bad things had happened in Brooklyn to people who had tried to do that. So, Lassen sold the land.

One night in Eatonton, Georgia Smith happened to be at the Tastee-Freeze, when a van pulled up, overly crammed with children. The markings on the van indicated it belonged to the Pyramid People. Smith watched as fourteen or fifteen children got out of the van—but there was something strange about their behavior. These kids were not jumping and squealing in anticipation of some ice cream. Rather, they were silent and rigid.

"Those kids never moved," Smith said. "Not one of them got out of line."

Later, Smith started seeing things that were more disturbing. At that time, she worked as a receptionist in a doctor's office adjacent to the county hospital. She saw frequent parades of groups of Nuwaubian women, going for treatment at the hospital. Most of those women were dressed alike in black, despite the Georgia heat. Many of the women pushed strollers with small children, and a startling number of the women appeared to be very young themselves and obviously pregnant.

"It seemed like so many of the girls were pregnant, but they walked along like they were proud of it," Smith said.

Overall, these early encounters with the Nuwaubians generated more head-scratching than alarm among the locals. In those first years after the migration, the prevailing attitude toward the Pyramid People was more curiosity than animosity.

"They intrigued us," said Steve Layson, a member of the county commission in the mid-1990s and the husband of Sheila Layson. There was "a bit of a fear factor," he said, when the local folks heard the newcomers spouting the strange claim that they were descended from superior beings who lived deep within the earth and were locked in conflict with evil creatures who ruled the earth's crust. It was also more than a little weird to hear these black folks from the big city claim they were members of a lost tribe of Native Americans who were descended from the prehistoric tribes who had inhabited this part of Georgia and had left their mounds at a place in Putnam County now called Rock Eagle.

Most people in Putnam County were just wondering, "Who are those people?" Layson said.

That puzzled group briefly included Howard Sills.

His first encounter with the newcomers was when he passed a group of black men coming down the courthouse steps.

"They were in cowboy attire, big hats and belt buckles, and vests," Sills said. "It would be very unusual to see white people around here dressed like that, but even more so with blacks."

At that time, Sills was chief sheriff's deputy in neighboring Baldwin County, and he was preparing to make a run for sheriff of Putnam County. He had moved back to his native Putnam in 1986.

Later, Sills would learn that his predecessor, Putnam County Sheriff Gene Resseau, had received some unsettling information about the newcomers from New York. A few people from up North had called Resseau, asking for help. They said their children had been brainwashed and had joined a cult that had moved to Putnam County. Some of the callers said their children had sold all their possessions when they joined the cult.

There really wasn't much Resseau could do, even if he had been disposed to intervene — which he was not. First, the parents were calling about their adult children, who were legally free to join a cult if they so chose. Second, Resseau had little interest in a group who rarely came to town, much less voted. Sills recalls Resseau being quoted as saying, "Long as they ain't messin' with my niggers, I don't care."

Resseau's use of the possessive in referring to Putnam County blacks reflects a relationship that was fairly common in small counties in Georgia, even into the 1990s. In such counties, the sheriff is frequently the elected official closest to the black community. The sheriff is the primary law enforcement official in most small counties. And as the person responsible for the operation of the jail, the sheriff is the main contact point for those who have relatives inside. The way it traditionally works, the white lawman – there are still only a small handful of black sheriffs – who can do the best job of establishing a working relationship with the black community is usually the one who can count on getting the black vote and becoming sheriff.

However, Resseau had bigger problems than race relations or cults. He was leaving office because he was the target of a federal corruption investigation. Resseau later pled guilty to diverting tens of thousands of dollars of public money to his private use, mostly to pay off gambling debts. He served five years in prison and died in 2004.

Shortly after taking over, Sills started receiving the same kinds of calls from worried parents that had come to his predecessor. A nearly frantic mother told him, "My daughter left Howard University to get on the spaceship."

Sills may have been more inclined to investigate than Resseau, but he faced the same legal limitations. He needed more than worried parents; he needed someone with direct evidence that a crime had been committed – and that he did not have. "There was absolutely nothing we could do," Sills said.

Cult consciousness among Putnam Countians was raised by the news coverage of the mass suicide of nineteen members of the Heaven's Gate cult in San Diego, California. Some people in Putnam County started surfing the internet, and they called Sills in alarm over what they found. While clicking around in the general area of cults, they discovered that there was one in their back yard. Some cult-watch websites had general information about the Nuwaubians, or, the latest version of Dwight York's formerly Muslim cult. These people called Sills to ask him what he was going to do about it.

One thing Sills could do was go to Oregon. With their talk about setting up their own government and the use of their festivals to encourage out-of-state visitors to register to vote in Putnam County, the Nuwaubians were starting to sound ominously like a blast of ill wind from Wasco County, Oregon's past.

In the early 1980s, a group who came to be called the Rajneeshees, a sort of sexually-oriented cult led by a native of India and self-proclaimed god calling himself Bhagwan Shree Rajneesh bought some property near the town of Antelope, in Wasco County.

The cult leader, dubbed "the world's most famous sex guru" drew attention to the group by flaunting his fleet of Rolls Royces and his predilection for flashy jewelry.

The Rajneeshees made a determined and highly dangerous attempt to take political control of the county in the elections of 1984. To swell their own ranks, they brought busloads of supporters in from major cities including Seattle and even San Francisco. They sought to register these people, many of whom were homeless, as voters in Wasco County.

In order to deplete the ranks of local resident voters, they resorted to terrorism.

Members of the cult had discussed contaminating the area's entire water system, but they settled for something only slightly less lethal. The cultists went to about ten fast-food restaurants in Wasco County and sprinkled salmonella bacteria on the salad bars. More than seven hundred people became ill.

Investigators from the U.S. Center for Disease Control at first blamed the restaurants' food handlers. It was only after another year or so, after the cult had been stymied in its growth plans, that some members dropped out and gave police the evidence they needed to tie the bacterial attack to the cult. The witnesses provided evidence that the cult had made up a hit list of public officials and journalists that the cult wanted to eliminate. Police also found vials of salmonella stored at the cult's property.

The "Bhagwan" was deported, and other cult leaders were charged with attempted murder, and the cult quickly collapsed. He died in India in 1990.

Leslie Zaitz, a reporter for the *Portland Oregonian,* wrote a detailed history of the cult in a twenty-part series. As described by Zaitz, the buildup of the Rajneeshee cult was eerily similar to the early years of the Nuwaubian cult in Putnam County. "If anything, the local news media were restrained and conservative in their coverage of the salmonella episode. There was nothing alarmist, nothing to trigger a public panic. More aggressive coverage perhaps would have heated up already tense community relations with the commune. Yet the benign treatment also gave the Rajneeshees comfort that they could get away with it," Zaitz later said.

When he went to Wasco County in October of 1998, Sills was struck by the similarities of this place to his Georgia hometown. The courthouse was probably even smaller than Putnam County's.

As he walked into the courthouse to meet with the sheriff, Sills noted a large statue of an antelope on the courthouse grounds. He didn't stop then to read the plaque beneath the statue. In his meetings with local police and prosecutors, Sills learned that Wasco County had spent millions of dollars in legal fees to fight off the political invasion of the Rajneeshees, challenging the cult's voter registration tactics and their commercial expansion plans.

The Oregon authorities told Sills that their most potent weapon against the cult had been their land use, or zoning, laws. For example, the cult had obtained a building permit for a greenhouse, which they promptly converted into a thriving, illegal collection of commercial shops. The county's use of zoning laws to shut down the mall cut off an important source of revenue for the Rajneeshees.

"Hold fast to your land use laws," was the parting advice Sills received from the Oregon prosecutor.

As he left the courthouse in the Wasco County seat of The Dalles, Sills stopped to take a closer look at the antelope statue. At the base of the statue, there was a plaque dedicated to "the people of Wasco County who stood against the Rajneesh in the attempted takeover of the county, 1981-85." The wording on the plaque also paraphrased the famous words of Edmund Burke, "In order for evil to prevail, good men should do nothing."

Throughout the coming battles, Sills would often reflect back to that plaque.

The trip to Oregon only confirmed the concerns that Sills had already developed about the Nuwaubians. Before he left, Georgia Smith had stopped in his office to tell him about all the young, pregnant girls she'd seen passing by her office. Also, some of the Nuwaubians, including York, had been making statements about establishing their own sovereign government. Even during routine traffic stops, Nuwaubian drivers claimed they were not subject to local laws. Like some of the early adherents of the Moorish Science Temple, they sometimes brandished their Nuwaubian identity cards and claimed they were not subject to local laws.

More importantly, Sills' inquiries brought him a copy of the 1993 FBI intelligence report on York and his followers and their activities in New York.

"I knew then I was fixin' to have some trouble," Sills said.

The troubles got uglier and more public after the closure of Club Rameses, and the period of puzzlement and tolerance between "The Pyramid People" and official Putnam County was over.

"We were under siege," said Frank Ford, an Eatonton attorney who represented the county in most of its legal battles with the Nuwaubians.

For a targeted group of white officials in Putnam County, the three years following the padlocking of Club Rameses was a time when they were regularly vilified by the Nuwaubian propaganda machine. For blacks who dared to oppose York, the name-calling was even worse.

The most boring of small-town governmental functions, like meetings of the planning and zoning board, were routinely turned into heated, tense confrontations with large groups of protesting Nuwaubians. Some female county workers were intimidated enough to ask for police escorts to their cars. Practically every new issue of the Nuwaubians' newspaper brought some new, anonymous, distorted rumor or outright slander.

Nuwaubian research squads descended on area libraries and records archives, digging for dirt with which they could smear their opponents. The public library in neighboring Baldwin County

York portrayed himself as prophet and savior.
From a Nuwaubian poster.

closed its conference room for a time, because the Nuwaubians had effectively occupied it.

Georgia Smith, who had founded a group called Mothers Against Crime and who had tried to oppose the Nuwaubians' takeover of the local chapter of the NAACP, was sometimes followed and taunted by carloads of Nuwaubian men. Sandra Adams and her children were targets of slanderous articles in the Nuwaubian newspaper.

Sills was a prime target. The Nuwaubians published his son's name and the name and address of the school the son attended, as if to show that they knew how they could hurt the sheriff. Also, they published vicious, unfounded rumors regarding the breakup of Sills's first marriage.

To most of the county officials who dealt with the Nuwaubians, it seemed as if the group never really wanted to solve their problems. Strangely, the more the county officials tried to show the Nuwaubians how to avoid conflict, file their papers properly, and resolve their problems, the more the Nuwaubians ignored their advice. "Everybody kind of bent over backwards to appease these people," Dizzy Adams said.

It became clear that York really wanted to maintain the atmosphere of conflict, so that he could portray himself as a black religious leader who simply wanted to live with his "family" on his land, but who was being harassed and discriminated against by the racist officials of Putnam County.

In the historical attempts to establish a Black Utopia, there had been real hostility by the whites who surrounded the black enclaves. Racial animosity served to strengthen the resolve of the Utopians, fostering an us-against-the-world mentality and bolstering the perceived need for a separate society. In John McCown's attempt to build a black-based economy in Hancock County in the Civil Rights era, he was met with blatant racism from whites – and not coincidentally, he was given millions of dollars of foundation money to make his dream work and to combat that racism. In Brooklyn, Dwight York did not have to manufacture stories of hostility towards Black Muslims; the newspapers were full of accounts of clashes between Muslims and the police, some deadly. So, in order to sell his version of the enduringly attractive dream he started peddling in Putnam County, York needed to be able to point to something similar; and if it didn't exist, he would need to make it up.

The blacks of Putnam County must have frustrated York even more than the whites. They didn't flock to his cult, nor did they fall in behind his banner of protest against the county officials and police. Maybe York's separatist vision had limited appeal to Southern blacks by the 1990s; and maybe they simply didn't appreciate being told whom to hate.

Nevertheless, some important people outside Putnam County appeared to buy into York's psychodrama. Some elected officials, including the governor of Georgia, gave at least partial credence to York's claim that he was the victim of small-town racists. A community relations specialist from the U.S. Department of Justice came to Putnam County to investigate York's allegations. Until the child molestation investigation developed into a case too strong to be ignored, federal officials were reluctant to pursue criminal investigations against York and the Nuwaubians. Nationally-known activists, including Rev. Jesse Jackson and Rev. Al Sharpton came to Putnam County to laud York and to criticize those who sought to enforce the law against him. *The Macon Telegraph* published an editorial in support of York's harassment claims.

"Extra! Extra! Extra! Mr. Jerome Dean Adams Obviously Comes From A Line Of Criminals! It's In His Genes!" screamed one of the York-front newsletter headlines. The accompanying article went into great detail regarding the legal problems of Dizzy Adams's son and daughter. Apparently, the reader was supposed to make some sort of linkage between the children's records – the matters involved a DUI charge and an admission of misuse of about $3,000 in public funds – and the father's mindset in discharging his duties as a county building and zoning inspector. By "exposing" the children, the newsletter writers sought to cast doubt on the father's integrity.

For his part, Dizzy Adams saw the smears for what they were: a crude attempt to get him to back off.

"They wanted to keep us from enforcing the law," he said. "And when it became evident that wasn't going to work, they tried threats and intimidation."

The threats were made clearly, though not in overtly criminal language, Adams said. One time, a Nuwaubian official became angry that Adams would not approve something he wanted approved. "You'll get yours," the Nuwaubian man told Adams.

Marianne Tanner said the Nuwaubians dropped all their pretenses of civility, after the Club Rameses incident.

"They got uglier, harassing us more," she said. "They started writing things about me," she said, referring to lies in the Nuwaubian newsletter regarding her sexual and drinking habits. "But I still had to turn them down." At the end of one heated argument in her office, a Nuwaubian man flung a set of building plans across a table at her, she said.

Once, the Nuwaubians sought to bring in a small traveling circus as part of their festival celebration. She gave them liability papers that the circus operator would have to sign. The next day, the Nuwaubians brought back the signed papers. Later, Tanner had to check something with the circus operator, but when she called the man, he told her he had never signed the papers she had given the Nuwaubians.

Not long after the closure of Club Rameses, dozens of Nuwaubians stormed a meeting of the planning and zoning board to protest the citations they had received for the multiple safety violations at the nightclub. "They talked on and on, all saying the same thing," Tanner said. All the Nuwaubians' talk was about how the citations were an example of racial harassment; nobody wanted to talk about fixing the wiring or moving the propane tanks to safer locations.

By the time of the next local elections, in 2000, the Nuwaubians started to mobilize to gain more political clout. A slate of Nuwaubians or Nuwaubian supporters filed for every local office, including sheriff. Their candidate for sheriff was quickly disqualified, due to residency requirements.

As the 2000 election approached, Tanner, acting as county registrar, found cause to challenge the validity of about 150 registered voters who also were Nuwaubians.

"We found as many as twenty-eight people listed as living at the same address," she said. There was a court hearing over the removal of the voters, and scores of Nuwaubians showed up to protest. Nevertheless, the court upheld the disqualifications.

Attorneys for the Nuwaubians filed a suit in federal court, claiming the disqualifications amounted to a denial of the individuals' civil rights. The Nuwaubians produced witnesses who testified they lived at the addresses as listed on the Putnam County voter registration rolls, but almost all of them could produce no documentary evidence to support their claims. The federal judge ruled in favor of Putnam County in approximately 120 of the 150 disqualifications. Again, the Nuwaubians protested, claiming racial discrimination.

"They were trying to improperly influence the election process, no doubt," Tanner said. "We'd never had anything like that in this county before."

For Georgia Smith, the hostilities started in the summer of 1998, when a delegation of seven Nuwaubians showed up at a regular meeting of the Putnam County chapter of the NAACP. A woman in the delegation stood up and identified herself as a retired school teacher with seven grandchildren.

"I would not let my grandchildren live in Putnam County, y'all are so backward," the woman scornfully proclaimed. "Y'all are still under the white man's thumb."

Smith took offense. "If things are so bad here, why'd you move down?" she asked the woman.

The woman ignored the remark and went on to demand that the NAACP chapter initiate a study comparing the wages of blacks in Putnam County to those of whites.

Smith responded that such a study wouldn't even apply to the Nuwaubians, since most of the Nuwaubian women she'd met were on welfare and not working at all.

"They wanted to change everything in the NAACP," Smith said. "There's a lot of things that need to be done here, but they didn't want to solve problems. They just wanted confrontation."

Actually, the Nuwaubians did take over the local chapter. At the next meeting, about two hundred Nuwaubians showed up and formally joined the chapter. About the only thing they ever did as part of the NAACP, however, was to march as a separate group in the chapter's annual Martin Luther King Jr. parade.

"They were all dressed in black. It was intimidating," Smith said.

However, the new members did not seem to be interested in the work of everyday advocacy for blacks, Smith said. "They never did much with it," she said.

They did, however, succeed in sowing discord within the organization. Smith said the older members argued among themselves about how to deal with the newcomers. Was there any merit to what they were saying? Or were they just trying to use the local chapter for their own cause? Some of the longstanding members simply stopped coming to meetings. The Nuwaubians hardly ever showed up, either. The chapter more or less faded away.

Smith's opposition to the Nuwaubians earned her the ultimate insult from one black person to another. In the Nuwaubian newsletters and newspapers, she was referred to as a "house nigger."

The name-calling angered her grown children more than it did her. Her son almost got into a fight with a Nuwaubian man whom he overheard disparaging Smith at the factory where both men worked. The two men had to be separated.

Tensions escalated, when Smith started to be followed around town by cars filled with groups of Nuwaubian men. "It seemed like every corner I went on, they were there too," Smith said. "They'd say things like, 'There she goes. That's the one we wrote up.'"

Smith said she never was physically harmed, nor was she ever intimidated enough to back down from her opposition to the Nuwaubians. Still, she said, it took an emotional toll. "By the end, they got kind of vicious," Smith said.

Smith's stand against the Nuwaubians did not mean she thought that complete racial harmony had already been achieved in Putnam County. "I know I've been discriminated against here," she said. "I was born here. I live on the same street I was born on. But all those people did was open up old wounds."

Gus Kilgore thought the Nuwaubians went way too far, with their anti-Christian rhetoric. As pastor of the predominantly-black New Life Christian Outreach Center in Eatonton, Kilgore was outraged at the way York appeared to be setting himself up as a god.

"People are always looking for a savior, but Mr. York is not a savior," Kilgore said.

Also, the way the Nuwaubians tried to attract recruits from the members of his congregation, particularly the younger members, went far beyond the bounds of religious competition, he said.

"They were showing a hostile spirit," Kilgore said. "They came in and told us, move over, let us have our own way, and if you don't give it, we'll take it."

He also suspected them of going beyond the bounds of the law. He received reports from local people that the Nuwaubians were attempting to peddle pirated music tapes.

Furthermore, others complained to him that low-income tenants of rental properties in Eatonton and other nearby cities were being evicted by their landlords, because the newly-arrived Nuwaubians needed places to live and were willing to pay higher rents.

Kilgore tried to rally opposition to what he viewed as the Nuwaubians' attempts to stir up racial animosity in Putnam County. He used his pulpit and his time on a weekly radio program to preach against the Nuwaubian's doctrines and tactics. He warned his congregation members not to go out to Tama-Re, and he started forming an alliance of local ministers to oppose the cultists. In return, he received anonymous threatening letters.

"I was crying out for the people and the pastors to come together to fight this stuff," Kilgore said. "I was really concerned about a racial war."

The smear campaign directed at County Commissioner Sandra Adams was especially dirty.

Besides slapping her with the "house nigger" defamation, the Nuwaubians used their propaganda organs to suggest that she was indifferent to violence against blacks.

One Nuwaubian newsletter charged that Adams "forgot she is Negro, and they lynch her kind."

The Nuwaubians also made ridiculously false allegations about her family. They stated that her daughter was half white, implying that Adams had had an illicit relationship with a white man. Adams said she nearly laughed at that one, since her daughter's complexion is quite dark, and no one could mistake her features for Caucasian. There were also libelous, unfounded allegations that she had used her influence to shield her son from legal problems and to obtain a construction contract for her ex-husband.

"They really hated me," Adams said. "They thought because I was black, I should automatically jump on their black bandwagon."

But she viewed her opposition to the Nuwaubians as a simple matter of colorblind enforcement of some very basic, easy-to-follow laws. "Buddy, if I want to put a porch on the back of my house, I have to get a permit, just like everybody else," she said.

She was furious over the personal insults published in the Nuwaubian newsletters. "Those are fighting words," she said. But who was she supposed to fight? The offensive materials were printed anonymously. She could sue for libel, but there would be a problem in proving that York was orchestrating the propaganda campaign.

Sheila Layson said the atmosphere of relations between the Nuwaubians and courthouse workers got significantly more tense, after the Club Rameses incident. The Nuwaubian research squads began spending more and more time in the courthouse. Nuwaubian cameramen videotaped nearly all their encounters with the courthouse office workers, as if any routine transaction might quickly escalate into a racial complaint.

"They just stayed in the offices all the time," Layson said. "Mostly, they were digging up dirt on people. They always came in numbers, never alone. Sometimes, they used fake names."

Once, a Nuwaubian man became angry with her, because he wanted a case file that had been sealed. She couldn't give it to him, but he wouldn't accept her explanation. He backed her into the office vault, demanding the file. She refused, and he left.

The Nuwaubians filed numerous document requests under the Freedom of Information Act, and they spent significant sums of money for copies of court documents and files. Their requests took up so much of her staff's work time, that she increased the per-page charge from twenty-five cents to one dollar, as allowed by state law.

Layson said she never saw the research squads' efforts produce valid documents they could use against their enemies, but they were rather effective at harvesting the gossip grapevine.

"They had an uncanny ability to find rumors," she said. They even came up with a minor-league "scandal" involving her and her husband, Steve. Years earlier, they had been involved in a project to sell candles, as a civic-club fundraiser. Some of the proceeds had been lost. Somehow, the Nuwaubians found out about the candle sale and printed an accusation that the Laysons had misappropriated the money. No one took the accusation seriously, but it was sort of creepy to have people probing so deeply into her past and trying to use such trivial material to attack her integrity.

Even when she was able to comply with the Nuwaubians' demands for court records, they were seldom satisfied. "They were always thinking we were trying to hold back on them," she said. "It made some people a nervous wreck."

One woman in her office became a target of racism charges in the Nuwaubian newsletter, after she told a Nuwaubian that she could not stamp a document that the Nuwaubian wanted stamped. The woman was so upset by the charges that she transferred to a job where she wouldn't have to deal with the public.

Still, Layson said she and her office workers tried to accommodate the increasingly confrontational Nuwaubians as much as they could. "We were trying to be fair, to treat them like everybody else," she said.

Steve Layson said the Nuwaubians' tactics met with increasing resistance. After the Club Rameses incident, the county commission decided to enforce their zoning ordinance more stringently.

"That's where we drew the line in the sand," he said.

Part of it was because some people were afraid. There was talk of Nuwaubians going to gun shows and buying all the ammunition they could. Their annual festivals drew thousands of people from out of state, and some of those people were apparently staying to fight for the Nuwaubian causes.

"Some people thought we were going to be inundated," Steve Layson said. "Some wanted to go out there and take care of business and tear those buildings down."

Instead, in May 1998, the county sued the Nuwaubians' property manager for repeated violations of the zoning ordinance. Dorothy Adams asked her husband, Frank Ford, to represent the county.

"Frank is a litigator; I wasn't," she said. The judge ruled in the county's favor and fined the property manager $100,000.

From that point forward, Ford became one of the Nuwaubians' primary targets. They sought to make a legal issue of his participation in the case, complaining privately to Jimmy Davis, a black commissioner who had been their ally in their early years in the county. Dorothy Adams had to explain to the board of commissioners that bringing in outside counsel was a common and perfectly legal occurrence in such cases.

Then, in December of 1998, Ford filed a civil suit against the Nuwaubians on behalf of Putnam County. The issue was a matter of journalistic fraud. The Nuwaubians had published an issue of their propaganda newspaper, claiming that it was the legal organ for the county, that is, the newspaper designated for the publication of legal notices. To bolster their claim of legitimacy, the Nuwaubians copied the masthead of the local newspaper, *The Eatonton Messenger,* onto their phoney newspaper. Ford was granted the injunction he sought against the Nuwaubians.

In early 1999, Ford filed another civil suit on behalf of the county against the Nuwaubians. This suit asked for a moratorium on all construction activity on the Nuwaubians' property, due to the history of repeated zoning violations and of the Nuwaubians' practice of ignoring the previous judgments entered against them.

During the course of that case, the Nuwaubians' attorney asked the judge to compel the county to make a detailed list of everything the Nuwaubians needed to do to be in compliance with county zoning laws. Ford spent days doing that, and the judge thought the matter was settled. However, the Nuwaubians simply ignored the terms of the settlement, Ford said. They continued to build without proper permits and inspections, and then they persisted in complaining that they were being harassed.

The truth, said Dorothy Adams, was that the Nuwaubians were getting special treatment. They were getting away with defying the law, and still county officials were trying to appease them. "We went way beyond what we had done to help anybody else in the county," she said.

Ford said it became clear to him that the Nuwaubians were not interested in any form of compliance. They wanted a perpetual state of conflict, to support their claims of harassment, he said.

"They wanted sovereignty," Ford said.

As the county persisted in its litigation against the Nuwaubians, their propaganda machine heated up. One Nuwaubian publication characterized Ford as "Frank Ford the forgery expert."

A Nuwaubian attorney published a list of Ford's private clients, implying that Ford's integrity was somehow besmirched by his representation of people accused of crimes. It amused Ford to be accused of being a criminal defense attorney, since that's what he was.

Another time, the Nuwaubians used their cinematic talents against Ford. A Nuwaubian official had barged into Ford's outer office, and when he was told to leave, he claimed he had a right to be there. Ford then ordered him out, and poked his finger into the man's arm or chest for emphasis.

The Nuwaubian man turned this encounter into a charge of assault against Ford. That evening, a television station reported on the incident, using videotape supplied by the Nuwaubians. However, the Nuwaubians had spliced on extra scenes, showing the man stumbling and falling in the street and then seated in a wheelchair in the hospital.

The next day, there was a court hearing on the assault complaint. The judge quickly threw the case out, noting that the added scenes were obvious attempts by the complainant to dramatize the event.

Soon after this incident, the Nuwaubians distributed a flyer with a pointed warning for Ford: "You hurt us; we're going to get you back."

The threatened payback would later become real. One night, Ford stopped at a supermarket on the way home. He noted that a car pulled up near him, parking at an odd angle. Ford went into the store, and when he got out, he saw that the tires on his car had been slashed.

There were witnesses to the tire-slashing. Two teenagers had pulled into the supermarket lot just in time to see a man get out of the oddly-parked car and slice Ford's tires. The man got back in his car and drove off, but the teenagers followed him. They also used their cell phone to call police, who arrested the suspect. The man convicted of the crime was a ranking Nuwaubian.

Dorothy Adams recalled with a shiver the morning she went outside their house and discovered the gutted carcass of a dog that had been left in the street near their driveway.

On another occasion, a rock was thrown through the window of their downtown law offices.

But for her, the worst parts of the siege were the everyday anxieties. Normally routine meetings became occasions of tension and barely-subdued rage. Adams was given police escorts to her car, anytime she left the courthouse after dark. She regarded the precautions as necessary annoyances.

"The Nuwaubians would come en masse to the court hearings and commission meetings," she said. "To leave, you had to wade through a bunch of people who were muttering things about you."

For her birthday in 1998, Ford bought Adams a gun. He said he got tired of the intimidation tactics.

"My spine stiffened," Ford said. "They were relentless, and everything they did was to intimidate people. Their tactics may have worked with some people, but they also found we have some people with character here."

Ford said the Nuwaubians' campaign of increasing hostility turned out to be their biggest mistake. "It created a negative public reaction," Ford said. "The more people they added to their 'hit list,' the more people started saying, 'These people are nuts; they're nasty people.'"

The nastiest of the Nuwaubians' attacks were directed at Sills. He was repeatedly called a racist in the Nuwaubian publications. He received dozens of anonymous death threats.

Once, Sills was at a downtown Atlanta mall with his wife and son. He saw a group of men standing nearby, and recognized some of them as Nuwaubians. He told his wife to take his son and go quickly to their car. In moments, he was surrounded by ten or more of the men, who got as close to him as they could and muttered curses and veiled threats. Sills broke out of the circle and the incident ended without violence.

There were times, though, when York prayed that violence would befall Sills. Witnesses later told investigators that York had frequently led groups of Nuwaubians in praying for Sills's death. York told his followers that Sills needed to go, because Sills had figured out that York's real plan was to create an autonomous, independent state; and as long as Sills was around, he would be an obstacle to that plan.

A few times, York would rebuke his followers, according to the witnesses, because they had not acted to bring an answer to his prayers. York scolded the Nuwaubians, saying that in the old days in Brooklyn, when he prayed for something, someone would demonstrate their loyalty to him by making it happen. But now, York chided, none of his followers was willing to suffer the jail time that might come from eliminating York's enemy.

Other times, York would tell his people to hold off on the assassination plan, saying that the crime might be too easy to trace back to its source.

Meanwhile, things that should have delighted York were happening on the political front. The unity among the Putnam County commissioners lasted only until the next election. Though the commission had voted unanimously for the zoning-enforcement resolution that started the battles with the Nuwaubians, they split apart over the issue of whether to keep the pressure on the cult.

Steve Layson ran for county commission chairman in 2000, challenging Ralph Perdomo, a former private investigator and an ally of Sills. Whether it was intended or not, the race was framed by the Nuwaubian issue: hardliners vs. the can't-we-all-just-get-along crowd.

Steve Layson said he started gravitating toward the latter group, after a tense, highly-publicized hearing – which will be described in detail in a later chapter – which resulted in a court-ordered settlement of the zoning disputes. Layson said he took the court's admonition to heart; besides, he was tired of the tension and the brinksmanship.

"I didn't want to be in the courthouse when it was blown up," he said. In addition, he was concerned that the Nuwaubians were preparing to drag the county into federal court in a civil rights case.

During the campaign, he paid a visit to the Nuwaubians on their property. He said he told them he intended to try to work things out with them, as long as they did their part. "I decided to back off," Layson said. "Some people still had hard feelings towards them, but at that point, I decided just to get out into the audience and watch the play."

Layson said he offered no quid pro quo for the Nuwaubians' support, but they did campaign for him, and he did win the election. The Nuwaubians videotaped their meeting with him, so Layson noted that if he had made any promises and then failed to follow through, the Nuwaubians surely would have made it public.

The supposed détente worked only in the sense that there was a drop-off in the level of open hostilities. The fact that York was spending most of his time in a $500,000 house he bought in Athens probably had a lot to do with that.

In Putnam County, the rest of the Nuwaubians continued to flout the county's zoning laws. "They said they wanted to cooperate, but nothing happened," Layson said.

What Layson and most others did not know was that as the zoning battles receded, a much darker, though secret, phase of the saga was beginning.

Sheila Layson got a hint of what was going on, when she took a phone call from a nervous-sounding woman, who had asked to speak with her personally. Sheila Layson didn't recognize the caller's voice. The caller started talking about child molestation that was going on at the Nuwaubians' property, and Layson told her to go to the authorities.

On September 25, 1998, social welfare officials in Putnam County received the following anonymous letter:

"I read the article "Racial, Legal Issues Cloud 'Egypt'" in the *Atlanta Journal-Constitution,* dated Sunday, September 20, 1998, concerning the Dwight York cult.

"I am an ex-member whom [sic] questioned the sick-minded and theocratic hold that Dwight has over the thoughts of his followers.

"Recently, Dwight has been becoming God himself to veteran members, subsequently exercising more divine rule to do whatever he wants to young girls below 16 yrs. of age, young boys of the same age group, and a "herd" of concubines of a wide variety of ages that he "stables" on the property for free labor and sex.

"These facts, until very recently, were very closely guarded secrets. Even amongst the residents of the compound, few knew how often and with which "adopted daughters" York was having sex.

"Well, now they are pregnant. Some of the concubines are so young that his sexual perversions have surpassed being criminal. Because they are loyal to him, they may well deny all these things, but science will not tell a lie.

"Children with children should be tested for paternity. Girls that are now 18 yrs. old that have children more than 5 yrs. old are examples of who Dwight York really is to the compound members: an abuser.

"Of course, the young girls who are not pregnant yet should be tested for sexual tampering. Children Services [sic] will surely find that they have been penetrated by a full-grown male.

"No men on the compound are allowed unsupervised communication with Dwight's concubines, unless he is the law, an "outsider" that York has to impress or deceive, or a relative of the girls in question.

"Strangely enough, many support the abuse and a very skillful line of questioning is necessary to first establish that there was not any prolonged, unsupervised exposure to any other of the compound's males that York may try to pawn.

"His twisted affair will be unmasked. Once, when the GBI (Georgia Bureau of Investigation) went to the compound, he was informed beforehand that they were coming, and busloads of young boys and girls were temporarily shipped to Macon, Georgia, to mask the overcrowding and rape.

"Please save these children. My ability has been exhausted from trying to advise some of the girls who have left the organization to speak up.

"We are afraid. We feel alone. We need help."

As soon as the letter was passed to Sills, he opened a new case. It would become the largest child molestation prosecution in United States history, in terms of numbers of victims and potential numbers of crimes, ever directed at a single suspect.

York's many costumes from the Nuwaubian era.

CHAPTER 6
True Believers, False God (1993 - 2002)

I came giving you what you want so you would learn to want what I have to give. – Dwight York, *The Holy Tablets*

While she was sorting York's mail, one of his girl concubines found a love letter to him from her younger sister. She tore it up.

"I didn't want her to go through the same thing I went through. Not my little sister," the older sister, named Areebah, later told investigators.

The stories of Areebah and those of the other victims recounted in this chapter are taken from interviews with this author, their statements to police investigators and from court documents. They tell what was going on inside York's secret chambers, during the years when most people outside the cult thought the primary issues were zoning violations.

Areebah was five when her mother moved with her and her younger sister Karida into York's Brooklyn community. York was actually her stepfather of a sort, since her mother later bore York a child. In those years, she saw her siblings and her mother usually about once a week, on the day designated for family visits. Her mother earned York's displeasure somehow, and they were sent to the Philadelphia community, where they stayed for about six months, until they were summoned to Camp Jazzir.

Areebah was school age by then, and the Sullivan County school officials were pressing York to send the children living with him to school. Rather than do that, he sent Areebah and Karida back to Brooklyn, where school officials were apparently more compliant. The girls' mother and half brother stayed with York.

Areebah recalled taking this separation in stride. "I was kind of used to it, because I didn't see my mother that much, anyway," she said.

In the late spring of 1993, Areebah and the rest of her family were allowed to move to Georgia. There were two houses where most of the women and children lived, she said. One was for the more highly-favored concubines and their children. It was the former main house of the property, and it was in good repair. It was called "100" and by the time Areebah got there, about fifty people were living in it.

The other residence building was called "103." It was for the less favored, and conditions there were squalid. Usually, about twenty people were assigned to live there.

During those early months, York lived primarily in a trailer. His permanent private quarters were being built as an addition to the main house.

Not long after they got to Georgia, one of York's favored concubines, Basheera, came to Areebah with a proposal. She wanted to know if Atyah, who was thirteen at the time, was interested in having sex with "Doc," the name many of the followers used for York. Basheera was one of the older girls, when Areebah was growing up in Brooklyn.

"I was shocked for the most part, because to me, he was like my Dad, and to me he was like God," Areebah said. She asked for a little time to think about it; Basheera told her Doc would be waiting for an answer.

She used that time to talk with her friend Azizah, who was about her age and had received a similar proposal. They'd both been warned not to talk about this with any adults, so they had to try to sort it out themselves. They both knew that other girls their age and older were having sex regularly with York.

"It was like wow, so it was just basically like – it was like that. It was weird," Areebah said. "It just took all of the, I guess, all the good and nice ways how I felt about him away. It must be degrading. I didn't think anymore about it."

Her mother suspected what was going on, but she didn't expressly forbid Areebah to go to York. That would have been open treason. Instead, she started cautioning Areebah about where she was hanging out and whom she was hanging out with.

When York learned of these subtle efforts to sabotage his desires, he responded by kicking Areebah and her family off the land. They were sent back to Brooklyn, where only a few families remained from the old days of Ansaru Allah Community.

About a month later, Areebah had her fourteenth birthday. York invited her to come back to celebrate the occasion with him and her other friends. However, the invitation was for her alone, not for her mother or siblings. Again, her mother did not forbid her to go, but she advised against it.

For Areebah, though, most of her friends were in the Georgia settlement. She decided to go. Her mother gave her a cryptic warning: "You're going to have to learn on your own."

She was required to write a letter to York, apologizing for all the trouble she'd caused and begging for the privilege of returning to the

Spaceship hovers behind York, represented here as the man from Planet Rizq.

land. She did that, and she was welcomed back with gifts of jewelry and special privileges. "You didn't have to do nothing but basically hang out all day, watch TV, go out and have fun, and that was basically it," Areebah said. "But only until I gave in to what he wanted. Then all of that would just be gone. So that was basically it. Everybody was basically getting pimped."

Areebah played coy as long as she could. Basheera pressed her for an answer. Areebah said she hadn't made up her mind. Once, during a shopping trip with York, she thanked him for the clothes he'd bought her. "Oh, it's not free," York answered. "You're going to have to pay for that."

"I didn't know what to do," Areebah said. "I felt lost. We just wanted to keep going out and keep getting clothes." She and another on-the-fence girlfriend, Alimah, made a pact: if one would do it, so would the other. Neither wanted to go alone.

In November of 1993, York took Areebah and Alimah out for a shopping trip, complete with dinner at a restaurant. It was Alimah's birthday. They came back late and went with York to his trailer. There, Basheera told them York wanted them to stay, and then Basheera went to a back bedroom, leaving the girls with York in the living room.

York pulled out the convertible sofa, making a bed. "It's getting late. When are we going to do something?" he told the girls.

Areebah was still hesitant. "I was fourteen. I didn't know what to do," she said.

York showed them. He pulled out his genitals and instructed the girls how to perform oral sex on him. They followed his instructions, and then he moved on to sexual intercourse.

"He kind of positioned us in the position he wanted and just took our virginity," Areebah said. "It felt weird. I was in pain for most of it. I didn't know how to think of him anymore."

For most of the next three years, York called Areebah to him regularly and frequently, every other day or so. During that time, he expanded their sexual menu to include anal sex and group sex. Areebah was present while York had sex with girls who were seven or eight years old at the time. On some occasions, York's "main wife," Kathy Johnson, would participate in the sexual molestation. On one occasion, Areebah went to clean York's sauna, and she saw York receiving oral sex from a thirteen-year-old boy.

Once or twice, Areebah said, York suggested making videotapes of their sex acts, but she refused. Some of the other girls had told her that they had allowed the taping. York frequently supplied pornographic tapes for the girls to watch.

When asked to list the names of the other children she had witnessed having sex with York, Areebah said, "Like, everyone." Then she listed about twenty names.

When she was seventeen, Areebah started pulling away from York and refusing to go to him. But at the same time, her younger sister Karida was approaching fourteen, close to the age at which Areebah had become York's concubine.

One of Karida's letters got through to York, and she was allowed to come to Georgia. Areebah handled the sensitive situation much as her mother had three years earlier. She tried to watch over Karida and limit the time the younger girl spent around York.

But York sensed what was happening. He would say things to Areebah like, "Oh, you've got your sister up under you. Let her be free. Let her hang out with the other girls."

Gradually, the younger girl allowed herself to slide into York's inner circle, enticed by the same special treatment that had enticed Areebah. The older girl warned her sister not to stay late at Doc's place.

York assigned the sisters to separate houses, and he verbally attacked Areebah in front of Karida. "He just didn't want me to get in the way basically.

So he just started telling her that I was crazy and I'm a bitch," Areebah said.

Nevertheless, Areebah realized that she had lost the battle for her sister.

"It's like the same – it's a cycle," she said. "She started getting the diamond rings. She started getting gold. She started getting clothes. She was at his house all night."

After another girl confirmed to her that York was having sex with her sister, Areebah wrote York a letter of protest. "I told him not to mess with my sister, and he called me a liar. He said I was a whore, that I was a bitch, I was going crazy, and he didn't do anything to my sister, and I just need to chill out."

When Karida told her that she, too, was now a concubine, Areebah made up her mind to tell her story one day. It would be another three years before she got the chance. Before she could bring herself to tell what had happened, she went through a period of denying the too painful truth.

At an age when most children are still fans of Sesame Street, Jokara was made to watch pornography. One of York's concubines would show her tapes of adults having sex and tell her that "Baba," or York, wanted to do those things with her. These special showings started when Jokara was about eight. She had lived inside Ansaru Allah Community since she was two, with her mother and three siblings.

After her family was moved to Camp Jazzir, York started to find out what the little girl had learned in porno class. First, he fondled her through her clothes and exposed himself to her. Then he told her to perform oral sex on him, and she complied.

The intensity of the sexual encounters increased once the group moved to Georgia, Jokara later testified.

Once, the older concubines told her and her girlfriend Azizah to undress, and then they took videotapes of them. Within a week or two of their arrival on the land, York escalated his demands. "He had sex with me in my butt," Jokara said.

She and Azizah, who was about a year older than she, were often summoned to York's trailer together, and York would have anal intercourse with them both; one or two of the older concubines were sometimes present. When she was about thirteen, York started having vaginal intercourse with her. The summons to York usually came in the form of a request to come clean his quarters. This pattern continued for about the next three years, at which time Jokara started becoming interested in boys her own age.

"Well, I stopped going there that much, like because I didn't talk a lot, so he thought I was crazy, and we wasn't allowed to hang out with boys," she said.

"I guess he didn't want us, you know, to have a boyfriend. So I was hanging out with the boys or whatever, and I guess he thought that I was being bad, so he didn't have me around him."

Jokara was taken on one of York's reward trips to Disney World. She got carsick on the way there, so she was able to avoid being called to York's bed during the stay at one of the resort hotels; but she did see one of the other girls perform oral sex on York, while he watched television.

There were consequences for turning down York's advances, she said. "Well, you weren't given no clothes. I got in trouble for something, and I didn't get no clothes until like three years later. So I was basically wearing the same clothes I got and they were like too small for me, you know. Or, he wouldn't take us out. Sometimes he would put us on punishment and we can't leave the house."

Jokara's brother, Rafiq, remembers receiving some really nice gifts from York on his seventh birthday. They were living at Camp Jazzir at the time. He got a Batman costume and a toy billiards game, plus other neat stuff.

Before he turned eight, Rafiq had become a human toy in York's sex games. Rafiq recalled one night when one of the concubines took him into a room and played a pornographic video on the television. The concubines performed oral sex on him, and while this was going on, York came into the room, undressed and watched.

After the move to Georgia, an older boy took him to York's chambers and started touching him sexually. They went to another room, where they were joined by York and one of the concubines; all four continued the petting. Then York tried penetrating him anally, but he was unable to do so.

After that, Rafiq was summoned to York about once a week. He performed a variety of sex acts with York, the concubines, and other boys. This continued for about a year, until he was sent to Macon for a few months. He was not told why he was exiled, nor why he was summoned back.

But when he came back to the land, his attitude toward the sexual encounters had changed. He was about ten by then.

"I started realizing what was really going on. When it happened, I was like so young, so it was like I didn't really know what was really going on. But when I got older and started realizing, I tried to like keep my distance," Rafiq said.

As Rafiq withheld himself from York, York would withhold the little rewards from Rafiq. York would point out the gifts he was buying for the more compliant children. He would say to Rafiq, "Well, maybe if you would come around more, then you could get what I bought them."

Rafiq's sexual encounters with York declined in frequency, but for the next three years or so, he never told his mother what was happening. "I didn't know what was going on was something you were supposed to tell your parents," he said. "I didn't know that it was something that's not supposed to be happening. It was like something he inbreeded in me that it was a secret. So I didn't really go around blabbing my mouth."

Azizah liked to play with her friend Jokara, and York liked to play with the two of them together. The little girls were about six and five, respectively, when York began fondling them at Camp Jazzir, Azizah recalled.

The older girls would summon the little girls to York's chambers. On a few occasions, the concubines would tell the girls to undress, so that they could take videos and pictures of them.

The older girls never protested about the abuse of the younger girls, but Azizah said she understood. "They would've gotten into trouble if they did," she said. "They would stop getting talked to, or their food would be taken away from them."

The temptation is to become frustrated with explanations like Azizah's. Why didn't the children run screaming to their mothers? Why didn't the mothers run screaming to the police?

That nobody ran to anybody with the ugly story indicates how deeply enmeshed they all were in York's web of psychological and physical dependency and exploitation. Those who lived with York accepted him as the center of their existence. He provided whatever food, shelter, and clothing they received. To submit to him meant becoming closer to their god, or to the father that most of the children never had. The rewards they obtained for compliance may seem meager, but they were both the fulfillment of real needs in an environment of enforced want, and a sign to all that they were favored by god.

Theoretically, any of them could leave at any time. Some did. But most of the ones who stayed firmly believed that, as bad as things were on the inside, things were worse on the outside, where the demons ruled. And as for the children, where could they run?

Those who stayed and tolerated York's abuse were frequently reminded by him how worthless they were. He told them they had no skills to survive in the outside world. He neglected to tell them that it was part of his scheme to keep them believing that they had value only to him.

York also never told them how contemptuous he was of them. He considered them fools, and in unguarded moments he would laugh at those who had been most loyal to him. He wanted them to think, however, that he was their best chance for happiness.

Azizah recalled a time when she and Jokara were being fondled by York.

He said the touching was only a preview of better things to come. Once they graduated to real sex, he told the girls, they would keep coming back to him, and they would like it. York turned out to be only half right.

Azizah said that after the move to Georgia, "Things got worse than before." York would demand oral sex from her or the other girls in the expanding clique nearly every day, she said.

She can vividly recall the pain of the first time York performed anal sex on her. He kept demanding it on an almost daily basis, and it kept on hurting, she said.

York kept the bedroom of his trailer dark, with black sheets on the beds and lights from candles only, Azizah said. The room also had the leopard skin pillows that Azizah remembered from Camp Jazzir, the pillows on which she'd been told to pose nude. There were nude statues around the room, and York kept a large supply of dildos there.

When she was about twelve, Azizah worked up the courage to confront York. She was angry about how York had raped her friend Khalid (not his real name), the young son of his most-favored concubine. She had been in an adjacent room and heard Khalid screaming in pain, and she saw the boy come out of the room crying.

Azizah openly defied her god. "I told him we didn't want him touching us anymore," she said.

York shot back, "Who do you think you are? I'm the king, and I'll tell you when we stop having sex," she said. (Khalid was later questioned by police about this incident. He broke into tears, but he denied that it happened. Other children, however, told police that he had been repeatedly molested by York.)

The next day, Azizah said, Khalid came to the window of the room where she and the other girls slept. She went off to talk with him, and he told her that he wanted to run away. He was angry with his mother for letting York assault him.

But the escape plan never materialized. They had nowhere to go, no one to help them. They were ignored by York for a short time, but then he summoned them again, and they went to him.

Azizah said that York attempted to have vaginal intercourse with her, but was unable to penetrate her at first. He turned to the other girls for a time, but he wasn't through with Azizah.

When the couple from Trinidad referred to earlier in this work divorced in 1994, their ten-year-old daughter Ramillah wasn't happy about the custodial arrangements. Her mother took her and two of her sisters with her to York's farm in Georgia. York was the father of Ramillah's oldest half-sister. It had been her mother's insistence on moving from Trinidad to Brooklyn to be with York that ultimately led to the divorce.

"I didn't want to leave New York," said Ramillah, who had been living with her father, Asad. "I missed my best friend and my Barbie dolls."

Once in Georgia, Ramillah went straight from Barbie dolls to pornography. She was assigned to live in a house with other girls of her age group, including her new friend, Jokara. During her first few months there, one of York's concubines showed her a pornographic magazine. She was invited to come to York's house and watch television. While she was doing that, York, whom she viewed as a stepfather, would ask her about her boyfriends and what she might let them do to her. She told him she didn't have a boyfriend.

When she was twelve, Ramillah was escorted by a concubine to a darkened room adjacent to one of York's offices. The concubine told Ramillah to take a dip in the Jacuzzi tub in the room, and while she did, the concubine played a pornographic tape on the television.

Then, she was escorted by another concubine into York's chambers. She remembered how dark the room was. She stumbled over a pillow and fell to the floor. Then she heard York's voice calling to her from the bed. Then he performed anal intercourse on her.

After that, sex with York became almost a nightly event for a year or so. York often told her that sex with him was her ticket to salvation.

"If you do this, you'll go to heaven, you'll be saved," he told her. "This is a good thing. You're lucky."

Ramillah knew better. "I knew it was wrong from the get-go," she said.

Nevertheless, she submitted to him. Though she saw through his come-ons, she firmly believed his threats to punish her, if she told her mother. "If I told her, she would've gotten into trouble," Ramillah said.

In return for her submission, Ramillah got one of York's cheap diamond rings, like many of the other girls wore. Once, she recalled, one of the older concubines got angry with the younger girls and took all their rings away.

Ramillah started to whisper to the others about her desires to leave. For this, she was reported to York, who wrote her a scathing letter banishing her from the inner circle to one of the squalid trailers. After a few months of exile, she apologized to York and asked to be taken back. This time, he complied.

Writing a letter to "Doc" was the accepted way to try to regain his favor. Whatever the girls or concubines had done, they had to acknowledge that it had been their fault. Typically, they expressed their fanatically deep devotion to him and begged for a second chance. Some of those letters became evidence.

"My love," began a letter from a concubine named Yamha. "Once I met you I gained respect for you as Alla (sic) in the flesh...I never had a brain, just my love and concern for you...I didn't see myself as a bad person or anything, and I didn't have anything to hide, other than my early pregnancy, and I didn't think that warranted me as a bad person...I know you have a job to do and don't have time for this sorry stuff. I just need to know what you want." The letter came in an envelope addressed, "To God, From Yamha."

Another letter, from a woman or girl named Zahirah, was addressed to "Atum-Re" one of the Egyptian deity names York used from time to time. She wrote, "I want to thank you for letting me go shopping today. It was a wonderful experience This whole pregnancy has been a wonderful experience for me. And I just want to thank you, because you made my dreams come true. Love, Zahirah."

A concubine named Hanifa wrote, "Dear Doc, I know you think, well, know, that I am crazy, and I am. I'm crazy about you. Could you mold me into whatever you wish? Could we have more than a blow here and there?...I also want Falak to get to know you and you to know her...Can I get closer to you? Can Falak (her daughter by York) and I move to 100?...Can I please come up under your wing?"

"Dear Baba," wrote a young woman named Ghadya. "I apologize for opening my mouth. I really miss you very much...I remember all the good times you and I had together, but I guess I mest (sic) up that time. I want to be around you...I don't want to hang around with boys forever. I want to be around you."

Zahirah wrote another letter saying, "Doc, I know what you said about people coming at night. I'm not one of those people. I see an opportunity to take care of you, and I feel the need to take care of you, when I have the chance. I'm not coming for SEX, FOOD, or MOVIES. Just to make it clear."

A young woman named Banan had apparently done something to displease York, when she wrote this letter: "Yes, I made a stupid and detrimental mistake, and I didn't realize how detrimental it was to our relationship. I know you don't care to hear it, however, I apologize...I love you with all my heart and I hope and pray to gain your love and respect one day...Thank you for giving me the opportunity to express myself without hitting me (At this point of the letter, Banan drew a smiley face on the page.) Please forgive me for talking crazy today. I honestly want to grow old with you for another 13 years and an eternity...I am happy that you feel good, you look radiant and no one can hold a candle to your looks."

In another letter, Zahirah sought to make amends for some infraction: "Doc, I would like to thank you for everything you have done for us. Without you, there is no guidance, light through this dark tunnel...Doc, I really am sorry for the incidents that have been taking place. I think for a long time I was holding a lot of stuff in, and that was my breaking point...I don't care what feeling I have about things not going my way, you are still my first priority. Because without you there is nothing in my life. You are our children's father. Believe me, I can't lose you. Please find somewhere in your heart to forgive me. Please." Then she added a postscript: "P.S. You said you were going to forgive me if I gave you a B.J. WHAT HAPPENED Do you need another one?" Just before the question mark, she drew a smiley face.

As desperate as some of these girls and women seemed to be to stay in York's favor, some of them were equally desperate to get out of the less desirable communal housing. In October 1997, Nasira wrote a report to Kathy Johnson on the conditions at 103, or the Girls House. She served as a sort of housemother at that time.

The report consisted of a room-by-room list of problems:

"Big Bathroom – Both sinks leak, the whole wall next to the toilet is gone, the bottom of the shower collapsed, the toilet doesn't flush (has to be flushed with a basin of water).

"Kitchen – One large hole in floor (boarded right now, cat came through), the oven doesn't work, the door is falling off, the refrigerator doesn't work (drips freon, food spoils fast).

"Dining Room – One boarded up window, holes in bottom parts of wall.

"Living Room – One large hole in inside wall.

"Laundry Room – Neither washer nor dryer works, need a new door (The door is nailed onto the house with two fence posts, but it is not closed. Small animals could come through).

"Small Bathroom—The floor is warped, the toilet doesn't work (recurring problem), large hole in wall to small bedroom, the shower leaks, hole in tub (You can see the ground under the house, water pours out to the side of the house).

"Large Bedroom—Hole in the floor, hole in the wall.

"Sun Room—One boarded-up window, hole in wall below window, double doors fell off.

"Bedroom next to small bathroom—Hole in the floor, hole in the wall, electricity problem (You have to unscrew the bulb to turn the light off and on).

"Other small bedroom—two holes in wall, small holes in floor, needs a door.

"Other—Vents are rusted, curtains, need more dishes, silverware, ironing board, tables, heat problem (The pilot light doesn't stay lit and no propane), no carpet in the living room, sun room and dining room and Big Girls room. We no longer have a mice problem (We caught 20). Carpet (which gave the house an odor) was removed."

She ended the report by saying, "Please fix our house." Then she added seven smiley faces.

Only a few people living at Tama-Re even suspected that horrible crimes were being committed in York's private chambers. Nearly all the people living on the land or coming there to hear the Master Teacher spent twelve to sixteen hours of their days toiling for York. They had joined the community as adults, most of them seeking spiritual growth and thinking they would find it at Tama-Re.

Doc wants lobster for dinner, the caller told Marc Hill. Doc, aka Dwight York, was on Tama-Re, in Putnam County. The young man who received the call was in Atlanta, 120 miles away.

Hill was being offered the privilege, or, more precisely, suffering the demand, of dropping whatever he was doing, finding some fresh, live lobster, buying the lobster with whatever of his own money he had not yet given to York, and then making the trip to bring York his entrée of choice.

Of course, Hill promptly jumped into his beat-up car and began the crustacean hunt.

Hill went to the northern suburbs of Atlanta to find live lobster. He bought more than $100 worth – a small fortune for an incense salesman. When he was about half way to Tama-Re, he got a call from one of York's concubines. It was getting sort of late, the caller unnecessarily reminded him, adding that Doc's hunger had gotten the best of him, so he had found something else to eat. Don't bother bringing any lobster, Hill was told.

At that time, in the mid-1990s, Hill had dropped out of college to become a Nuwaubian. He was sleeping mostly in the back rooms of one of York's bookstores in Atlanta, and he would sneak back into his college dormitory when he needed a shower. All the long hours of his labors were devoted to York, either selling York's books, teaching classes on York's latest re-casting of his black separatist cult, or standing in shopping mall parking lots peddling the cheesy incense or personal care products packaged at Tama-Re by other York devotees.

Nevertheless, Hill did not allow himself to become angry that he had wasted scant resources, not to mention the better part of an evening, trying to satisfy York's whim for lobster. Nor was he outraged that York had cancelled his order so casually and with so little regard for Hill's efforts to please his savior. No, Hill just turned his overtaxed four-cylinder automobile around, went home and cooked himself and his friends a lobster dinner.

What was a smart young man like Marc Hill doing in a cult like this?

That's one of the easiest questions to ask about the characters who played supporting roles in the Nuwaubian saga, yet it's also one of the most difficult to answer.

A significant fraction of the Nuwaubian followers of Dwight York were people like Hill – young, articulate, educated, and possessed of options to pursue lives in the mainstream world.

Instead they chose to enslave themselves, often for years. They devoted practically all of their time, talents, energy, and personal resources for the personal gain and pleasure of Dwight York.

It may be easy to write off such people as misguided dupes, or even scorn them for failing to see York for the evil shuck-and-jive artist that he was. Those who followed him certainly should have known better, it would seem.

To dismiss these believers, however, would be to fail to understand both their motives and the power of the dream York was selling. As tawdry as the reality was, many of the Nuwaubians sincerely believed that they were part of something noble, that they were building something good. Some of the answers to the riddle of the Sphinx, the polyurethane foam Sphinx, that is, can be found in the stories of Marc Hill and Nuwaubians like him.

Black separatism was as close as the street corner, in the Philadelphia neighborhood where Marc Hill grew up. The area was a stronghold of the Nation of Islam. Hill's older brother joined another separatist movement called the Five Percenters, a black Muslim sect splintered from the Nation of Islam.

The Philadelphia branch of York's cult, then called "The Ansars" locally, peddled their products and books on the streets.

As a high-school student, Hill was looking for something to help him define his racial identity. "Traditional religion wasn't doing a good job explaining the world to me." He drifted away from the faith of his church-going, professional parents.

Some of the other students at his school were attracted to Islam, partly as a way of distancing themselves from Christianity, which they saw as a religion devised and dominated by whites. There was a variation of Islam being peddled on the corner of 52nd and Market by an Ansar whom Hill recalls as "a gentle guy, who liked to listen to and talk with me."

The man gave Hill one of York's books, entitled *360 Questions To Ask A Christian*. Some of those questions were like the ones Hill was asking himself.

The definitive, defiant tone of the book appealed to Hill. Perhaps he had found someone who could answer his questions. "It was like Doc would be explaining the world to me," he said.

After high school, Hill went south to Morehouse College in Atlanta. He had high expectations of playing varsity basketball at college; however, he failed to make the team.

The day he got cut, he was in a state of deep dejection. He took the Atlanta subway, called MARTA, heading for a bookstore in a mall. On the train, he was working on an assignment for his class in Arabic. A stranger approached him and struck up a conversation about the language. After offering a correction to a mistake he'd noted in Hill's Arabic, the man gave him one of York's books.

The book re-kindled Hill's interest in York's teachings, and he soon enrolled in a class to learn more. He was attracted to the way York seemed to take the best from all the established religions. Hill was inspired to change his major to religion.

"Doc honored all the holy books," Hill said. "He didn't make me choose. He allowed me to do everything, believe in everything. That was the brilliance of it."

The fact that he'd met an attractive young woman in the Nuwaubian community only increased his enthusiasm.

In February of his freshman year in college, Hill filled out the nine-page application to join York's group. At that time, the Nuwaubian trappings had not been fully deployed, so the working name of the organization was the Ancient Mystical Order of Melchizidek, Lodge 19.

The cover of the application was dominated by a large picture of York, identified as "The Grand Master Teacher." Above the picture was an inscription written in pictographs, below that a line in Arabic, and below that a line in English: "Only Fools Duck When The Truth Is Thrown At Them."

The application was a probing document, seeking to know highly personal details of the applicant's life. It also sought to establish that the applicant was fully prepared to walk away from whatever he or she had been, in order to enter a new and dramatically different way of life.

In a section called "Marital Status," the applicant was required to list "former religion and type of marriage ceremony performed, if married."

The questions continued: If divorced, do you have divorce/separation papers? If separated, will it become a legal divorce? When?

Do you have children by ex-mate? How many? Who has custody of children?

Does ex-mate pay child support? His/her feeling about children joining?

There was a page for questions about family members, and questions about the applicant's educational background and about any special skills, professions or trades they possessed.

In an essay section, applicants were asked to describe their feelings about Dr. Malachi Z. York, the name Dwight York had taken at that time.

How do you feel about his mission? In what ways do you feel you could assist in his mission? Do you have any questions, feelings, curiosities, worries, or discrepancies that you would like to share with us beforehand?

The applicants were asked to list any military experience. Female applicants were required to list all live births, miscarriages, and abortions.

Under a section labeled "Personal," applicants were given a large blank space to answer the question: Do you have any ties in the world that you feel you cannot break? Explain. Also in this section, applicants were asked to list details of any bank accounts in their names.

The applicants were required to have their signatures notarized. They were also required to include four passport-sized color photos of themselves, as well as copies of the results of a recent physical exam, and copies of their Social Security cards, birth certificate, and driver's license or other picture ID.

Under the signature blank was a statement in which the applicant agreed to abide by all rules of the organization.

Hill submitted his papers, waited for a few weeks, but received no response. He inquired at the bookstore where he'd filed the application and was told that his papers had apparently been lost, and that he'd have to file a new application, with all the supporting documents, as well as the $50 application fee. In retrospect, Hill suspects that the paperwork problems were just a ruse to get another filing fee from him. Nevertheless, he submitted a new application.

This time, Hill was quickly accepted. He started going to the Putnam County property for Sunday evening classes. At this stage, York's appeal became less philosophical and more personal.

York wouldn't appear at every class. The newcomers could only hope that they'd be graced by an appearance of the Master Teacher in the flesh. Most often, another teacher would start the classes.

"Then, suddenly, Doc would come in, with his security guards and four or five women," Hill said. For a while, York would stand quietly in the back of the class.

"Then, somebody would ask a question, and Doc would jump in," Hill said. "His thing was about surprising people."

During this period, York would preach and lecture about "the space stuff," Hill said. York presented himself not as a deity but as "The Reformer." He often told the students, "I'm here to get you ready for Jesus."

York's followers also needed to prepare themselves for the end of this world, which, York then predicted would come sometime early in the year 2000. The students were supposed to develop the notion that York was "their last chance," Hill said.

As the lessons went on, York seemed to be defining himself more as a savior than as a teacher.

"The deeper in you got, the more it became, He is God," Hill said.

Hill stayed with the program, captivated more by York's style than by what he was actually saying.

"He wasn't this fiery, dynamic preacher," Hill said. "He was charming, an entertainer. His voice would always hit me. It was very seductive and attractive."

Once he was on the inside, Hill's perspective began to change. The importance of believing his words and admiring his style started to fade. Gaining York's favor became the primary goal.

"In the beginning, it was all about the books," Hill said. "Then it became all about being near Doc, serving Doc."

Getting closer to York was directly tied to a student's success at bringing in money for York, and to the student's capacity for blind acceptance of York's pronouncements.

"If you weren't buying whatever Doc was selling at the moment, you weren't in the community," Hill said.

Hill became an enthusiastic and productive peddler. He worked out of York's bookstores in Atlanta and peddled York's products in shopping mall parking lots. As he grew in York's favor, his interest in college declined.

When he talked to York about whether he should stay in school, York told him, "Why waste the time?" The world was ending in a few years, York proclaimed, so what good was a college degree?

When he finished his first year at college, Hill called his parents and told them he wouldn't be coming home for the summer, as planned. Instead, he'd be spending the summer at this exciting new place that he'd discovered in the country.

As it turned out, the summer was no picnic for Hill. He was part of the crew that erected the first of the pyramids at The Egypt of the West.

"We were like the Egyptian slaves, except they probably didn't get any sandwich breaks," Hill said.

During that summer of 1997, York staged the largest Savior's Day celebration up to that time. Thousands of followers attended what was essentially the debut of York's Nuwaubian line of books and costumes.

Hill recalled how York led the parade out of the pyramid, resplendent in his new, pharaoh-like robes. As he walked through the crowd, York smiled and pointed at some of his followers. Those who were pointed at took the gesture as a signal that they had gained York's favor, that they would be among the saved, Hill said.

"The persons he pointed to were going to Paradise, the others to Hell," Hill said.

Towards the end of the summer, Hill went home to Philadelphia for a visit. His parents were worried about him, and they agreed to pay his rent if he would return to school. He came back to Atlanta and re-enrolled in college, though he changed his major to religion.

In the Nuwaubian world, though, he was still regarded as something of an outsider, and his decision to stay in school kept him on the outside. So, he dropped out, demonstrating his commitment by becoming a full-time Nuwaubian.

He couldn't shut off his inquiring mind. During a class at Tama-Re, Hill interrupted York to ask a question. It was the first time he'd done that, and once he did, "Things were never the same," Hill said.

Before he spoke out, Hill had wondered in silence about York's mispronunciation of some frequently used names in the lesson. "You should know how to pronounce the name of your own tribe," he said.

York's new claim to be a Nuwaubian Moor and a supernatural being from another planet puzzled Hill, since York had claimed for many years that he was a descendant of the royal family of Sudan. Hill wanted some clarification, so he asked York to explain how his new lineage could be reconciled with the old.

York didn't become angry; he became sad, and that hurt Hill even more.

The Master Teacher responded with a plaintive request to the whole group. "Can't you all just trust me this one time," he said. He was letting everyone know that he'd been wounded by Hill's question.

It didn't matter that Hill's question had been a valid one. Hill instantly wished that he'd never opened his mouth, because it was his words that had hurt the savior. "It broke my heart," Hill said. "I felt guilty."

From that moment on, his status within the group dropped dramatically. "I became 'The Guy Who Asked That Question,'" Hill said. "Everything I worked for was in jeopardy."

The Nuwaubians who had regarded him as an outsider now added "slanderer" and "troublemaker" to the whispered charges against him. Some of the Nuwaubians clearly did not want to be seen with him.

In the following months, Hill worked extra hard to redeem himself. He had a car and he lived in Atlanta, so he gladly offered to bring in people and things from the big city. He would go to the Atlanta airport to meet some of the entertainers booked into the new Club Rameses and bring them out to Tama-Re. Even things like the cancelled lobster dinner did not faze him. There were days when Hill would make three round trips between Atlanta and Tama-Re.

Gradually, the stigma from having challenged York began to wear off, Hill thought. Once, after one of his trips from Atlanta, Hill received a warm handshake from York. "I was in heaven," Hill said.

As evidence of his return to York's good graces, Hill was invited to share Thanksgiving dinner with York and the inner circle. They enjoyed a pleasant dinner, and Hill was invited to stay overnight in the guest house.

The next day, Hill worked with the other men and then returned to Atlanta for the night. On Saturday, he returned to Tama-Re, anticipating another day of work. He needed something for a chore and went looking for it in the nightclub building.

Inside, Hill saw York surrounded by about fifteen children, all of whom were wearing roller skates. Apparently, they were going to use the dance floor as a skating rink. Hill found what he needed and left.

But as he walked away from the building, one of York's security guards gruffly stopped him short. "You can't do that!" the man shouted at him.

Hill didn't know what he'd done, but he vowed to himself that, whatever it was, he'd never do it again.

He wouldn't get another chance to step out of line. The next time he returned to Tama-Re, about four days later, he was stopped at the gate.

"Marc Hill, you've been whitelisted," the guard told him.

There was no discussion, no appeal. Hill simply drove away from the pasture with the pyramids he had helped build.

Later, he managed to get a phone call through to York's offices. The only explanation he received for his ban was that he was considered a "bad influence" and that he was suspected of drug use.

To clear himself of the latter charge, Hill had himself tested for drugs. He faxed the results to York's office, proving that he was drug-free.

After receiving no response for about two weeks, Hill called the offices at Tama-Re. Yes, they'd received the drug test results, and yes, they were sorry that Hill had been falsely accused. But no, he could not come to Tama-Re. The ban remained in effect, permanently. Again, no discussion, no appeal.

Hill was devastated. He thought he had given all he had to give to advance Dwight York's dream. "I'd been fighting for a bed in a barn, for a plate of rice," Hill said.

He stayed in Atlanta only long enough to have his car repaired for the long drive home. Back in Philadelphia, Hill resumed his education. He is now on the faculty of a northeastern university, where he teaches African-American studies.

In retrospect, Hill believes the criminal case against York was a valid one. He never saw any direct evidence of the child molestation, but he did see how York almost always surrounded himself with young women and children.

He also saw the way York's selected girls acted around men other than York. He recalled a time when a male entertainer at Club Rameses passed among the crowd, hugging or touching hands with the members of the audience. York's girls, sitting in a group, backed away from the singer, as if they'd been forbidden to touch another man.

Also, Hill had seen the children roller-skating with York. It was outwardly innocent, but he believes someone must have worried that Hill might begin to suspect that York was doing more than skating with the children. So, Hill was banished.

Despite all that, Hill still values parts of his Nuwaubian experience.

First of all, there was the sense of accomplishment, the feeling that he and his fellow Nuwaubians were working together to live out a shared dream.

"We believed we were building something good," Hill said. Theirs would be a community built by black hands, where blacks made the rules and lived by a spiritual code devised, they thought, by a black man. "We were sacrificing for something better," he said.

To make that dream come true, Hill was willing to work long hours for no pay in the heat of a Georgia summer, building a pyramid for a man who was his teacher and savior. At the end of those days, he and his young comrades would stretch out in the field and savor their hard work, maybe sharing a bottle of cheap wine as they relaxed.

"All we had was each other, but we had fun together," Hill said. "In fact, I had more fun that summer than I'd ever had in my life."

Even though he now views York as a criminal receiving a just punishment, Hill can also see good in the dream that inspired him and the others.

"There's a part of me that still roots for Doc, even though I know now it was all fake," Hill said.

There's another part of Hill that bears a permanent symbol of his misplaced devotion. On one of his shoulders, he has a tattoo of a crown – the same crown design that can be found on the inside cover of *The Holy Tablets.*

He didn't know what to call it at the time, but the teenaged street hustler experienced an apotheosis. He found someone who could fill his spiritual and intellectual void, someone in whom he could believe.

For Derrick Hodge, the apotheosis was the elevation of the man Dwight York to the status of a god. Hodge was still in high school in Columbus, Ohio, when he started coming to the classes offered by York's followers.

In the books and tapes, York efficiently brought down the gods of other religions and installed himself in their place. For example, the Christians' Jesus was presented as a worthy prophet who was neither crucified nor raised from the dead, and he went on to have a rather normal family life. More importantly, the "real" Jesus wasn't like the one depicted in most of Western art.

"I said, 'Whoa! Jesus was black!'" Hodge said. The more classes he started attending in the early 1990s, the more York seemed to become a Jesus for modern blacks. "What actually appealed to me was the picture of a prophet with a positive black image."

Hodge saw York's doctrines as an attractive "fusion of Islamic and Hebrew." This was the theme of *Whatever Happened To The Nubian Islamic Hebrews?*, one of Hodge's favorites among York's books, and a tract that explained how York's belief system offered the best of the old religions in a new package.

The books, tapes, and doctrines all paled, however, in comparison to the man. York had style, flash, and all those women. He seemed to be a living embodiment of Hodge's teenaged dreams.

"It wasn't what he did, or even what he wrote. It was who he was, the whole lifestyle," Hodge said.

When York spoke so confidently about the flaws in other religions, it was easy to believe him. Similarly, it was easy for Hodge to allow York to fill the vacuum of doubt that York had created.

Hodge became an enthusiastic "street preacher" for York, he said. He would "propagate and peddle," recruiting students for York's classes, while he sold them incense or oils. Sometimes, he would give York's books away. They were hard to sell, but, as a gift, they would hold the customer at his table long enough for him to sell something else.

At school, Hodge wasn't afraid to advertise his affiliation with the Muslims, and that appealed to a white girl named Shanda, who sat next to him.

"He wore his robes to class. Nobody else did that," Shanda said. She was attracted to the black youth who wasn't afraid to be different. They began a relationship.

Derrick and Shanda had long conversations about his membership in an Islamic community and what that would mean for her, if she stayed with him. She read the books he gave her and found them interesting. She was undeterred by York's characterization of whites as inferior beings.

"I was going to be the one to prove them wrong," she said. "I wasn't racist."

Shanda started wearing a veil and attending the Friday evening services at the house in Columbus that served both as living quarters and as a mosque for York's community.

The mixed-race couple was not invited to move into the community's house, however. They were warned that if they did move in, Shanda might be "mated" with a man other than Derrick. Also, they learned that the women of the community were less than thrilled at the prospect of having a white sister.

So, they lived apart from the others but worked for the common cause. Derrick gained recognition for being an outstanding salesman, recruiter, and teacher. Derrick and Shanda had their first child in 1992.

Then, in 1993, everything started changing. The communal houses in Columbus and other cities were shut down. The bookstore operations were to be continued, though the overtly Muslim titles had to be discarded, since the cult was evolving into something new.

York gave his overall enterprises the name "Holy Tabernacle Ministries." Derrick was invited to move to Atlanta and start an HTM bookstore. They couldn't afford such a move, but they did agree to start a bookstore in Columbus.

The chain of bookstores was a rather unorthodox enterprise. The operators not only had to cover all their local expenses, they had to pay York for the books. Derrick went several times to York's old base in Brooklyn, searching the old mosque, which had then been converted into a storage facility, for books that he could bring back to Columbus to sell. On top of all that, he was expected to travel to York's property in Putnam County every two weeks, bringing money for York with them.

In the beginning of this period, he was expected to bring at least $250 for York each trip. Over the next two years, the amount would double, then triple. There were times when Derrick's sales did not meet the quota, so he would make the remainder by soliciting donations from people in his classes and other members of the community.

Derrick and Shanda were married in 1994, and soon after, he took her to Georgia to meet York. "I'm going to introduce you to the Lamb of God," he told her.

Shanda said that first meeting was "very pleasant." York told her that she was the fulfillment of one of his prophesies – "that the colors would mingle in the new community."

Still, to many of those who lived on Tama-Re, Shanda was an "Amarite," a member of the despised race of white people. York scolded some of the women who spoke against her, but that only made them more hostile to her. When they asked York about their prospects for eventually moving onto Tama-Re, he told them, "You don't want to live here."

The Hodges stayed in the cult for about five more years, and for all that time, they were the only mixed-race couple. They never lived on Tama-Re, however, nor did they bring their children with them for any extended visit.

Some of the aspects of the emerging new community started to trouble Derrick. What was all this cowboy stuff about? Derrick didn't particularly like cowboy attire, nor did he appreciate having to travel to Atlanta to buy the stuff.

The new books York was churning out were even more troubling. Derrick said he was asked to bring a selection of New Age books to York's offices, for research use by York's concubines. He started noticing close similarities – in some cases identical reproductions – between the books he supplied and the books being published with York as the purported author.

In late 1996, the Nuwaubian identity had been fully adopted by York and his followers. At York's request, Derrick and Shanda closed their Columbus bookstore and moved to Warner Robins, a small city in central Georgia dominated by a military base. They rented a kiosk in a local mall, where they sold York's books and personal care products.

They had their own apartment, which they were later asked to share with some Nuwaubians from the Macon area. They agreed, and before they could object, sixteen people had moved into their place. "They were filthy degenerates," Shanda said. Life in the overcrowded apartment soon became intolerable to the Hodges. They moved out and found another place of their own.

They were still loyal followers of the Master Teacher, but they also started noticing more of York's human flaws.

Derrick recalled a time when he was standing beside York at the back of a room at Tama-Re, while a class was in progress. A man in the class was giving what for him was a heartfelt personal testimony, proclaiming that he was unworthy of being a Nuwaubian, since he often failed to live the Nuwaubian lifestyle away from Tama-Re.

York seemed to be amused by the man's confession. While the rest of the group was listening attentively to the man, York turned to Derrick and whispered, "The monkeys will do this. Watch."

York then started applauding, and in a moment, the rest of the people were clapping, too.

At some of these gatherings, York would appear, holding a walking stick that also functioned as a flask. Though York preached abstinence from liquor, what he was drinking from the hollowed-out walking stick was definitely alcoholic, Derrick said.

Derrick worked on the construction crews that built Club Rameses, and after it opened in 1997, he and Shanda went there on weekend nights, when the place was packed with 1,000 or more revelers.

Shanda recalled how York manipulated the women of the community about their behavior at the nightclub. On Saturdays, York would encourage the young women to go to the club, and to dress and dance provocatively.

Then, on Sundays, York would berate the same women. He would tell them things like, "You were dancing like whores," she said. "It got to the point where we wouldn't dance anymore."

Derrick also started noticing inconsistencies in some of York's presentations. Once, he mentioned to York that he had said something that was contradicted by statements in some of his books. York responded, "If you don't know something, just act like you know it," Derrick said.

Derrick started attending fewer and fewer classes and buying fewer and fewer books, some of which carried price tags up to $50.

He was also increasingly repulsed by York's sexual practices. York would claim that when he had sex with another man's wife or mate, he was doing a favor for the couple by performing a sexual healing. When some of these married women became pregnant with York's children, Derrick was shocked to see how the husbands responded by taking the women back and raising York's children as their own.

The contradictions between what York preached and what he practiced became too much for Derrick to accept. He finally confronted York, after he heard York proclaim that Jesus and the prophets had never existed. In many of his books, York had frequently stated the total opposite and had written at length about the lives of Jesus and the other prophets, and how they fit into his belief system.

"Right Knowledge is supposed to be absolute," Derrick told York. "What's all this about Jesus doesn't exist, and Abraham doesn't exist? You taught about all those prophets, and now you say they didn't exist."

York didn't even bother trying to explain himself. Instead, he later approached Shanda and told her, "You're married to a demon." He also made a thinly-veiled suggestion that Shanda might want to consider becoming one of his concubines.

At this point, the Hodges were already close to ending their life as Nuwaubians.

In September of 1999, they were offered the privilege of working for free on Tama-Re. They moved into a home in Eatonton, sharing the rent with an older male Nuwaubian. Not long after that, someone from Tama-Re called and asked if they'd take in a sister. The sister turned out to have been rejected by her Nuwaubian mate. She had three children and no money. The Hodges helped her for awhile, but then they asked her to leave.

Their male housemate left as well, and not long after regaining their privacy, a stranger came to their door, asking to look at the house for rent. Shanda was eight months pregnant with their third child at the time. They called the landlord, who informed them that he no longer wanted them as tenants, since their former housemate had told the landlord some very uncomplimentary things about them.

When they called York's office to report that they were losing their home , they received some expressions of sympathy and a have-a-good-life dismissal – but no offers of help.

That was the last straw for Shanda. "All I could think about was the thousands of dollars we'd used to purchase overpriced books, the times we'd buy dog food for York's mutts, the times they called us and asked if we could run to Ingles (a supermarket) to buy Baba some veal," she said.

The Hodges headed home for Ohio. "We left with no regrets," Shanda said. "We don't regret ever being a part of it, and we surely don't regret leaving. We had some amazing life experiences that we won't trade for anything – but we are very grateful to be out of that cult."

For Derrick, the reality of life as a Nuwaubian was a betrayal of the dream of a Black Utopia that he bought into as a teenager. It turned out to be "volunteer slavery, cloaked as building a nation," he said.

It lasted as long as it did, he said, because York was able to impose a communal lifestyle that did not recognize the value of the family or of private property. None of the societal norms in sexual relationships applied on Tama-Re.

"As a result, the ruler of this Utopia justified, encouraged, and catered to the acceptance of such deviant sexual behavior as pedophilia, promiscuity, and rape," Derrick said. "York made evil seem fair."

In her search for black power, she found black servitude.

"I was born into the Nation of Islam," said Sahar Ba'ith. When she was growing up in New Jersey, her father was an active member of the Nation. She read some of his books on black separatism, including some of Dwight York's tracts. "I was always interested in the struggles of our people," she said.

For the most part, she accepted the negative view of Christianity that York and other Muslim groups promulgated. "Christianity was given to the slaves by the slavemasters," she said.

When she was still in high school, she visited York's Ansaru Allah Community in Brooklyn. She was impressed that they offered "a different look at how our culture was created."

However, she was more deeply impressed – in a negative way – by the attitudes she saw among York's flock of women. "They only cared about what they were going to eat next, and who was going to have the man's next baby," she said.

After her graduation, she moved with her father to New Orleans, where she found one of York's satellite communities and started taking classes. The New Orleans community then consisted of fifteen to eighteen people living in two double-wide trailers.

Ba'ith saw a significant difference between the Brooklyn and New Orleans communities. As small as it was, and without York's regular presence, they were more free to make their own rules. In practice, this meant that women were given much more responsibility for the main work of the community – making money to take back to York and finding new recruits to do more of the same.

"They needed as many people as possible to push those books," she said.

"And I was a good saleswoman."

Ba'ith had been a track star in high school, and she might have been a strong candidate for an athletic scholarship to college. Instead, she joined the Holy Tabernacle Ministries in 1994 and moved into their trailers. She accepted the group's notion that higher education was just another trap of a society they sought to reject. The prevailing belief was: "Education was the white man's education."

She didn't stay long in New Orleans, since all of York's communal houses were being shut down about the time she joined. She was assigned to move to Atlanta and then to sell York's books to travelers at the Atlanta airport.

"It was awkward at first, but I found I could turn the people on to something," she said. She set the prices where she thought she could move the most books. "You want to buy this book? $10? $5?" was her pitch. Her bestseller was a York tract entitled "Who Is God?"

On just about every Wednesday night, she and the other Atlanta area followers of York would make the trip to York's land in Putnam County to take part in classes. There were often as many as one hundred people in the classes, some of them from as far away as California and London, England.

Her first opportunities to see York in an informal setting were revelations for her. "I still thought Doc was holy, until I got to the land," she said. For a holy man, York had some quite common habits, and he seemed to slip frequently into profanities.

"I didn't think he would curse. I thought he wouldn't eat pizza," she said. But she saw him do both those things regularly, as well as other habits she had thought were restricted to mere mortals. "That's cursing!" she thought to herself with some alarm, when she heard York's profanity-laced speeches. "I got spooked out."

York's preoccupation with finances was also on prominent display. "His whole purpose was to bring in more people to get that money," Ba'ith said. "There was always more to sell."

During this time, York "mated" Ba'ith with a male in the group, and she accepted the arrangement. The couple was assigned to start a bookstore and recruiting station in Monticello, the county seat of Jasper County, just to the west of Putnam. Her mate could cut hair, so they opened a barber shop, where they also offered a selection of York's books for sale.

Monticello turned out not to be fertile territory. Most weeks, Ba'ith sold only a few books. Their income came mostly from the haircuts, but whatever they earned beyond their basic living expenses, they dutifully took to York.

"I never took out a dime," Ba'ith said. She believed in York's version of the black utopian dream, and that's where she thought her money was going.

"We were going to do our thing, have our own society, with our own doctors, our own teachers, everything. We wouldn't need the white man for anything," she said. "We felt we had something nobody else had, and we wanted to share it with the world."

York's brand of black separatism appealed to her, because she saw it as less threatening than some of the other movements. "It was like following Malcolm X, but without the violence," she said.

Her mate was dispatched for an extended trip to New Orleans, where he was ordered to sell pirated music tapes that were being churned out at Tama-Re, she said. While he was gone, she was invited to move temporarily to Tama-Re. No one had consulted her mate about this plan, and he was unhappy about it. "I know what he wants from you," her mate told her.

Nevertheless, she went to stay on York's property. She was assigned space in what was called "the favored house," where she saw firsthand the way that the women would compete for York's favors. She also saw how York stoked and enflamed this atmosphere of competition.

Some evenings, York would walk through the house, selecting the women and girls who would come with him on an excursion to the outside world, say, a Chinese restaurant. York would point to the women he chose for his companions, saying, "You, you, and you."

"Everybody else would be left behind to eat rice, beans and cornbread," she said.

She also saw what happened to women who fell out of York's good graces. They were shipped to what was called the "punishment house," where conditions were "totally disgusting," she said.

York tried to talk her into staying at Tama-Re. He pointed out her mate's faults, and he asked her how strong their relationship was. He asked her, wouldn't she prefer to "walk with The Lamb?"

When her mate returned from New Orleans, his jealousy was unabated. They argued about York and whether he was trying to insert himself into their relationship. She left him, and he left the cult.

Ba'ith was then assigned to go back to Atlanta and work in one of the bookstores there. She became interested in a man in the group, someone whom York had not sanctioned as a mate for her. She wrote the man an affectionate letter, which was found and ultimately turned over to York. As punishment, she was told she had to move to Philadelphia and sell York's books there.

She again flourished as a saleswoman. She helped open new bookstores in Mt. Vernon and Yonkers, New York. "I was a top propagator, and I was getting talked about," Ba'ith said.

She also got pregnant, by a man who left her and the cult, as soon as she told him the news.

Despite her relationship problems, she re-gained her status as one of York's favorites. When she made the bi-weekly trips to Tama-Re, she was treated as a special guest.

York acted like a father to her. He seemed to enjoy her company. She made him laugh, and she laughed at his jokes. He frequently selected her to accompany him on his dinner outings. "He thought I was cool," she said.

As a token of his affection, York gave her a ring, like the one he gave to his special girls. This caused some of his concubines to become more jealous of her; some of them thought her ring was nicer than theirs.

One of the concubines charged that Ba'ith had used sex to win York's attentions. "You must have gotten your knees dirty to get that," one woman said of her ring. "He just wants to fuck you."

Ba'ith said she was repelled by the women's attitudes. One of York's favored concubines warned Ba'ith against trying to replace her. "This was the same woman who was pimping her son to York, so they could go to Disney World," Ba'ith said.

However, Ba'ith said she never had to turn down York's advances, because he never made any toward her. Besides, she was pregnant. York mated her with another man in the community, and they were ordered to move to Milledgeville to open a bookstore. The man, a trained medical professional, was supposed to work at a job arranged by a doctor who was friendly with York.

The bookstore never opened, and the promised job never materialized. "It was a total disaster," Ba'ith said. The recently-mated couple was broke and their relationship quickly soured.

In August 1996, Ba'ith went into labor. She first tried to deliver the baby at Tama-Re, with the help of a midwife in the community. But there were complications, so she went to the public hospital in Milledgeville, where the baby was delivered by Caesarian section.

Before the operation, Ba'ith followed orders she'd been given at Tama-Re and instructed the nurses to save her placenta, so that she could take it home with her. She had been told by cult members that if she left the placenta at the hospital, white doctors would use it for medical experimentation.

After the birth, she called home for help. Her father, who by then had moved back to New Jersey, came to Georgia and took her and the baby home with him.

Ba'ith wasn't ready to leave the cult just yet. She accepted an assignment to work at a bookstore in North Carolina, and in a few months, she moved back to Tama-Re and attempted a reconciliation with her mate. That didn't work, but she was allowed to stay on at Tama-Re and was given an office job. She was also

York's image graced the covers of most of his books and tapes.

assigned to the more desirable living quarters.

She made the serious error of trying to maintain a friendship with a woman who'd been banished from the inner circle, despite the fact – or perhaps because of the fact – that the woman was pregnant with one of York's children. Ba'ith had met the woman earlier, and she saw nothing wrong with associating with a woman who'd been moved "up the hill" to the dilapidated housing given to the women York no longer wanted.

Ba'ith was appalled by the treatment her friend was receiving. "They were trying to starve her, and we were right down the hill, eating like fat cats," she said.

Once, Ba'ith was invited to go out for pizza with York and a group of selected girls. She asked if she could bring her friend, who was pregnant and hungry. For making that request, Ba'ith was punished by being ordered to move to the house where her banished friend lived. She was also demoted to a less desirable job in the mail room.

The banishment allowed her to spend more time with her friend. The two women were able to talk, while they worked together in a small building used to store old papers and books. There, her friend told her something that was becoming an increasingly ill-kept secret at Tama-Re.

"She told me that York was having sex with the children, some as young as nine," Ba'ith said. "It was the first time I'd heard that."

Also, her friend told her, York was trying to impregnate as many of the young women and girls as he could. One of York's missions while he was on Earth was to make as many part-Rizqian babies as possible, in order to combat all the evil influences in the world – at least that was what he was telling the women he was treating as brood mares.

Some of the parents knew or suspected what was happening, Ba'ith's friend said. Some of them rationalized or excused York's behavior, on the grounds that York was a supernatural savior, and anyone who wanted to be saved had better accede to his demands.

Her friend also told her that for years as they grew up, some of the children had been groomed by the older women to become York's sexual playthings. "They can't wait till they're ten, so they can sleep in Baba's bed," the woman told her.

As Ba'ith's status declined, so did the level of care given to her infant daughter. It became common for her to come to the infants' quarters after working a twelve-hour day, only to find that her baby's diapers had not been changed all day.

"It was one thing for me to get punished; it was another thing for my baby to suffer," she said.

She told one of York's concubines that she wanted to leave. York found out and tried to dissuade her, saying, "We need you here."

Despite York's personal plea, Ba'ith felt like "an outsider on the inside." She confided in her mate that she wanted to take her daughter and leave. The mate told the higher-ups, and there was another round of efforts to talk her into staying.

Ultimately, she was offered a ride north with some members of the group who were going that way. She left York and her York-sanctioned mate behind, this time for good.

Ba'ith was able to resume her education while she raised her daughter. As of 2005, she was working towards a law degree.

Looking back, Ba'ith can see how York was able to appeal to people like her, people who had educations or careers. She also can see how most of those same types of people came to be deeply disillusioned by him and his teachings.

"The way he boosted people's self image and self awareness is what was profound about the man," she said. And as much as she now repudiates York, she believes there was validity in the dreams he peddled to people like her.

Still, she cringes now when she thinks of how long and how hard she worked to advance York's cause and to line York's pockets.

"The man was disgusting, and there I was, standing on the street and professing for him," she said.

"I thought it was going to be a great thing. It's just a shame the way it turned out," she said. "I was selling The Man From Rizq, but he was just a pervert."

Diallo Seabrooks wanted to be an artist. Instead, he became a model dupe for a master con artist.

As an aspiring art student in Florida, Seabrooks found his favorite subjects and themes in black people and the way they lived. His portraits of young black men were intended to be uplifting depictions of the strength of his race.

When he first encountered York's books and tapes, Seabrooks believed he'd found a kindred spirit. The materials seemed to make a strong appeal to the aspirations of young blacks like him.

"We wanted to think we were elite, that we stood out from the rest," Seabrooks said. "We were a built-in market, and York knew that, so he turned around and sold it."

At the classes he took at one of York's bookstores, he learned that people who subscribed to other religions were simply wrong. "He stripped us of everything spiritually, then he put in his own spooky stuff," Seabrooks said.

York's claim to be a supernatural visitor from another planet never appealed much to Seabrooks, but the dream of building a black Promised Land did.

"He asked people to give him their lives, and at the end of their lives, they would go to Kodesh," Seabrooks said, referring to a name York sometimes used synonymously with Paradise. "Kodesh was like no place on earth; it was like heaven, a golden city, a place with pyramids, a place that was not going to be destroyed."

That sort of vision has historically had a special appeal for many blacks, he said. "We've been taken advantage of for so long, we're always looking for some savior or messiah-type person."

The power of the vision was increased by the notion that it came in only one color: black. Kodesh would be a place for blacks, run by blacks. "This was for us, this was our thing," Seabrooks said.

Once he joined the Nuwaubians and moved to Tama-Re, however, the reality turned out to be quite different from the dream.

"We were slaves," Seabrooks said of the men and women who lived on Tama-Re. "The only difference was, it was a black man running it."

Seabrooks was given a place in the barn where most of the adult men slept. "It was Third World conditions," he said.

On a typical day, he said, he'd get up about eight a.m. "We'd work till noon, then decide whether to bathe or eat."

Often, there wasn't much to choose from, on either side of that ledger. There wasn't much to eat, and nobody was earning any money to buy food. The bathing facilities were primitive and frequently non-functional.

"Hell yes, I was hungry a lot," Seabrooks said. "You didn't eat much up there. There was no money and no access to money."

At times, he said, he was reduced to begging food from the people who would come from the outside world for the classes.

The only opportunities for getting any money came from "doing a bid," he said. This was when he and other men would be sent to the cities, usually Atlanta, on peddling missions. "We'd sell whatever we could get our hands on to make money," he said.

Of course, whoever went out on a bid was expected to bring their earnings back to York, usually at least one hundred dollars from a two-week "bid." Seabrooks said he and the others soon learned how to set aside some money to buy food that they would sneak back with them, when they returned to Tama-Re.

Seabrooks tolerated these miserable living conditions for about two years. Like the others who stayed, he believed that the best way to improve his lot was to do whatever he could to raise himself in York's eyes.

"Everybody wanted to be like the people on the inside," he said. "As hard and tough as it was, you wanted to stay, to get closer to Doc."

But the closer to York he got, the more flaws he saw, especially in the area of sex.

York would match the men with women in the community infrequently and primarily as a reward for loyalty, Seabrooks said.

"He might hook you up with one of his concubines, to make you feel like you're in the family," he said. "He'd call them his daughters. He'd probably slept with all of them."

Though he tightly rationed sex for the other men, York was clearly having all he wanted. "The men can't be with their women, but there were all these women walking around pregnant. How the hell does that happen?" Seabrooks said.

The women appeared to be attracted by York's flashes of wealth and the favors he could grant them, he said. Bearing York's children was just part of the bargain.

"His seed is supposed to be combating evil on the planet," Seabrooks said.

Seabrooks heard from some of the Nuwaubian women that York had made it a practice to conduct the sexual initiations of the young women and girls on Tama-Re.

"He would tell them, 'I'm your father. I need to be the first one,'" Seabrooks said.

Seabrooks never saw anything directly related to the molestation of children, but he was aware of an undercurrent of criminality at Tama-Re. Sometimes, he said, men would be dispatched to northern cities to sell guns that the Nuwaubians had purchased. It was also an open secret that York had sources of information within the Georgia Bureau of Information, he said.

He grew contemptuous of York's ideology, but at the same time, the criminal stuff started looking better and better.

"I got tired of the rhetoric and the repetitious stuff," he said. "I got tired of being poor." Seabrooks and at least five other Nuwaubian men joined a massive check counterfeiting ring that operated out of Atlanta. In describing the operation, federal prosecutors charged that members of the ring were sent to cities all around the South to cash the phoney checks; millions of dollars were fraudulently obtained.

In 1979, Seabrooks and the other Nuwaubians were among thirty people indicted for participating in the check-fraud ring. He pled guilty and served two years in federal prison.

Seabrooks said he was not ordered by York or anyone else to join the ring, nor does he know whether any of the illegal proceeds made it back to York.
What he does know now, he said, is that just about every facet of life at Tama-Re was a scam.

"It was all a hustle, a game," Seabrooks said. "Whatever happened to Kodesh?"

For Robert Rohan, the fifteen years of his life that he devoted to Dwight York began when some neighborhood toughs stole his sheepskin coat. He was sixteen years old at the time, the mid-1980s, living in a middle-class section of Staten Island.

He had two cousins he barely knew who lived near him. They were, he soon found out, stronger than the boys who'd robbed him. They had a stern talk with the thieves, and Rohan got his coat back.

His cousins gave him some books written by Imam Isa, York's name in those days. "My first thought was 'Wow! A black Jesus!'" Rohan said of his reaction to the books.

Soon, Rohan joined Ansaru Allah and started selling the books himself, often on his trips to Manhattan on the Staten Island ferry. He usually had no trouble making the fifty dollar daily quota, or even the later quota of one hundred dollars. He dropped out of his local high school, moved into York's Brooklyn community, where he studied Islam and the Arabic language.

During some of those classes, York would sit quietly in the back of the room. When someone posed a question, York would rise and give an authoritative-sounding answer. No one questioned the Imam. "Here's this one man answering all those questions," Rohan said.

He recalled being impressed by the order of the community, in particular by the groups of children marching from their schools to the mosque. One time, an AAC security guard mentioned to him, "These children are going to lead us to Paradise."

Rohan was less impressed by the disparity in living conditions. He was given space on the floor in what was essentially an abandoned building, unheated, cold showers only, and in general disrepair. When he was assigned to a crew who were moving some of York's personal belongings from Brooklyn to Camp Jazzir, he saw how the Imam lived.

"My mouth dropped open," he said, when he saw York's oversized Jacuzzi and other luxury furnishings. "We were living in Third World conditions, and he was living like that."

When he pointed this out to the Imam, York told him he was "thinking with the wrong part of your brain." Rejection of worldly comforts was one of the sacrifices that true Muslims were required to make, York told him. "This was how to become more spiritual," York said to Rohan.

Also, Rohan noted with some alarm that Imam Isa was becoming less and less devout in his practice of Islam. In the late 1980s, York started frequently skipping Friday services at his community's mosque, Rohan said. Dissension within the community grew, as York continued to distance himself from the Islamic faith he had preached so fervently for so many years, he said.

Rohan had married a woman of the community by this time, and when his mother-in-law visited and saw how they lived – and started making rather loud complaints about the situation – Rohan was quickly shipped out to the satellite community in Pittsburgh. His marriage fell apart soon after that.

Nevertheless, he remained loyal and accepted York's invitation to move to the new land in Georgia and become a Nuwaubian. He married another woman of the community, and they would have two children together.

For most of the next few years, Rohan and his second wife struggled to operate a Nuwaubian bookstore in Rome, a small city in northwest Georgia. There wasn't much of a market for things Nuwaubian there. Adding to the difficulty, he had to purchase the materials from York, try to sell them, and then bring the profits back to York.

Things got so tight, he said, that he and his wife and their children had to live for a time in the back of the store. Even so, he said, his wife insisted that they take very little out of their revenues for their own expenses, so that they could give more to York, he said. He took an outside job as a prison corrections officer.

"We went without many times to place orders (for Nuwaubian merchandise and books) with money we really did not have," he said.

When the bookstore failed, Rohan and his wife moved back to Tama-Re. By this time, he could no longer summon any loyalty to York, who called him a "black devil." His wife decided to stay on the land, but Rohan had had enough. He left the community in 2000.

"Everything had gone wrong," Rohan said. "I had no job, no money, no marriage."

Why did Rohan stay so long? Basically, he said, he believed in York's vision. "If he had done the right thing, it would've worked," Rohan said.

After disavowing York and the Nuwaubians, Rohan wrote a book about his experience, entitled *Holding York Responsible*. In it, Rohan issues an apology to the people and officials of Putnam County who were slandered by York and his Nuwaubian followers.

In his book, Rohan also states that he and other Nuwaubians must accept some of the blame for not stopping York sooner. "It was our responsibility to hold Malachi York accountable for his actions," Rohan wrote. "It was because we did not take action as the followers of Malachi York that Sheriff Sills and the federal government had to take on the responsibility for us."

These believers were remarkably like those depicted in one of the earliest scholarly examinations of black cults. In 1944 Arthur Huff Fauset, a black journalist and scholar, wrote *Black Gods of the Metropolis, Negro Religious Cults in the Urban North*. One of the cults he studied was the Moorish Science Temple, the forerunner of the Nation of Islam, and one of the groups whose doctrines and practices York copied heavily.

One common theme among these groups was that they flourished in the big Northern cities, while they had little or no appeal among the blacks who had remained in the South.

Despite the segregation and discrimination that predominated in the South in those times, Fauset concluded that it was not uncommon to find blacks who had been able to amass wealth there. However, he noted, blacks who migrated to the North were frustrated to find that the barriers they encountered to economic progress were only slightly lower than those in the South.

"Consequently, the Negro in the North, when compared with the Negro in the South, often appears to be 'all head and no body," that is, the Negro in the North frequently has much better intellectual equipment than his Southern brother, but in the absence of avenues of employment and lucrative revenue, he becomes an economic and political slave," Fauset wrote.

Fauset listed these factors, in order of importance, which he found common in attracting people to the cults he studied:

1. Personality of leader.
2. Desire to get closer to God.
3. Racial or nationalistic urge.
4. Dissatisfaction with Christianity.
5. Miraculous cure.

Decades after Fauset's study, these same factors worked to pull people into Dwight York's cult. Almost all these people were, like the blacks recruited into the cults of the early twentieth century, from major Northern cities.

Just as Fauset had observed in the 1940s, York's cult never found fertile recruiting grounds after it moved to Georgia. Most of the people who came to Tama-Re were blacks from the North.

Fauset's cult criteria for the groups he studied are similar to those defined by Robert Jay Lifton, distinguished professor of psychology at the City University of New York. In his 1981 essay, "Cult Formation," in *The Harvard Mental Health Letter,* Lifton wrote that a cult can be defined by three main characteristics:

1. A charismatic leader who increasingly becomes an object of worship as the general principles that may have originally sustained the group lose their power.
2. A process I call coercive persuasion or thought reform.
3. Economic, sexual, and other exploitation of group members by the leader and the ruling coterie.

By both Fauset's and Lifton's definitions, York's groups easily qualify for cult status. Nevertheless, York and his followers always bristled when people called his group a cult. They would assert that the word "cult" came from "culture," and if one meant that his group was its own separate culture, well then, you could look at it that way.

York angrily denied that his groups bore any relation to the suicide cults of Heaven's Gate and Jonestown; and in one important aspect, he was correct. York was never interested in killing himself or having his followers commit mass suicide. He was simply too interested in the sex and money of his lifestyle to take leave of it by his own hand.

However, there was a parallel in York's story to a phenomenon called "The Death Spiral" by cult researchers Flo Conway and Jim Siegelman in their book, *Snapping.* They identified a pattern of escalating chaos in their study of apocalyptic cults, satanic sects, and radical paramilitary survivalist sects, particularly in the story of David Koresh and the Branch Davidians at Waco, Texas.

"Repeatedly, we watched the same spiral dynamic draw everything into its path – individuals, families, communities, the media, law enforcement, and higher government officials – into a vortex that exploded in fury and left a trail of death and destruction in its path," they wrote.

In the case of Koresh, Conway and Siegleman described him as "a strange attractor, a one-man energy center." Koresh sealed his group off from the outside world, preached frequently about the coming Armageddon, amassed an arsenal of weapons, beat his followers and starved and sexually abused their children – all things that York did to some degree. Koresh foretold of a coming holy war between his cult and the surrounding world, and prepared for that war by stockpiling weapons, burying a school bus on his compound and stocking it with a year's worth of food, and prepared his followers for an apocalyptic end.

On February 28, 1993, the Waco death spiral went irretrievably out of control. Federal agents mounted a raid on the compound, to arrest Koresh on weapons charges. A gunfight broke out, and four federal agents were killed and sixteen wounded; inside the compound, six cult members were killed and Koresh was wounded.

After a fifty-one-day standoff, federal forces mounted a final siege, ramming the main house with a tank and pumping tear gas into it. Koresh then set his prophesied holocaust into motion. His followers set fires in several parts of the building, which was quickly consumed by flames. Those who did not die by fire were shot. Seventy-five Rafiqians, including Koresh, perished.

York's "death spiral" was more of a sexual descent. During his Brooklyn years, he excessively indulged himself by claiming sexual rights to any woman in his group. He apparently made some efforts, however, to limit himself to those women who were of legal age.

But then boredom set in. He started relaxing his age standards and inviting the teenaged girls into his Backstreet recording studios, exchanging special privileges and status for sex. After he bought the country property in Sullivan County, he made special arrangements to bring the Backstreet Girls up to the camp, where he was more free to entertain them in isolation from the rest of the community.

Then, when the Catskills retreat proved unsatisfactory, he moved to an even more isolated setting, rural Putnam County, Georgia. There he was free to indulge his darkest perversions. At Tama-Re, there were no age limits to his sexual predations and no taboos that could not be broken.

Notwithstanding the silly semantics games that York like to play with the word "cult," calling York's various groups "cults" is clearly belaboring the obvious. At the top there was an autocratic ruler who claimed god-like status.

People who joined were required to donate all their possessions and labors to the leader. Connections with the outside world were severed, and the member's pre-existing family structures were shattered, once they moved into York's domains. And, sadly, there was a mountain of evidence of sexual exploitation.

The Nuwaubian nation was "almost a caricature of a cult," according to Phillip Arnn, senior researcher for Watchman Fellowship Inc., a Texas-based organization that maintains files on five thousand cults and cult-like groups. In his group's files on the Nuwaubians, he said, there are reports of gatherings where cartoon-like figures representing beings from another galaxy were projected on the walls of the room.

York's claim that a definite number of people, 144,000, would be selected for transport to that far galaxy—and he would do the selecting—is what Arnn called a "classic anti-social, apocalyptic scenario."

However, establishing that the Nuwaubians and the Ansars and the Nubian Islamic Hebrews were all cults does not answer the question of why people stayed, especially those who were educated and articulate. Why did they subject themselves to such squalid conditions, some for years, some for decades? Why did they, knowingly or unwittingly, allow their children to be out of their care for extended periods and placed in situations where they could be preyed upon?

That sort of question is pertinent to any cult. Why did the people at Jonestown drink poison? Why did the members of Heaven's Gate commit mass suicide to catch a comet ride?

In all these cases, the followers must forfeit their free will, in deference to the cult's godhead. According to Bob Moser, a senior writer for the Montgomery-based Southern Poverty Law Center, once the Nuwaubians accepted York as their god, they followed him blindly. Moser came to Putnam County to study the Nuwaubians, and he interviewed former members and viewed tapes of York speaking privately to his followers.

"Once you accept Dwight York is special, then you automatically have to subordinate yourself to that authority," Moser said.

Part of York's pitch that brought him his followers and their money was racial hatred, Moser said. "It's definitely a black supremacist group, a mirror image of white hate groups," Moser said. Because of that, his center has placed the United Nuwaubian Nation of Moors on their hate list.

Margaret Thaler Singer, emeritus professor of psychology at the University of California at Berkeley, who studied cults for more than fifty years, devoted a chapter of her book *Cults In Our Midst* to answering the question often asked of former cult members: "Why didn't you just get up and leave?"

Singer listed the main factors that work together to make the cult member feel trapped:

1. Deception in the recruitment process and throughout membership.
2. Debilitation, because of the hours, the degree of commitment, the psychological pressures, and the inner constriction and strife.
3. Dependency, as a result of being cut off from the outside world in many ways.
4. Dread, because of beliefs instilled by the cult that a person who leaves will find no real life on the outside.
5. Desensitization, so that things that would once have troubled them no longer do; for example, learning that money collected from fundraising is supporting the leader's lavish lifestyle rather than the cause for which it was given, or seeing children badly abused or even killed.

Often, the more the follower has participated in the aberrant activities within the cult, the harder it is to break away, Singer stated. "You've been party to activities that in normal life you'd probably never have considered – acts that are morally reprehensible, actions that you never would have believed you could have carried out or witnessed. That kind of guilt and shame keeps people in cults," Singer wrote.

Singer never directly studied the Nuwaubian cult, but she served on the board of an institute founded by an anti-cult activist who did. In 1999, Rick Ross, founder of the Rick Ross Institute, gave a speech in Atlanta on the topic of violent cults. Afterwards, he was approached by two women who identified themselves as former Nuwaubians and told him that "something awful was going to happen" on the Putnam County land owned by York.

After that, Ross started monitoring York and the Nuwaubians. His New Jersey-based institute is primarily an educational service that compiles databases of information on cults and other controversial movements. Because of his experience as a cult deprogrammer, Ross was consulted by federal officials during the Waco standoff.

Ross said York probably benefited from the tragedy of Waco. "After '93, there was a reluctance on the part of most authorities to address cults," Ross said. Federal investigative agencies were effectively paralyzed by the negative fallout from the Waco disaster, he said.

In that period of relative immunity, York's character flaws festered. "York kind of became a victim of his own evil. All the people who worked for him, adored him, just reinforced his megalomania," Ross said.

Inside Tama-Re, York's followers were also paralyzed, in terms of their own ability to think, or to act against York's predations, Ross said.

"If parents had allowed their children to be molested, in order to face that reality, they would have to admit that they had surrendered their children's innocence to the dictates and appetites of this madman—and for nothing," Ross said. "They didn't want to know. If they knew, then what?"

CHAPTER 7
Savior Daze Showdown

My God, Howard! Are you going to kill people over building permits?
– Georgia Governor Roy Barnes, to Putnam County Sheriff Howard Sills.

There was more than a whiff of trouble in the air. The scent of honeysuckle couldn't mask it. The heavy dew on the courthouse green couldn't dampen it.

Not long after dawn, the first of five hundred or so Nuwaubian protesters began filling the lawn around the Putnam County courthouse in Eatonton. They were grim, silent, and dressed in black. Their ranks were patrolled by equally grim private security guards, who wore armbands to designate their command status.

No one in local law enforcement knew these guards, but everyone could see that they were big, strong, and possessed of clear and unquestioned authority over the Nuwaubians. When one of the guards told a protester to move two steps, the protester moved two steps.

Every sheriff's deputy was on duty, and extra deputies had been borrowed from a dozen surrounding counties. In case the trouble was more than this force could handle, more than two hundred state law enforcement officers were being held in rough-and-ready reserve at the National Guard Armory, just outside of town.

The rear entrance to the courthouse was closed to the public. Police cruisers had pulled up near the doors. Metal barricades were erected along the two sidewalks that vectored diagonally across the green from that entrance to the courthouse.

The tension between the local and state police agencies was every bit as keen as the black anger piling up on the grass. The commander of the state forces had put the sheriff on notice: the state forces were under his command, not the sheriff's. Typical law enforcement protocol would not prevail on this day. If the state commander, a deputy director of the Georgia Bureau of Investigation, determined that the sheriff wasn't controlling the situation, his troops would wade into the fray – at his command.

There was a very real prospect that a bad situation would be made worse by animosities among those charged with keeping the peace. So, Sills dispatched a deputy to race to Atlanta with a last-minute plea for gubernatorial intervention.

Meanwhile, the crowd and the edginess continued to build. Inside the courthouse, metal detectors had been installed at the bottom of the stairway leading to the second-floor courtroom. About an hour before the scheduled 10 a.m. time for the hearing that was the cause of all this anxiety, deputies began allowing spectators up the stairs. A long line of Nuwaubians quickly formed, but they progressed very slowly through the inspection station at the staircase. Women had to empty the contents of their purses on a small table, visibly adding to the sourness of their dispositions.

A moving van drove repeatedly around the four streets that formed a perimeter around the courthouse. Police pulled it over and found the back loaded with about twenty Nuwaubian men. The last thing that the police wanted was a rapid-deployment force that might inflame any hot spot, so they ordered the van driver out of the downtown area.

Prospects of a bad day ahead seemed as certain as the thunderstorm building in the overcast skies. It all served to confirm a warning Sills had received a few days earlier from a federal mediator who'd come to town ostensibly to calm the situation. The mediator told Sills that if things didn't go their way in court, the Nuwaubians were ready to riot.

This was the day, June 29, 1999, when Dwight York stood a very good chance of going to jail.

The scene at the courthouse was the denouement of a two-week period of increasingly melodramatic farce, or, increasingly farcical melodrama. There was a fittingly bizarre cast of characters, including a white supremacist appearing as an ally to the black separatists, a squad of rogue bounty hunters on a mission to sabotage the sheriff, a small army of state troopers led by the top brass of the GBI, thousands of Nuwaubians who showed up in Putnam County to help York celebrate his birthday and who stayed on by the hundreds for the protest, a black state legislator from Atlanta who designated himself a spokesman for and defender of the Nuwaubian cause, and a brief but significant cameo appearance, staying just offstage, by the Governor of Georgia.

Things started off strange and proceeded further and further through the looking glass.

On June 12, Everett Leon Stout came to town, driving a car with a license plate that proclaimed him to be a "Common Law Judge." Stout had attached himself to white supremacist causes around the country. He came to the Putnam County Courthouse and filed a document vaguely resembling a lawsuit, something he called a "Voluntary Contract."

It listed thirteen defendants, including Sills, Frank Ford, Dorothy Adams, Jerome Adams, several of Sills' officers, and something Stout called the "Electric and Power Company." Stout listed himself and a group called "Citizens For Constitutional Justice" as plaintiffs. For good measure, the listing of plaintiffs included "All sovereign private civilian inhabitants."

There was another class of parties, called "offerers," listed in the document. These offerers included Dwight York, two of his main lieutenants, and four hundred John and Jane Does, presumably the Nuwaubian men and women. An unstipulated someone was supposed to pay the offerers a $150 recording fee; if the fee was not paid, the offerers would be free to ignore any response to the voluntary contract.

The complaint was that the "human and civil rights" of York and the other offerers had been violated. The manner of said violations was not stipulated. However, the defendants were specifically charged with treason and kidnapping; and a group of unnamed attorneys and judges were charged with "incompetency, mental and physical disabilities, corruption, gross immorality, and acts of genocide."

After depositing his ten-page pile of twaddle on the desk of a deputy court clerk, Stout headed out to Tama-Re. The Nuwaubians notified the local news media of Stout's availability for a press conference, at which Stout claimed to have formed a common cause with the group of blacks, who were only trying to live as they pleased on their own sovereign land, free from government oppression.

Stout's antics could be easily ignored, but he had previously succeeded in making a real nuisance of himself. He had been associated with anti-government groups who used the tactic of filing liens against the properties of their enemies, the judges, prosecutors, and local officials who failed to recognize the validity of their claims.

If nothing else, it was an eye-catching spectacle. A white man who preached hatred of blacks was aligning himself with a black man who preached hatred of whites. A few days later, Stout drove his common-law-mobile out of Georgia. It turned out that he was a fugitive from a warrant in Tennessee; he was soon arrested in Alabama and sent to federal prison.

At about this time, an even stranger alliance was taking shape in Atlanta. The agents of that alliance would inject themselves directly into the legal and racial turmoil going on in Putnam County – and they would undertake their mission with the belief that they had the blessing of the governor.

York had a special political friend, State Rep. Tyrone Brooks, who represented a predominantly-black district of Atlanta in the legislature. It was Brooks who became most directly tied by documentary evidence to the decision to send the "Georgia Rangers" to Putnam County.

The Rangers were an unlicensed group of enforcers-for-hire, who'd earned a reputation as quick-on-the-draw urban cowboys from their work as private security guards. Their turf was some of the toughest parts of Atlanta, mostly apartment complexes and housing projects on the south side of the city. As bounty hunters and private security guards, they were not constrained by legal niceties that burdened real police officers, such as arrest warrants, probable cause, or Miranda warnings. They were pretty much free to bust whomever they wanted, wherever they wanted; then, the real cops could sort things out.

They rode around in cars with phony, police-like markings, including "Federal Ranger Services" across the tailgate of the vehicle. They carried phony, official-looking badges, marked "Ranger – Department of Public Safety."

Their guns, though, were quite real.

The commander of the Rangers was "Major" E.L. "Ed" Coughenour. His business card identified him as "Criminal Division Commander" and "CRT Team Leader, Violent Crimes And Drug Interdiction Unit."

Coughenour, a wiry man with the look of a high-school cross-country coach, was actually a bounty hunter and skip tracer (a person who tracks down defendants who have "skipped town," leaving their bondsmen liable for the full amounts of their bonds). Coughenour was also on parole from an embezzlement conviction in North Carolina. At the time when he first met Tyrone Brooks, Coughenour's Rangers had all the security work they could handle; but Coughenour was looking for a political connection to work that was, well, more reputable.

The head Ranger had already come a long way from the job he held in the mid-1990s, working as a skip tracer for a bail bondsman in Bartow County, about fifty miles north of Atlanta.

One of his skip-tracing assignments had taken him to an apartment complex in Adamsville, one of the grimmer parts of Atlanta. "I was some white guy riding into the middle of the ghetto," Coughenour said. He got his man, and the no-nonsense way he handled himself earned the respect of the manager of the apartment complex. As Coughenour prepared to head back to Bartow County, the manager asked whether he might be interested in some full-time security work.

That seemed like a step up to Coughenour, so he recruited three friends, moved to Atlanta and set up shop as the "Georgia Rangers." The Rangers patterned their tactics after the "Red Dog" police units, known for their aggressive patrolling of high-crime areas.

"We were rough-and-tumble," Coughenour said. "You didn't come over messin' with the Rangers, and if you did, the Zone took care of it." The "Zone" was a reference to the zone officers of the Atlanta Police Department. Coughenour was proud of the strong cooperative working relationship the Rangers had with the local police. "We got along great with the beat officers," he said.

As an example of how that relationship worked, Coughenour cited the time when an investigator from the office of the Georgia Secretary of State – the agency charged with professional licensing in Georgia – started pestering some of the Rangers about their lack of state licenses. Coughenour said he made a call to a friend in the APD, and the investigator never bothered them again.

They had similarly cozy arrangements with the Fulton County Sheriff's Office. If the Rangers made an arrest and the APD was too busy to send an officer to take over the case, the Rangers were allowed to take their man directly to the Fulton County Jail. The real police would come in later to straighten up the paperwork.

Private policing had its advantages. "We didn't need a warrant to walk in your door," Coughenour said. "We had a lot more teeth than the police to bite with."

If a Ranger saw someone who even looked like they might be involved in something illegal, the Ranger would simply tell the suspect to clear out of the area. If the person failed to respond, the Ranger could just conjure up some charges and make a citizen's arrest. "We'd lock 'em up for any cheesy charge – disorderly conduct, fighting words," Coughenour said.

Word got around, and the Rangers took on more and more clients. As the turf they guarded expanded, the types of crimes they dealt with grew more serious.

"We took drugs off tons of people," Coughenour said. "I've seen more dead bodies than I care to remember." Still, he recalls those days as good times. "We were doing what we enjoyed doing, and getting paid for it."

They certainly strove to look like police officers. They had cars with police-style markings, police-style radios, top-of-the-line handcuffs and body armor. They called Ranger Headquarters "Fort Adamsville."

Their ranks expanded as well. About two years after moving to Atlanta, Coughenour headed a force of about two dozen Rangers, most of them men with backgrounds like his and most of them black. In some of their patrol areas, the Rangers had more men on the streets than the APD, he said. They drew perhaps more attention than they wanted.

"The next thing you knew, we were on TV," Coughenour said, referring to a report on an Atlanta television station that raised questions about the Rangers's aggressive tactics. "It was getting out of control."

One reason the Rangers gained notoriety, he contended, was that their tactics worked. He boasted of federal crime statistics that showed a 50 percent drop in serious crime in the neighborhoods where they patrolled. "While I was there, the kids could play outside," Coughenour said.

In 1999, a group of owners of the apartment complexes patrolled by the Rangers formed the Martin Luther King Property Owners Association. Coughenour said this gave the Rangers a little more legal cover. As employees of a private business entity, the Rangers would not be subject to the same state licensing requirements as they would if they had formed their own security company. Still, Coughenour was looking for something even better.

"We were trying to move the Ranger concept into the light of day, make it something more legitimate," Coughenour said. "We were trying to line ourselves up with someone who could help us."

Some high-octane help was on the way. At a community safety meeting held by the property owners association in June 1999, Coughenour was pulled aside by an Atlanta city councilman. "There's somebody you need to talk to," Coughenour said the man told him. The person to be contacted had a problem, something to do with black folks being oppressed somewhere in rural Georgia.

Shortly after that meeting, the councilman left Coughenour a message suggesting that he call State Rep. Tyrone Brooks. On the morning of Friday, June 18, Coughenour made the call.

Coughenour's recollection of that phone conversation is that Brooks told him of the plight of a religious group in Putnam County called the Nuwaubians. They were being harassed by a redneck sheriff.

"If you send me down there, I'll do whatever I can do," Coughenour said he told Brooks. He also asked Brooks to give him some form of written authorization.

In response, Brooks faxed the following letter to Coughenour, handwritten on paper with the letterhead of the Georgia Association of Black Elected Officials:

"To: Maj. Ed Coughenour, Ranger Services.

"Thank you for calling. Indeed we are very concerned that county officials in Putnam are trying to force the Nuwaubians into a violent confrontation. Whatever your agency can do to convince the county to just let these people live in peace will certainly be in the best interest of Ga.

"Peace and justice,

"Tyrone Brooks"

Later, Brooks would contend that he had been hoodwinked by Coughenour. Brooks said he assumed the Rangers were legitimate police officers. He wasn't quite sure which agency, only that they must have been some kind of "federal folk."

Nevertheless, the Rangers had their commission. Coughenour and another Ranger headed down to Eatonton that same day. They flashed their badges to a female deputy clerk, who later stated that she thought they were police officers. Next, they went to another clerk and asked for documents related to the Nuwaubian property. This clerk later stated that Coughenour told her that he was "just here to keep the peace."

The Rangers asked questions like, "Were there any criminal charges against the Nuwaubians?" and "Why is the sheriff so vehement about going after them?"

Coughenour left town, and the locals managed to maintain the peace on their own throughout the weekend. By then, Coughenour had decided he needed to know a little more about what he was getting the Rangers into.

Accoding to Coughenour, he requested a personal meeting with Brooks, and they met Monday, June 21, in the Atlanta office of a car dealer who was also a major Democratic contributor.

Coughenour told Brooks that he'd done some legal homework, and he thought he'd come up with some grounds on which to attack the sheriff's handling of the Nuwaubian matter. It was his conclusion that Sills had been acting illegally in enforcing the county's zoning ordinance. Coughenour had viewed a videotape supplied to him by the Nuwaubians, which showed Sills and Dizzy Adams making an inspection of some construction on the Nuwaubians' property. To Coughenour, it was clear that Sills was calling the shots.

If he was correct in concluding that Sills was acting beyond his authority, Coughenour told Brooks, then Sills' state certification as a sheriff could be legally challenged. Maybe, the state's police certification agency would even pull his credentials, and Sills would have to leave office, Coughenour surmised.

"By this time, I thought Howard Sills was probably the meanest s.o.b. I'd ever had the opportunity to deal with," Coughenour said.

For his part, Brooks characterized the problem as "a white cracker sheriff messing with the Nuwaubians," Coughenour said.

Coughenour said Brooks assured him that the Rangers would have high-level political cover for their operation. "He made it very clear that the governor's office was behind it," Coughenour said. "He told me, 'You don't have to worry; the governor's office is involved.'"

With backing like that, Coughenour said he viewed the assignment as "a cute little covert situation."

Cute or ugly, the job had to be a strictly freelance assignment. Under Georgia law, state officers are typically allowed to operate in a county only at the invitation of the county sheriff. Sills had no intention of inviting the GBI into Putnam County. The GBI doesn't need an invitation to conduct investigations of alleged criminal activities by local officials, but at this stage of the game, no one on the state level wanted to open an official investigation of Sills or of the other Putnam County officials involved in Nuwaubian affairs. Better to send in the Rangers.

Coughenour had no reservations about accepting the assignment. "We were working under the assumption that we were protected by the Governor of the State of Georgia," he said. Otherwise, there was no way he would have undertaken the mission, he said.

"We made some stupid mistakes in this incident, but we would never have been stupid enough to take on a county sheriff, if we didn't think our butts would be covered by a higher power," Cougenour said. "I thought I was doing the right thing for the right people."

At this point of the meeting, Brooks excused himself, and another man, someone Coughenour did not know, came into the room. The man did not introduce himself, but he seemed to be quite aware of what was going on, Coughenour said. Coughenour noted that the man was the same as the man in a picture hung on the wall of his host's office. The inscription on the picture said, "Best wishes. Your buddy, Bobby."

Speaking to Coughenour, the man said, "If you can handle this, we'd really appreciate it." Then, Coughenour said, the man handed him four tickets to an upcoming fundraiser for Governor Roy Barnes. The tickets were valued at $250 apiece.

Those tickets were the only payment Coughenour ever received for an assignment that would end up costing him dearly.

Later, when Coughenour was in the Putnam County Jail, with plenty of time to ponder how his top-secret, state-sanctioned mission had blown up in his face, he was watching the news on television, when he happened to see a man he recognized as the man who'd dropped in on his meeting with Brooks. It was

Bobby Kahn, chief of staff to Governor Roy Barnes.

A subsequent GBI investigation of the Georgia Rangers episode did not mention this meeting; and Kahn, in a 2006 interview, denied ever meeting with Coughenour.

However, Brooks said in a 2006 interview with this author that he recalled asking Kahn to meet with the Rangers, and that Kahn agreed to do so. Coughenour insists that he told GBI investigators about this meeting, but they apparently chose not to include it in their report.

If Coughenour's involvement in the case seems strange, Brooks's was only slightly less so. Brooks represents a predominantly-black section of Atlanta in the state legislature. His credentials as a state-level black leader come primarily from his presidency of the Georgia Association of Black Elected Officials, a group he founded. Other than his desire for peace and justice, he has offered no explanation for his recurring public support for the Nuwaubian causes. He denied that he was ever paid for his efforts on York's behalf.

Brooks said he was brought into the Nuwaubian situation by Joe Beasley, the Atlanta-based regional director of Rev. Jesse Jackson's Rainbow-PUSH Coalition. Beasley was convinced that Sills was trying to provoke the Nuwaubians into a violent confrontation, Brooks said. "There's a serious situation brewing in Putnam County," Brooks said Beasley told him. He did not say whether Beasley also told him about the real estate deal in Atlanta that Beasley and York were involved in. Beasley was part of an ownership group that had sold an apartment complex to York.

Brooks said he had made three visits to Tama-Re, to discuss the political situation and to join in their celebrations. He said he was favorably impressed by the people and the community they'd built. He was part of a group of black political officials and activists who met with York and attended a "Moorish Feast" at Tama-Re in the spring of 1999. The event included a fashion show, entertainment, and a meal catered by an Atlanta restaurant.

"This is awesome," Brooks said of his impression of Tama-Re. "This could be a major tourist attraction."

Also that spring, Beasley, Brooks, and two NAACP officials held a two-and-a-half-hour meeting with Sills in Eatonton. "We begged the sheriff to back off," Brooks said. However, he added, Sills seemed resistant to their suggestions. By the end of the meeting, Brooks said, he had concluded that "the sheriff had a personal vendetta against the Nuwaubians and York." All Brooks wanted, he said, was to find an answer to the question, "What can we do to keep the peace in Putnam County?"

Peacekeeping, Brooks claimed, was still his top priority, when he slipped into Governor Barnes's Ford Crown Victoria on Tuesday, June 22. This was the day after Brooks met with Coughenour in Atlanta—the meeting when the man Coughenour later identified as Bobby Kahn dropped in.

Brooks had received a phone call from the governor's office, asking him to join Barnes and Barnes's wife, Marie, while Barnes was riding to the airport. By this time, Brooks had given Kahn a copy of the commissioning letter he had given to Coughenour and a copy of Coughenour's business card—the one with the bogus claims of office and rank. The GBI investigation indicated that Barnes had a copy of Brooks's letter and Coughenour's business card with him in the car.

An aide later asked Barnes what he did with Coughenour's card, and Barnes said he probably threw it in the trash.

During the limo ride, Brooks briefed Barnes on his view that the Nuwaubians were a peaceful group and that it was Sills who was stirring up the trouble. Brooks also stated that Barnes suggested that Brooks contact Leroy Johnson, a former state legislator who represented York on other legal matters, and tell Johnson to seek to have the zoning case moved out of state court and into federal court.

If Barnes had any reservations about York or the Nuwaubians, Brooks did not mention, during his interview with the GBI, that Barnes expressed them. Nor, according to Brooks's statement, did Barnes raise any red flags, or even ask any questions, about what the heck they were doing, sending a bunch of bounty hunters into what all parties agreed was a highly-tense, racially-charged mess of a situation. Barnes was not interviewed by the GBI during its investigation. However, in a later email to this author, Barnes stated that he told Brooks his primary concern was that no one would get hurt in the planned protest in Eatonton.

Meanwhile, the tension levels in Eatonton were being ratcheted up. On the same day that Brooks took his ride with Barnes, Circuit Court Judge Hugh Wingfield publicly stated that he'd had enough of Dwight York's hide-and-seek games. At the end of what was supposed to have been a contempt of court hearing on the Tama-Re zoning violations case, Wingfield stated that he had issued an arrest warrant for York, who had not deigned to attend that day's hearing, as had been ordered by the court.

Wingfield instructed York's attorneys to have their client in court on the following Tuesday, June 29. If York did not appear, the judge stated, the warrant would be executed and York would be arrested and jailed.

Onto this animosity-drenched stage strode the Georgia Rangers. On Wednesday, June 23, two carloads of Rangers, seven in all, crossed the Putnam

County line. Their first stop was Tama-Re, where the Rangers received a tour of the property. The Nuwaubian tour guides mentioned to Coughenour that they were bringing in an extra contingent of security guards for next week's showdown at the courthouse in Eatonton; the guards were supposed to be coming from a Los Angeles-based security firm, called The Royal Guards of Amon-Ra, which was owned by movie star Wesley Snipes. (Snipes' name would surface in a later segment of the Nuwaubian saga.). Coughenour said he left two of his Rangers at Tama-Re, while he and the others proceeded to Eatonton.

Once inside the courthouse, Coughenour and the other Rangers started asking the same sorts of questions they had on their prior visit. "We were talking off the cuff with the clerks, asking what kind of problems these Nuwaubians had gotten themselves into," Coughenour said.

Coughenour also talked with Dizzy Adams, who told him that the best person to answer their questions would be Sheriff Sills.

By this time, Coughenour said, he had started to develop some doubts about his mission. He hadn't encountered the sort of overt racism that the Nuwabians and Brooks had described. Maybe, just maybe, the sheriff was only trying to do his job. Even though his own badge wouldn't get him into the Police Auxilliary ball, Coughenour considered himself a lawman at heart. He worked well with the police in Atlanta, and he understood how difficult it was to be a cop. He'd bent a few rules himself, in the quest for peace and justice.

"There's a fine line between being oppressive and being proactive," Coughenour said. "It was starting to look to me like Sheriff Sills was more on the proactive side."

The best way to settle it would be a lawman-to-lawman – well, perhaps wannabe—lawman-to-lawman—meeting, he decided. So, Coughenour radioed the two Rangers back at Tama-Re and told them to meet him and the others at the Sheriff's office.

At this point, Coughenour was close to a decision to abort the mission. "If this was what I was beginning to think it was, I was ready to roll out of there, never to return," he said.

His queasy feeling that he might have been cast as the patsy in this little melodrama became more intense, when the Rangers rendezvoused at the parking lot of the sheriff's office and jail, about a mile south of the courthouse. In an open space about twenty yards away from the parking lot, a Nuwaubian film crew had set up their cameras and trained them on the Rangers.

Coughenour knew that he hadn't told any of the Nuwaubians that he was going to see Sills. Also, he was pretty sure they hadn't overheard his plan when he called his Rangers he'd left at Tama-Re. That call had been made on the Rangers new, encrypted-signal radio. Coughenour was particularly proud of those radios; he'd bought them as recent trade-ins from the U.S. Secret Service. How had the Nuwaubians known, and what were they thinking of, showing up with their videocams?

Whatever happened in the parking lot, it would clearly be caught on tape. Coughenour certainly didn't want any Rangers to get into a fight with any sheriff's deputies; it started to dawn on him, though, that someone else just might want to have trouble break out for the cameras.

Coughenour and his second-in-command went inside and spoke briefly to a detective. Then they were asked to come to the sheriff's office.

The conversation with Sills started pleasantly enough. The two Rangers presented their credentials, such as they were, to Sills. In an affidavit he later filed to support his request for a search warrant of Ranger headquarters in Atlanta, Sills stated that Coughenour told him that the Rangers had been sent on the mission to Putnam County by Bobby Kahn.

Then, Coughenour attempted to persuade Sills to do what his sponsors back in Atlanta wanted Sills to do, that is, back off the Nuwaubians. He started to explain his legal analysis of the situation, to wit, his opinion that Sills was acting beyond the scope of his legal authority in the zoning disputes.

Sills was not amused. He did not appreciate being lectured on the law by this stranger with clearly bogus law-enforcement trappings. The mood in the office took an even sharper decline when a deputy entered and informed Sills that the men in the Ranger vehicle were armed.

All pretenses of cordiality vanished. Sills ordered all the Rangers to come inside the building. Probably to the disappointment of the Nuwaubian film crew, they complied quietly and quickly. Sills confiscated the weapons and ordered the men to produce identification.

He had them wait, while his deputies ran records checks on them. The checks revealed that four of the seven Rangers were felons, convicted on charges ranging from manslaughter to impersonating a police officer.

Sills informed the Rangers that he had the legal authority to arrest all of them on impersonation charges. However, he wasn't ready to do that right then. He told the Rangers he'd let them go for now, but he also advised them that their days of freedom might be numbered, and in the single digits.

The Rangers immediately headed out of Putnam County, and as soon as he crossed the county line, Coughenour pulled into a convenience store and made a call to the governor's office. The call was accepted by Penny Brown-Reynolds, who was then legal counsel to the governor.

"You'd better get the GBI down here," Coughenour told Brown-Reynolds, who assured him she'd pass his message along.

It must have been passed along very quickly, because that same night,

Coughenour said, he received a home visit from Vernon Keenan, then the deputy director of the GBI. Coughenour briefed him on the latest exploits of the Rangers in Putnam County.

Keenan, now the director of the GBI, confirmed Coughenour's account of the sequence of events that night. In a 2007 phone interview, Keenan said he received a call from Brown-Reynolds, who asked him to meet with Coughenour. At that time, he said, he had never met Coughenour nor heard of the Georgia Rangers. His purpose was to try to sort things out. "Everybody wanted to know who the Rangers were," Keenan said. One thing that was immediately obvious to Keenan was that the Rangers were not cops. Later, GBI agents would participate in the arrests of the Rangers, though the only prosecutions of those charges occurred in Putnam County.

The Rangers's mission was over. The next time Ed Coughenour came to Putnam County, it would be in the back seat of a police car—a real police car.

The next morning, Thursday, June 24, Sills received a call summoning him to the governor's office. There was to be a high-level meeting about the Nuwaubian situation.

Before Sills arrived in Atlanta, the other participants of the meeting gathered in a conference room. In his statement to the GBI investigators, Brooks said Barnes was part of this group. Barnes asked Brooks, "Tyrone, you've been down there. What's going on?" Brooks said he'd been told the sheriff had subjected the Nuwaubians to "racial profiling of the worst kind." Sometimes, Nuwaubian drivers were stopped and their belongings scattered on the roadside during police searches, he said he'd been told by Joe Beasley.

Brooks recalled Barnes saying that if trouble broke out, it would be an embarrassment for the entire State of Georgia. Brooks expressed the view that the Nuwaubians wouldn't be the ones to start any trouble, but they would defend themselves. As far as he was concerned, the Nuwaubians were peace-loving people; they didn't drink hard liquor, and they simply wanted to build their Egyptian-themed community the way they wanted.

Brooks stated that he then asked the GBI officials present whether they had experienced any serious problems with the Nuwaubians, and two of Georgia's top law enforcement officers said they had not.

By the time Sills had arrived, Barnes had left for other business. Those left at the meeting included Brooks, Kahn, Brown-Reynolds, and the two GBI men. To Sills, the gathering had the feel of a star chamber, and the heat was on him.

It was a strange feeling, Sills said, because he had always held Barnes in high regard. He said he considered Barnes a fair-minded legislator, who had always been a reliable advocate for issues important to law enforcement. Sills had even made a statement in support of Barnes' policies, which was used in Barnes's successful 1998 campaign for governor.

Shortly after Barnes assumed the office of governor, Sills tried to alert him to the potential for big trouble with the Nuwaubians. In a letter to Barnes dated March 9, 1999, Sills wrote that the Nuwaubians had been conducting a campaign of defamations and "utter fabrications" against him and his office for the past year.

Sills also reported on the findings of a trip he'd make to New York to meet with agents of the FBI's Terrorist Task Force. "The activities of York's group during the years when they were headquartered in Brooklyn were frightening to say the least," Sills wrote. "Information we have obtained in the last several months is even worse."

In the letter, Sills told Barnes that he believed the Nuwaubians were deliberately trying "to racially divide the citizenry of this county." He reported on the "hit list" of public officials and journalists that the Nuwaubians had published, in their search for defamatory information that could be used against those listed. He told Barnes how the Nuwaubians had used vile racial slurs against black leaders in Putnam County who refused to support them.

He asked Barnes for a face-to-face meeting, where Sills could brief Barnes on his ongoing criminal investigations of the Nuwaubians. "Governor, I have been in this business every day of my adult life, and I can categorically state without hesitation that a great propensity for the development of a dangerous incident involving the group is imminent," Sills wrote.

Despite putting his concerns in writing, Sills was concerned that his message was not having the desired impact on the governor. Instead, he believed, Barnes was being influenced more by input from people like Tyrone Brooks, who sought to label Sills as the villain in the piece. That view was reinforced by GBI officials, who were describing him to Barnes as a "loose cannon," Sills said.

Shortly after writing the March letter to Barnes, Sills got the opportunity for a brief personal exchange with Barnes. It quickly became apparent to Sills that Barnes did not place much credence in Sills's assessment of the situation.

"My God, Howard!" the sheriff recalled the governor saying to him. "Are you going to kill people over building permits?"

One thing that everyone in the meeting at the governor's office could agree on was that the threat of a violent outbreak was real.

Brooks laid the blame for the situation at the sheriff's door. He admitted commissioning the Georgia Rangers to go into Putnam County, but he repeated his claim that he had been deceived into believing the Rangers were federal agents.

To Sills, Brooks was trying to make a racial issue out of a law enforcement problem. "The race card was being played, and Tyrone Brooks was the dealer," Sills said later of the atmosphere at the meeting.

Brooks seemed to have the backing of the GBI officials at the meeting, one of whom expressed the belief that Sills was going off on a tangent in his pursuit of the zoning violations against the Nuwaubians, Sills said.

What Sills could not say then was that he was investigating York for crimes far more serious than zoning violations. He didn't trust the GBI; he'd been told that York had a source inside the agency.

Later, Sills would reflect on the bitter irony of his being accused of harassing blacks, while he was actually pursing an investigation of some hideous allegations of molestation of black children. "The only racial issue was that every victim York preyed upon was black," Sills said.

Despite the unspoken agendas, the focus of the meeting turned to the problem at hand, preventing violence at next week's court hearing. Sills requested that a force of state law enforcement officers be sent to Eatonton, to be held in reserve. He was told to put the request in writing.

Sills said he left the meeting with the distinct impression that he had been put on notice, that he was the one being watched. He was also convinced that York had some people in high places watching out for him.

"The only thing that was clear to me was that the governor was trying to influence me to walk away from the zoning issues, to get me to back off," Sills said.

On the same day as that meeting in the governor's office, the Nuwaubians opened up a second-front public relations initiative of their own. They called a press conference at Tama-Re. There was a crowd of one hundred or more Nuwaubians in attendance, some of whom were early arrivals for the Savior's Day festivities, which would begin in earnest the next day.

At the news conference, Ozell Sutton, regional director for the Department of Justice's Community Relations Service, was pressed forward by the Nuwabians to make a statement. He didn't quite produce the ringing condemnation of Sills that the Nuwaubians wanted. "I don't know that there is a racial problem," was as far as Sutton would go in a public statement. He said he would talk to people on both sides of the issue and offer his help in resolving the disputes.

The spokesman for the Nuwaubians, a long-time member of the group named Marshall Chance, was not nearly as restrained. Chance, who had bestowed the title "Pastor" on himself, proclaimed that the Nuwaubians were being harassed, because the local establishment saw them as a political threat.

The prevailing "racial attitudes" were so harshly anti-Nuwaubian that their Master Teacher, York, had decided to spend less and less time in Putnam County. Also, York had received an unspecified number of death threats, Chance claimed.

The federal mediator never reported finding any substance to the Nuwaubians' claims of racism, nor was he ever invited to participate in any mediation activities. He did, however, get a message to the sheriff before he left town. "If the judge puts York in jail, they're going to riot and burn Eatonton down," Sills said the mediator told him.

By the end of the day on that Thursday, the governor's office put out a response to the press inquiries they'd received about the Georgia Rangers' foray into Eatonton the previous day. "We didn't send the Rangers there," a spokeswoman for the governor said. "We're trying to find out who the Rangers are."

The 1999 Savior's Day festival started the next day, Friday, June 25. The celebration was quiet and wet. Possibly due to the intermittently heavy rains, the crowds were smaller than in past years, the estimates ranging from two thousand to four thousand attendees. The hillside used for a parking lot at Tama-Re was slippery and wet most of the weekend, and the traffic left a trail of red mud for hundreds of yards in either direction of Shadydale Road. As far as police-blotter incidents, though, all was quiet on the Egyptian front.

"Frank...Roy Barnes." The greeting from the governor on the other end of the phone line was a bit unsettling for Frank Ford. As Republican Party chairman for Putnam County, Ford wasn't used to fielding calls from the Democratic governor. As the attorney preparing to represent the county in a potentially explosive hearing in the Nuwaubian case, Ford thought it more than a little inappropriate, when he heard the governor apparently attempting to influence his handling of the case.

"What're you people doing down there?" Ford said Barnes asked him, in a clearly disapproving tone. Just in case his message wasn't getting through, Barnes crystallized his position, saying, "Y'all just need to back off."

Ford regarded Barnes' phone call as an extraordinary and unwarranted intrusion into a highly sensitive case. In Ford's estimation, Barnes had weighed in on the side of a group that had repeatedly thumbed their noses at the county's laws. That group's leader was already in contempt of a judicial order to appear in court.

Aside from the issue of who was right and who was wrong, how in the world did it become the governor's business?

"Can you imagine, the Governor of the State of Georgia calling a lawyer

Governor Roy Barnes, center, with Nuwaubian Anthony Evans to his right, in a 2002 photo taken in Barnes's office.
At that time, Nuwaubians represented themselves as a Masonic-style group.

in one of the 159 counties in the state on a zoning matter?" Ford said.

That same day, Monday, June 28, Sills met with a delegation of officers from the Georgia State Patrol to make logistical arrangements for the backup force for the next day's hearing. They decided to use the local high school gym as the staging area for the one hundred or so officers Sills anticipated. The state patrol officers asked whether Sills would supply any food for the reserve force. Sills assured them that he would. The agreed-upon menu: soda and sandwiches.

The next morning, while the assembling protesters were still making tracks as they crossed the dew-covered courthouse green, Sills got a call from the deputy director of the GBI, Vernon Keenan. The call was another summons for Sills, this time to the National Guard Armory not far from downtown Eatonton.

When he arrived, Sills saw a force of about 250 state patrol officers and GBI agents. They'd brought along a FEMA field kitchen (so much for Sills' sandwiches) and were setting up a full-fledged command post, wired by communications gear imported for the occasion.

Keenan proceeded to lay out the rules of engagement for Sills. "We're not going to do anything, unless your people can't handle it," Sills said Keenan told him.

However, the ultimate decision on whether to call out the reserves was going to be Keenan's, not Sills's. "If you don't ask us to come in when you should, we'll go in on our own," Keenan told Sills.

Sills left the state command post in a barely-contained fury, convinced he was being set up to take the blame, if things got ugly.

"It was going to be my fault, no matter what happened," Sills said. "It looked like I might have to fight the GBI and the State Patrol."

The exchange only strengthened Sills's desire to call the whole thing off. He had previously argued that this hearing should not be held so close to the Savior's Day events. He didn't want the hundreds, or maybe even thousands, of visiting Nuwaubians to be around to swell the ranks of the protesters he would have to contain. But the judge who had put York on notice to appear was not about to initiate a postponement at this late hour.

Sills had only one move left to attempt. He dashed off a letter to Milton Nix, then the director of the GBI. Sills had been instructed by Brown-Reynolds, the governor's counsel, that he should direct any communication regarding the Nuwaubian situation to Nix. Sills gave the letter to one of his deputies, instructing him to use the police prerogative of ignoring all speed limits and to deliver the letter personally to Nix.

In the letter, Sills expressed his concerns about the strained relationship between the state and local police forces deployed in Eatonton. "I have the distinct impression that there is at least some reluctance on the part of the executive branch of the state government and its law enforcement personnel in providing assistance here in Putnam County today," he stated.

Sills also wrote that he was "to say the least, appalled" that there had been a news leak from his meeting at the governor's office during the past week. A local news reporter had called Sills to ask about a comment Sills was supposed to have made at the meeting, regarding the judicial handling of the case. The reporter said his source was someone in the Nuwaubian community. There hadn't been anyone at that meeting who had professed to being a Nuwaubian, so the only way the reporter could have gotten his information – or misinformation, in Sills's view – was if someone at the meeting talked out of school to the Nuwaubians.

Given all that, Sills wanted Nix to encourage Barnes to invoke a state law that gave the governor extraordinary powers to act to prevent a potentially violent situation. Even at this late hour, Barnes could cancel the hearing, ban the protest demonstration, and even order the county to dismiss its lawsuit against the Nuwaubians, Sills contended in the letter.

The letter failed. Barnes did not intervene. The show was on.

It didn't last long at all, at least not in the intended venue.

Judge Wingfield gaveled the courtroom to order, and the two hundred or so Nuwaubians who packed the spectator gallery immediately fell silent.

Somberly resplendent in a black fez and an all-black outfit accented by a bucketful of gold jewelry, York took the witness stand. The first order of business was supposed to be York's explanation for why he hadn't bothered to show up for the previous hearings on the disputes over the zoning issues on his property.

The only problem – and it was a big one – was that Dwight didn't live there anymore.

After stating his name, York was asked to state his address. He said he lived in Athens, Georgia, three or four counties away from Shadydale Road.

"I move around, because I want to stay out of someone's focus," York proclaimed. "I move from place to place."

When Ford attempted to question York further, York invoked his Fifth Amendment right against self-incrimination.

This defendant had been testing Wingfield's tolerance for weeks. Now that York had finally shown up, the judge wasn't about to let him play games in his courtroom. Wingfield immediately gaveled the hearing into recess. He ordered York and the attorneys for both sides to convene in his chambers, and he ordered the bailiffs to clear the courtroom.

The Nuwaubians were not keen on moving. They'd stood in line for their seats and waited for more than an hour in them for the proceedings to begin. An angry buzz went up among them. Was this some sneaky tactic to send them off, while the white-devil sheriff whisked The Lamb off to jail?

Tyrone Brooks, playing the peacemaker, moved up to the wooden rail separating the spectators from the parties to the case. He called out for the people to stay calm and leave quietly, and, with the extra urging from the bailiffs and their own marshals, that's what they did.

The protesters re-formed on the courthouse green, where they would keep a vigil for the next two hours.

Inside the judge's chambers, Wingfield pushed the parties to make a deal. First though, Frank Ford took the opportunity to ask York directly about the stream of personal attacks against county officials in the pro-York newsletters and newspapers. York claimed he didn't know anything about any of that.

Outside, the protesters were drenched by a violent thunderstorm. Hardly any of them sought shelter, though. Neither did they talk amongst themselves or splash in the puddles. At times, they held up their hands, chanting and praying. They moved when and where their marshals told them. The scene was not unlike a bad zombie movie.

Two hours after the courtroom had been cleared, the rains ended, the clouds parted, and York appeared triumphant at the courthouse doors.

"Peace is made," he proclaimed with a smile. Then a phalanx of security guards wedged him through his cheering and adoring crowd. He slipped into the back seat of a waiting black SUV and drove off.

The crowd broke up and the small army of law enforcement officials could go home. No one had been hurt, and there would be no riot footage on the 6 o'clock news. That was a victory of sorts.

As he left the courthouse, Wingfield commented that he believed the deal reached in his chambers marked a resolution of the long zoning battle. "It should be over now," he said. "It's up to the two sides to live up to it."

Basically, the deal was that the county and the Nuwaubians had agreed to cooperate better in the future. The key element in making that happen was that York effectively removed himself from the fray. He legally transferred the deed to Tama-Re to a group of nine of his followers. No money changed hands; but now, York was no longer the titular owner, so the county wouldn't have to worry about dragging him to court or about all the turmoil that would entail. No more mass protests, and no more tense standoffs between the law and the Nuwaubians.

To Frank Ford, the change in York's status as a property owner was the only significant change. "We've had this same deal two times before," he said.

Tyrone Brooks courted the television cameras and claimed a great victory for peace and justice.

County Commissioner Sandra Adams said the whole day had been nothing more than a publicity stunt by the Nuwaubians. "When you play the race card, everybody stands at attention and listens," she said. However, it bothered her that the news coverage of the protest might transmit the false impression of Putnam County as a place where blacks needed to march in the streets to obtain justice. "We're not tyrants," she said.

There remained a few loose ends for Sills to tie up, namely, the Georgia Rangers.

On the night of July 3, Ed Coughenour had his door kicked in by some uninvited guests with badges. "The next thing I knew, I had Howard Sills's gun in my face," he said. Sills also wielded a search warrant for Ranger headquarters and a warrant for Coughenour's arrest.

The charges included impersonating a police officer, using a vehicle similar to a police car, crossing a guard line with a weapon (at the Putnam County Sheriff's office and jail), and possession of a firearm by a convicted felon. The six other Rangers who had ranged into Putnam County were also arrested on similar charges. During the search of Ranger headquarters, police found the four tickets to the governor's fundraiser. The Rangers hadn't used them after all.

Coughenour languished about four months in the Putnam County Jail, awaiting a bond hearing that never seemed to get scheduled. His friends in high places let him sit. He never made bond. Instead, he was dispatched back to a North Carolina prison. His arrest had been a violation of his parole on the embezzlement conviction. He entered a guilty plea to the Georgia charges, and served that sentence concurrently with the year-and-a-half remainder on his previous sentence.

The Georgia Ranger fiasco became the subject of a GBI investigation. In documents from that investigation, both Bobby Kahn and Penny Brown-Reynolds denied having anything to do with sending the Rangers to Putnam County. However, Kahn did admit to knowing about the scheme before the Rangers' last trip, because he stated that he passed copies of Brooks's letter and Coughenour's card to Barnes. Brown-Reynolds acknowledged that she had accepted the phone call from Coughenour that preceded his de-briefing by the GBI.

Brooks insisted to the investigators that he had been duped into thinking the Rangers were federal agents. He professed to have become angry when he learned that they were not really police officers of any kind. When he was asked why he thought the Rangers came to him in the first place, Brooks offered the miserably lame explanation that they might have seen him on television and therefore known him as an advocate for the rights of black people.

However, the investigative file does not contain any explanation for why a group of people at the top level of state government allowed some cowboys with play badges to ride into the middle of a feared impending race riot.

Coughenour continues to insist that he told the GBI agents who interrogated him before his arrest about the meeting where the man he believed to be Bobby Kahn dropped in and tacitly approved the Ranger mission.

During a 2001 interview regarding the Ranger incident, Barnes stated that no one in his office was involved in sending the Rangers to Putnam County.

In the end, nothing came of the GBI investigation of the Ranger incident. In retrospect, Keenan said the case illustrates the difficulty in applying the concept of justice to matters that appear to be religious in nature. "When someone wraps themself in the cloak of religion, law enforcement can sometimes become cautious." Keenan said.

The Rangers themselves, however, were out of business, permanently.

The role of Roy Barnes in the affair is a curious one. When this incident occurred, he had only been in office for about six months. He had been elected with an overwhelming majority of the black vote, so it seems natural and proper that Barnes would have listened to someone like Tyrone Brooks, a long-time legislator bringing him a tale of oppression of blacks in a rural county. Nevertheless, Barnes seems to have accepted the stereotype – redneck sheriff tromping on the rights of black folks – with little or no questioning, even though the sheriff involved had previously informed him that the stereotype just didn't hold in this case.

Rather than entertain the notion that a black religious leader might actually be the villain in this drama, Barnes and his subordinates appeared to be operating on the assumption that York's claims of discrimination, as relayed by Brooks, were automatically valid. Of course, similar assumptions had been made by politicians and law enforcement officials throughout York's tenure in New York. In Georgia, the scam was altered slightly, but it still worked.

But if Barnes was relying on political support from people like Brooks, he was disappointed. Even though he led comfortably in the polls right up until election day of 2002, he was defeated in his bid for re-election.

Barnes contends that he was most concerned with preserving the peace. In an email to this author in 2006, Barnes stated, "I was confronted with a building permit dispute that was quickly being elevated to a race riot. I have been practicing law for 35 years, and I have never heard of force being used or threatened in such a dispute. The only thing I told Brooks to tell York is that if a police officer was ever hurt, I would send the National Guard in there to take over." Barnes turned down the author's request for an interview on the topics covered in this chapter.

Even though violence was averted in Eatonton on the day of the showdown on the courthouse green, the event did become a milestone of sorts in relations between the Nuwaubians and Putnam County officialdom. After that, both sides seemed to grow weary of the protracted battle over zoning.

For the Nuwaubians' part, there were no more construction projects to fight over. There would be no new pyramids on Tama-Re. York really had moved to Athens. He began spending more time at the $500,000 home he'd bought in the Athens suburbs, and he would move some of his business operations there, taking selected concubines and child victims with him. He would return regularly to Tama-Re to hold classes for the new recruits, but he would also work to develop new bases in cities, including Athens and Macon. They never attempted to re-open Club Rameses.

For their part, the members of the Putnam County Commission did back off from their confrontational stance toward the Nuwaubians. In 2000, the local elections resulted in an effective new majority on the board. The county's zoning lawsuit against the Nuwaubians was dropped, and Dorothy Adams was fired as county attorney.

Without the expressed backing of the county commission, Sills no longer involved his office in zoning matters. There were much more sinister allegations against York for him to investigate.

And as for York, the victory he claimed on the steps of the Putnam County courthouse was just another of his illusions. His empire had already started to collapse from within.

Tama-Re in ruins. Photo by Anderson Scott

CHAPTER 8
Exodus From The Egypt Of The West (1999 - 2002)

I have witnessed the affliction of my people in Egypt and have heard their cry of complaint against the slave drivers. So I know well what they are suffering. Therefore, I have come down to rescue them from the hands of the Egyptians and lead them out of that land into a good and spacious land, a land flowing with milk and honey. – Exodus 3:7,8

The girl sent out her cry in the middle of the night. Ramillah sneaked into the offices of Tama-Re and made a phone call to New York.

"Daddy, come get me. I want to leave," she said.

She wanted to get out of Putnam County. Even more, she wanted an end to what had been three years of frequent, repeated, sometimes nightly, sexual assaults upon her. Ever since she was twelve, the fifteen-year-old Ramillah had been used as a sexual slave by Dwight York, a man forty years her senior.

Her father, Asad, left immediately from New York with two of his grown children. He expected some trouble. The last time he'd been down to Tama-Re, more than a year earlier, he had not been allowed to see his daughter. So, this time, he drove a different car, thinking that might help him get past the guards.

Their plan was to arrive at Tama-Re at a pre-arranged time, then wait for Ramillah at the playground just up the hill from the entrance.

When they arrived, the guard did not recognize Asad, who had been listed as one of York's enemies. Ramillah was there waiting. She had a bookbag and the clothes on her back, and that was all.

Ramillah had failed to keep her departure a secret. She had tried to leave twice before, so she was on a sort of escape watch. One of York's concubines had learned of this latest plan and had come to Ramillah to try to persuade her to stay. Ramillah was adamant.

As the girl proceeded to the waiting car, her mother came to the playground. The mother had brought Ramillah and two of her other daughters with her to Tama-Re. The older woman had borne York a child back when she was about the age Ramillah was now; and even though she later married Asad and had six children with him, she remained devoted to York. She had become one of his most trusted concubines, and she would remain at Tama-Re.

The mother and daughter exchanged no words or farewell embraces. Ramillah had been warned by York never to tell her mother what had happened to her. What was there to say to her now?

The girl got into the car and left.

For a long time, Ramillah did not tell her father about the abuse. Her moods and behavior, however, informed him that something was wrong. Ramillah was frequently withdrawn, sullen, and rebellious.

"I knew something bad had happened to her, but I didn't know what," Asad said. Not long after taking Ramillah away, he moved to Florida. He made arrangements to have Ramillah's younger sister sent to live with him there.

Later, Asad overheard Ramillah talking with her sister about having been abused by York. He confronted Ramillah, and she finally told him the ugly truth.

Asad was enraged. He had believed in York. He had raised York's child as his own. Now, he was faced with the reality that not only had his marriage broken up due to his wife's return to York, his daughter had become York's victim.

"He took advantage of my little girl," Asad said. "Her innocence was grabbed away from her by this man. He's the devil in fancy African robes."

Asad called the police in Florida. They told him he would have to report the crimes to authorities in the place where they had occurred. His next call was to Putnam County Sheriff Howard Sills. The next day, Asad took Ramillah to the Orlando offices of the FBI, where they were interviewed by Sills and several federal agents.

This was the way York was finally exposed. Throughout the thirty-five-year run of his various cults, he never really lost his political support. For different reasons, he had also never been indicted, even though he had been the target of several criminal investigations.

In the end, it was Ramillah and the girls and boys like her who stood up against him. York had abused and impregnated and discarded scores of young women during his long ride at the top of the cult. For the most part, they just slunk away and never troubled the great man again.

But these little girls were different. Most of them were born in the cult or had been brought into the cult as young children. They had grown up being told that whatever York wanted was good, that York was their god and substitute father. They had been lured by York's cheap diamond rings, candy, good food, trips to restaurants, and movie privileges.

As they grew up, however, they wised up. York's child victims became adolescents who were old enough to realize that what happened to them was wrong, and sick. Some of them told their mothers, and the news shook those women out of their cult-induced stupors enough for them to get their children out of York's clutches. Some of the other victims simply found their own way out.

This was no mass exodus. The victims left silently and separately and, for the most part, secretly. They did not run straight from Tama-Re to the police or to the press. They scattered to whichever friends or relatives would take them in. Their departures started not long after the big demonstration at the courthouse in Eatonton in June 1999; but it was almost two years after that when the first of the victim/witnesses gave her statement to the FBI.

Aludra was among the first of the old Backstreet Girls to break away. By 1999, she had reached her mid-twenties. All but the first five years of her life had been spent in the cult. York had started molesting her when she was fifteen, but now that she was grown, there was a new crop of girls for him to play with, including her younger half sister, Jokara.

"I knew that when I got too old, he'd just give me to a brother," she said.

She was deeply depressed, but she couldn't see through her depression to a way out. Instead, she started thinking that suicide was her best option. "I'd rather think of killing myself than leaving," she said. "I was miserable, but I got used to it."

It was watching the younger girls getting called to Doc's rooms for the same treatment she'd received that snapped her our of her funk. "It became apparent that it was just a vicious cycle," she said.

But there was something different about this group of girls; they weren't submitting as meekly as the older women had.

Aludra started to gain strength from their spirit of defiance. The younger girls were deliberately doing little things to annoy York. They didn't seem too terribly upset when York punished them or temporarily banished them. "They started wearing pads and telling Doc that they were having their periods, so that he wouldn't want to have sex with them," she said.

Aludra talked with one of York's highest-ranking concubines, Basheera, about the growing resistance of the child victims. Basheera was having her own issues with York; she had two children with him. He wasn't going to support them or fund their education. Besides, Basheera was stuck in the concubine rankings behind his favorite, Kathy Johnson. Aludra and Basheera decided that they could be as uppity as the girls. "We decided we needed to do the same things," Aludra said.

She started her serious getaway planning after she received a visit from her grandmother, whom she hadn't seen for at least fourteen years. The grandmother brought her a picture of her biological father, a man Aludra had never known. The older woman also gave her contact information for her father's side of the family.

Soon after that visit, Aludra wrote a letter to an aunt, seeking help in locating her father. It angered her mother, Nasira, to find out that Aludra was trying to establish contact with the outside world; but Aludra persisted in her search.

After the 1999 protest at the Putnam County courthouse, York started pressuring Aludra and the other women her age to get out and find jobs in the area. Of course, he expected them to turn in nearly all their earnings to him. To Aludra, that order was a sign of her declining status in the cult.

She was only infrequently included in the groups of girls and women driven in vans to York's "mansion" in Athens, where the more important work of the cult was increasingly being done. She was clearly no longer among York's special girls.

Aludra had no high school diploma and no driver's license. She joined some of the other women doing telemarketing work, which was about all she could do.

Her growing discontent must have been obvious. "People started gossiping about me," she said.

York learned that she had been talking to Jokara and some of the other girls, and that angered him. Aludra was called into a disciplinary meeting and informed by one of the concubines that she was in danger of being kicked off Tama-Re. The girls she'd been talking with were also punished; their little treats of food and movies were temporarily suspended. The threat of expulsion didn't terrify her anymore.

Finally, in late 2000, Aludra was summoned to a meeting with one of York's main concubines. "Doc says you have to leave," the woman told her. She was forbidden to have any contact with her siblings at Tama-Re; however, her mother came to her and tried to persuade her to stay. Perhaps if she wrote a letter apologizing and begging for Doc's forgiveness, York might allow her to stay.

By this time, though, Aludra actually welcomed the expulsion order. She had located her father, who was living in Atlanta, and he had agreed to take her in.

On the day that she was to be transported to her father's house, her belongings were searched, to make sure that she wasn't taking any money or extra clothes or potentially incriminating pictures with her, she said. So, she left her mother and her four siblings at Tama-Re and walked away from the cult that had been her home for twenty years.

Once with her father, she told him what had happened to her and the other members of the cult. "He got upset. He hated Doc and he didn't even know him," she said. Her father told her to go to the police. She would, she promised, but first, she had to attend to some family matters.

Her first priority was to get Jokara out of Tama-Re. Her next objective was to make sure her mother knew what was going on right under her nose.

She made a visit to Tama-Re. She was denied access to Jokara, but she was able to talk with her half-brother Rafiq. Both of them had been York's victims, but they didn't talk in detail about that. They didn't need to; there was a shared understanding between them. As Rafiq later recalled their conversation, "She was like, I know what you're doing down there. And we basically knew what each other was talking about."

Through Rafiq, Aludra got word of her plan to Jokara. A time was set when Aludra would come back and take Jokara away. In preparation, Jokara packed a few belongings and hid them.

When the day of the planned escape came, Jokara said she was taking trash out to the dump area in the woods. One of the trash bags contained her things she wanted to take with her. She hid her bag in the woods, then came back to the house. A little later, she announced that she needed to make another trash run.

Jokara grabbed her bag and scampered through the woods to a spot down the road, where Aludra was waiting for her.

Soon after that, Aludra wrote a letter to her mother. She didn't go into great detail; it would have been too painful. But she made it clear that bad things had happened to her and the other children at Doc's house. She sent the letter to the Eatonton post office box that her mother kept, as a way of ensuring that the Social Security payments she received for her daughter with Down's Syndrome

– York's daughter – would not be confiscated by York.

"I was devastated," Nasira said of her reaction to the letter. Aludra's letter made it impossible to deny that three of her five children had been repeatedly molested over a period of years by the man who'd fathered her other two children.

In her state of shock, she couldn't see an immediate way out. Where would she go? How could she provide for her four underage children? She knew that she'd probably be kicked out soon. After Aludra and Jokara left, York had demoted her from her office job at the Athens house.

Still, she wasn't capable of outright defiance. She'd joined York's cult twenty years earlier. She stayed within the chain of command, writing letters to York and to Basheera, stating her desire to leave. She told them that she'd discovered what had happened to her children, though she too refrained from putting the details in writing.

Basheera called Nasira in for a meeting, though she didn't try to change the older woman's mind. She questioned Nasira about how she felt, regarding what Aludra had told her. Would she report any of this to outside authorities?

Nasira reassured Basheera that the only thing she wanted to do was to leave and take care of her children. Basheera gave Nasira $1,000 from York, and told her that York wanted her to come to him, if the children ever needed anything. However, that money was the last she'd ever receive from York.

Even though she was supposedly leaving with York's permission, Nasira made the arrangements in secret. She called Aludra and set up a rendezvous. Then, she got a woman friend at Tama-Re to take her and the three children she still had with her to Eatonton, where Aludra met them and took them to Atlanta. From there, Nasira took Jokara, Rafiq, and the two younger children and returned to Brooklyn.

Azizah had committed a major offense – behaving like a normal thirteen-year-old girl. She started becoming more interested in having a boyfriend her own age than in submitting to the sexual desires of a man in his early fifties, Dwight York. At the Savior's Day festival of 1999, Azizah was caught spending time with a boy.

She had already acquired the reputation of a troublemaker. She was the one who had confronted York for sexually assaulting a boy her age. She was the one who'd tried to hide from York in the Athens house by sleeping under her bed.

Also, she was worried about her little sister. One night in York's bedroom, she overheard one of the older concubines telling York that Azizah's mother wanted money for a birthday present for Azizah's younger sister. York asked how old the girl would be on her birthday, and he was told it would be her twelfth.

"You know what that means," York said. "It's going to be her time." Azizah knew only too well what it meant.

One of York's concubines ordered Azizah not to be caught again in the presence of her young boyfriend. If that happened, the boy and his family would be kicked off Tama-Re.

"All I did was that I saw a boy that I liked," Azizah said. "I didn't like it that they told me I couldn't see him again."

So, Azizah started making some threats of her own. She began talking about going to Sheriff Sills and telling what was happening to her and the other girls on Tama-Re.

York personally reported her transgressions to her mother, Badra. "Oh no, your daughter's in trouble again," he told her. "Do you know your daughter got caught up the hill with a boy?" Somehow, the girl's spending time with a male other than York was as serious a violation as threatening to report York to the police.

Badra was dispatched to deal with her disobedient daughter.

"Why do you want to get your father into trouble?" Badra asked Azizah. Sadly, York was as close to a father figure as the girl had ever had, and she had been trained to think of York as her father.

"My father!" spit back the girl. "My father has been having sex with me since I was five years old!"

Azizah followed that verbal stun-gun shot with more, telling her mother about how she was only one of many little girls that York repeatedly molested. The news was more than Badra was willing or able to process at that moment. All she could do was tell the girl to stay away from Doc.

"Don't go near him. Don't let him touch you," she told Azizah. She promised to start working on a plan to get them out.

At the same time, York was pressuring Azizah, trying to deter her from acting on her threat to go to Sills.

"He told me that if we run our mouth to Sheriff Sills, he'd get somebody to come down from New Jersey to shoot us, and he'll throw us behind the deer pen," she said, referring to an area in the deep woods where the previous owner had held game animals.

Azizah said York's death threats did not really frighten her. "He doesn't have the guts to do stuff like that," she said.

Nevertheless, Badra wanted to get herself and her two daughters out of there as quickly as possible. She managed to smuggle money out of the office where she worked, a few hundred dollars at a time. She befriended a male Nuwaubian whose assignments took him off the property frequently. He agreed to deposit the money in a bank account in her name.

Over the next months, she had managed to smuggle about three thousand dollars. In April 2000, she was seriously injured in a car accident while running an errand for York. For months, she had to wear a cast that covered most of her chest and neck. Her injury slowed her plans to leave but did not relieve her of her duties to York. While she was still in a neck brace, she was ordered to drive York to Washington D.C.; while she drove, York relaxed in the back seat.

York discovered that she had a male friend in the community who was helping her. York made the man publicly confess his guilt, and then he kicked the man out. He also started getting rough with Badra.

"I know you know what I did to your daughter," she said York told her. "If you ever say anything, I'll have the same thing done to you; and if I'll do it to you, I'll do it to her, and you'll have to watch it."

Badra knew their time at Tama-Re and her fifteen years in the cult were quickly coming to an end. Badra overheard York telling another of the concubines, "If she(Azizah) doesn't straighten up, we'll just ship the whole family out."

Azizah refused to "straighten up." A few days after the girl's last rejection of York, a concubine came to Badra and told her, "You have to leave."

Badra and her two daughters were driven to a motel in the next county. Their parting payoff: one hundred dollars. Badra's sister was able to arrange for a rental car, and they cleaned out her bank account and drove home to Virginia.

When she was seventeen, Areebah lost her battle to keep her fourteen-year-old sister out of York's clutches. When she was about to turn eighteen, she resolved to start fighting for herself. She was growing up and getting out.

Areebah was then one of the workers at the Athens "mansion." At times, there were as many as fifty people staying in the house. Rotating groups of the younger children were brought into Athens for York's sexual pleasure. Sometimes, fifteen-passenger vans arrived at the house loaded with thirty passengers.

Neighbors might complain, but they couldn't see what went on at night inside the house. Areebah saw, as could anyone else who was in the hallway of the bedroom area. York habitually left his bedroom door open, so that anyone in the hallway could see him having sex with the girls.

Areebah could no longer tolerate the abuse. She refused to make herself available to York, the man she'd been told to worship since she was four years old. Some of the other girls her age were making the same sort of decisions.

"See, most of us started having sex with him at an early age. So when you was about seventeen or eighteen, most of us started, like, awareness, self-awareness," she said. "You know, we're not ugly, we're not stupid. We've got brains."

The young women started to sit together in groups more often. York tried to break them up, but they re-formed their group as often as they could.

York also sought to set them against each other. When one of the girls was apart from the group, York would criticize her in front of the others. "So, it was like we were at war with each other, but after a couple of years, we all just started waking up," Areebah said.

As punishment for the growing resistance, York ordered Areebah and some of the other recalcitrants to move to "103," the worst female living quarters on Tama-Re. "There was a big hole in the wall. You could see right through the bathroom. It was mildewed. It was sewage leaking out every day. It was just nasty," she said.

York told the young women, "All of you have to suffer together, because y'all like each other."

Areebah started hearing more repetitions of the rumors of York having sex with the children. Even though she had seen it herself, even though she knew it was happening to her younger sister, and even though she had been a child victim herself, Areebah's first response was to defend York and try to quash the rumors.

"I caught myself saying, 'What! That's not true!'" Areebah said. "But deep down inside, it was true, and I was trying to figure out, Why am I saying it's not true?"

There could only be one explanation for her denying the evil she had personally suffered. "I was programmed. I was brainwashed," she said.

York had programmed her and the others to believe that their real parents cared nothing for them, that he was the only one who loved them, that the only way they could survive was to remain dependent on him.

"It was emotionally confusing, first of all because he was telling me, 'You're stupid, you're never going to make it, the only people who make it is people who sleep their way to the top,'" she said.

"So, I was really confused in the head," Areebah said. "And that's when I realized that I don't belong here, because if I'm defending this man knowing he's doing those things, something must be wrong with me."

Along with the confusion came fear. Areebah had the same sorts of impulses and interests most girls her age. She liked music, she wanted to wear pretty clothes and makeup, and she wanted to read something other than York's often incomprehensible tracts.

But she had been programmed to believe that such desires were evil, so she must be evil. Besides, she was afraid to find out what was out there in the real world, because she had no clue how she would survive in that world.

"And it was like, you didn't know nothing about the outside world, because

The ruins of Tama-Re. Photo by *Anderson Scott*

you grew up in this environment all your life," she said. "So, I was really afraid. I didn't really know what to do, so I was trying to figure out how to leave."

There was a guard gate and a fence between Tama-Re and the outside world. To Areebah, though, the biggest barriers were the psychological ones York had erected.

York believed he was immune from harm from his disillusioned or expelled followers. He boasted that none of those who left or were expelled would ever be able to harm him. "He used to always say that we're stupid and dumb and weak, that we're never going to do anything," Areebah said.

The mind games worked—and why not?—they'd worked for more than thirty years. When Areebah or one of the other girls broke a rule, York would threaten to kick them out, as if leaving him was the absolute worst thing that could happen to them.

"He was like, 'Oh, I'm going to kick you out; I'm going to let you go outside in the world, and somebody is going to kill you,'" Areebah said.

York sometimes followed through on his expulsion threats, even to women who were the mothers of his children. Mostly, these women just took their children and faded away.

Areebah and the cult-raised young women like her simply did not have the life experiences that allowed them to brush off the fears that York embedded in their minds.

"I didn't know nothing about the outside world," she said. "I had never been out there. So I believed him, and I was afraid."

As strong as her fears were, her determination to get out grew stronger. At the start of 2001, she made a New Year's resolution to walk away from the only life she'd ever known.

Making a plan was one thing; carrying it out was another. Areebah's whole family was in the cult. Who would help her? She didn't have anyone she could even ask. "If you wanted to leave, nobody was going to help you. You're going to have to find your own way out," she said.

And even if she knew whom to call, she didn't know how to make the call. She could use the computers in the office, but no one had ever taught her how to use the telephones.

It was her younger sister, the one she'd tried to keep away from York, who helped her take the first steps. She told Areebah to talk to a woman who worked with their mother in York's office. That woman might give her the name of someone who might come get her.

Her fears about the getaway plan proved groundless. Areebah talked with the woman, who gave her the contact name and showed her how to make the phone call. She punched a few buttons, and her life was changed.

Areebah's mother had the same fears about life on the outside, so she tried to persuade her daughter not to go. "She was just trying to watch out for me," Areebah said.

Still, her mother only added to her confusion. Though the mother had strongly disapproved of what had happened to her two daughters, she somehow tolerated it and accepted it as part of the price for being among the chosen people, the ones who had reservations on the spaceship to salvation.

"I think as she got older, she started to settle," Areebah said of her mother. "It was like, she's forty now, she's been here about all her life. I don't think she wanted to come out here and start her life all over again. I think she's just settling, so she didn't know what to tell me, but she knew the things that was happening."

When the day came for her departure, her bags were searched, and her extra clothing and jewelry were confiscated. "We had to walk out of there with nothing," Areebah said.

Even after she left, it was hard for her to sever her ties to York completely. She sent him an e-mail, asking how he was doing. "It's hard to break away from somebody you've known all your life, no matter what good or bad they do," she said.

It took about six months for her anger to break out.

"I wasn't mad until like in the middle of June, and I was at work and something in my head just clicked. I just started crying at work," Areebah said. She couldn't tell anyone else in the office what she was crying about, but she did pour her anger into a long, accusatory e-mail to York. She wanted him to know how furious she was with him.

"And he sent me something back like, 'God bless,'" she said. "I was like, 'Huh?'"

There were no witnesses to this exodus. During the time when York's victims started slipping away from Tama-Re, the publicly visible portion of the Nuwaubian saga was a series of publicity stunts, staged expressions of support for York by celebrity activists, and failed efforts by York to establish a new power base outside of Putnam County. All the while, York's front men continued the barrage of accusations that York and the Nuwaubians were the victims of a racist redneck Southern sheriff.

For his part, Sills was having his own troubles. For one thing, he had to try to convince federal officials that York was a dangerous criminal. The feds didn't seem to want to move against York, even though they were quite aware that the FBI had linked York to a number of serious crimes committed during York's Brooklyn years.

One federal law enforcement official who shared Sills' frustrations was Tom Diehl, a now-retired FBI agent who was then stationed in Macon.

"People don't have any idea what we had to put up with," Diehl said in a 2006 interview. Diehl was informed of the 1993 FBI report, and in conjunction with other federal agencies, he opened investigations of York, in the areas of firearms violations and illegal copying and distribution of tapes and videos and possible connections to Middle East terrorist groups.

He was more troubled by reports he was receiving about what was really going on at Tama-Re. He talked to a distraught mother in Maryland, who told him her daughter had left college and her family to join the cult. He learned that an inordinate number of women from the cult were having babies or abortions in nearby Milledgeville. There were other reports that children were being moved around to avoid interference from local authorities and that the people at Tama-Re were living in fear, he said.

The cases developed, but only to a point. Diehl said he was able to get two search warrants for York's property, but the searches failed to uncover illegal caches of weapons. There were significant logistical barriers to making a case against York; the group was practically impossible to penetrate with informants, and its isolated location on a large tract of private land made it difficult to set up surveillance, he said.

But the largest obstacle to investigating York, Diehl said, was the reluctance of Department of Justice officials in Washington, D.C., to sanction the aggressive investigation of York that Diehl thought was needed. "I couldn't get any support," he said.

In an effort to build up some support for cracking down on York, Diehl brought along a group of eight FBI profilers for one of the searches of York's property. Seeing Tama-Re made believers out of the specialists, he said. "They saw people who were like zombies," he said.

Even so, Washington was uninterested, to say the least. Mostly, Diehl said, there was an overriding fear of pushing a situation that could lead to another Waco.

Diehl remained convinced that York was a criminal who was simply trying to use race as a smokescreen for his plans to make Tama-Re the base for expansion of his criminal empire.

"When he came to Georgia, he was bent on changing his image," said Diehl, who retired from the FBI shortly before the ultimately successful investigation of York took shape. "But his plan was to own and control Putnam County. The thing that stalled him was Howard Sills."

York's image-polishing campaign shifted into high gear just a few months

The Reverend Jesse Jackson, second from left, and Macon Mayor Jack Ellis (who recently converted to Islam and changed his name to Hakim Mansour Ellis) fourth from right, at a 2001 event at Tama-Re.

after the protesters cleared the courthouse green. Rev. Al Sharpton, the New York activist who would later make an unsuccessful run for the presidency in 2004, came to Tama-Re in the fall of 1999. He denounced what he called the harassment of the Nuwaubians.

"First of all, there are plenty of groups that have property in Georgia that we ought to be examining, that are up on that property planning the harm of people based on race," Sharpton said. "This group is not planning anything, but trying to enhance their own people."

In April 2001 Rev. Jesse Jackson, a presidential candidate in 1988, came to Tama-Re, put on the same type of fez that the men of the community were wearing at the time, and extolled the virtues of the Egypt of the West. "The Nuwaubians are living the American Dream," Jackson proclaimed. That day, Jackson was accompanied by the Mayor of Macon, Jack Ellis, a black man who in 2007 converted to Islam and changed his name to Hakim Mansour Ellis. Later, the Nuwaubians circulated color brochures touting Jackson's appearance and claiming Ellis was a "fellow Nuwaubian."

Jackson's Rainbow-PUSH Coalition had already established itself as a prominent drum-beater for York's causes. In March 1999 Joe Beasley, the Southeastern regional director of Rainbow-PUSH, issued a press release headlined, "Racial Harassment And Abuse In Putnam County." In the release, Beasley stated, "We simply will not tolerate our people being harassed and having their citizenship rights violated."

Tyrone Brooks, the Georgia state legislator who had lobbied the governor on York's behalf, was described in one of York's newsletters as "one of the most powerful Nuwaubians in state politics." Brooks was quoted in the newsletter as stating, "It's time for the backward, racist officials to go. The Holy Land is beautiful, peaceful, and worth fighting for."

Some of the mainstream media printed or televised some of these statements. Some press outlets also seemed to be picking up the beat of the pro-York drums.

Charles Richardson, then an assistant to the editor of *The Macon Telegraph*, wrote in an op-ed column in February 1999, "In my humble opinion, the Nuwaubians have more to fear from the sheriff than the sheriff has to fear from them."

Two days after the showdown in Eatonton, the *Telegraph* published an editorial headlined "Fortress Putnam Survives York Visit." The editorial mocked the police preparations for a possibly violent confrontation, stating, "A tourist happening through Eatonton Tuesday might have concluded that he had stumbled across the site of a law enforcement convention. Only differences in geography and a few other minor details prevent comparison to the NATO peacekeeping presence in Kosovo." The editorial writer did not explain how a tourist might have stumbled into the inside of the armory, where the overwhelming majority of the police in town that day were being held in reserve.

My paper, the *Atlanta Journal-Constitution,* was at times aggressive and at times, I judged, passive in its pursuit of the Nuwaubian story. The *AJC* was certainly the first paper to report on the allegations of criminal conduct in York's past, and up until the indictment of York, it was the only large newspaper through those years to treat the Nuwaubian story as something more serious than a rural Georgia sideshow. Yet, I became frustrated with the paper's "go-slow" attitude.

The worst instance of journalistic reticence involved a story I wrote about two women who'd had the courage to make public accusations against York. They were Alima and Samarra, the first of York's concubines to come out of the harem in a public manner. Alima had come to York's Ansaru Allah Community as a seventeen-year-old runaway, borne York three children, and had been kicked out, pregnant and penniless. Samarra was one of the Backstreet Girls in Brooklyn who had come to Georgia with York; she had borne him a child at age eighteen.

The two women filed paternity claims against York, in an effort to have him support his children.

This author interviewed both women, and after some hesitation on their parts, they agreed to go on the record with their stories. They spoke of how York routinely debased them and the other women of the cult, how York used his male followers as unchained slave laborers, how most cult members lived in squalor while York lived in splendor, how York had fathered more than one hundred—and possibly more than two hundred—children and supported virtually none of them.

In agreeing to allow their names to be used, the women had to overcome some real fears. They had each been threatened against filing the paternity claims and against speaking out against York.

Unfortunately, the newspaper was not as courageous as its sources.

The story was written as the two women's account of life inside the cult. It bounced between the newsroom and the newspaper's lawyers for about two weeks after it was written. During that time, I, as the reporter writing the story, attempted to obtain a comment from York or his representatives in response to the allegations in the story.

As part of that effort, I went to his house in Athens, but I was unable to make it to the front door. As I approached the house, two security guards emerged and confronted me. I told them why I was there, but they demanded that I get off the property. They would not say whether York was at home or even concede that this was his house. I retreated to the street, and the security guards followed me. One of them jammed a video camera up to my face and called me a "racist."

Next, I placed more than a dozen calls to York's attorney in Atlanta. Finally, the lawyer's assistant told me that if I faxed her a letter outlining the content of the article, she would attempt to get someone to comment. I sent a letter summarizing the allegations made by the two women.

I never got a response to the letter, but the publisher and editors of my paper got an angry letter from Kathy Johnson, York's main concubine. She accused me of harassing York, intimidating Nuwaubian children and trespassing. She demanded that the newspaper take action against me.

I was not reprimanded, but my story was gutted. I was ordered to re-write the exposé into a tepid situation report. The primary focus of the re-written story was the apparent truce between the Nuwaubians and Putnam County officials. In it, I quoted the county's new building inspector saying he'd had no interference from the Nuwaubians during some recent inspections on their property. However, he also noted that the Nuwaubians had consistently ignored his admonitions to correct code violations.

The two paternity claims were briefly mentioned and the women were named, but virtually all their statements about mistreatment of people inside the cult were edited out of the article.

Both women said that all they got out of going public was more threats. One of them said she received a phone call from a man she recognized as a Nuwaubian; the caller simply said, "Bang, bang." They both decided not to press their paternity claims.

After that, no one else spoke out publicly against Dwight York, until well after the criminal investigation exploded his perversions into public view, almost a year later.

The kid-glove treatment afforded York by the two largest newspapers in Georgia was only the continuation of a well-established pattern. After York pulled out of Bushwick, *The New York Times* ran an article about the area, quoting some residents who wondered where the Muslims had gone and how they missed the calm, safe days when York ran things.

All this need not be viewed as evidence of the "liberal bias" that right-wing commentators are so quick to pounce upon. York's being granted the moral high ground by the media was partly due to laziness and sloppiness, partly to a reluctance to rock a boat with a black religious leader at the helm, and partly to the media's shortsighted determination to cling to time-worn racial stereotypes.

In New York, for instance, there had certainly been incidents between police and Muslims where police conduct could legitimately be called into question. But the police response to such questioning was to offer what was in effect blanket immunity to many of the Muslim groups. York simply figured out how to take advantage of the free ride.

In the South, it was similarly easy for the media to assign automatic validity to the strident claims of a black group that they were victims of discrimination by a rural sheriff and his minions. There was certainly a long and sometimes shameful history of such behavior in such places. Few, however, asked the crucial question of whether the stereotype was valid in this case. Instead, when even the national newspapers sent reporters down to Putnam County – and even after the *Atlanta Journal-Constitution* had broken the news of the federal investigations into York's past criminal enterprises – the stories they filed were basically "puff pieces," written with a slightly smarmy tone and focused on the strangeness of it all.

The statements by the visiting activists condemning the local officials were accepted at face value and printed or broadcast without bothering to ask for even the tiniest shred of supporting evidence.

This sort of tendency in the media was termed a "knee-jerk readiness to see racism in law enforcement and the administration of criminal justice," by author William McGowan, in his book *Coloring The News*.

"The journalistic establishment never tires of celebrating the Civil Rights

Movement, yet its own reporting would make it seem as if the struggle's gains have been minimal," McGowan wrote. "The press would have us believe that racism lurks everywhere, ready to violate nonwhites at any opportunity, and to erode the tenuous progress that has been made over the last 50 years."

There was no need for racial hand-wringing by media pundits, during the time when Tama-Re almost went Hollywood. There was a real-live celebrity involved. He happened to be black, but he was also big box office.

In the spring of 2000, action-movie star Wesley Snipes entered into negotiations to become the Nuwaubians' next-door neighbor. Snipes had become famous for his roles as a federal marshal on the run, a cop in trouble trying to thwart a presidential assassination, an FBI agent on a hijacked airliner, and a half-human, half-vampire warrior.

Snipes made an offer on a three hundred-acre tract of land on Shadydale Road, part of which adjoined part of the Nuwaubians' property. Sources familiar with the proposal said Snipes's offer was far above market value. According to documents filed with the county, Snipes's planned to use the land as a training camp for security guards.

He had already formed a security company called Royal Guard of Amen-Ra. Continuing in the Egyptian mode, Snipes's film production company was called Amen-Ra Films. The security company had posted a help-wanted ad on internet sites, seeking two hundred "highly trained men and women" for security operations that included "international and domestic risk management, executive protection to dignitaries and celebrities, counter-surveillance and counter-terrorism measures." Snipes's half-brother Rudy, listed in corporate documents as the general co-manager of the firm, had applied for a firearms dealer's license for the company.

The deal was contingent upon the then-current owner of the land gaining the needed zoning variances or re-zoning from the county. The plan submitted called for building a lodge for the trainees and an arsenal for weapons storage. The plan was denied by both the county building and zoning commission and by the county commission. The Snipes affair quickly became another opportunity to trot out the allegations of racism.

The Nuwaubians embraced Snipes as one of their own. In an interview with *The Macon Telegraph*, a Nuwaubian spokesman claimed Snipes was "actually an avid Nuwaubian." The spokesman went on to claim that Snipes was among "a few Nuwaubian millionaires from the music industry, the movie industry, business, finance, different aspects," who were planning to invest big-time in Putnam County.

The Hollywood connection was trumpeted even louder on the Nuwaubians' website, where Snipes was termed "a proud Nubian/Nuwaubian." The posting also claimed that the people on Tama-Re eagerly anticipated having a commando camp next to their property. "All Nuwaubians will join his elite force for training. We will stop at nothing to drive the evil out of Putnam County," the posting proclaimed.

In one of York's newsletters of that period, the tone became even more shrill. In an article headlined "Racism Chases Millions Of Dollars Out Of Georgia," it was stated that Snipes was being joined by singer Stevie Wonder, singer/actress Erykah Baydu, dancer Debbie Allen, and other luminaries of the entertainment world in making large, jobs-generating investments into Middle Georgia. They were being deterred, however, by the prevailing racist attitudes in Putnam County, according to the article.

Once all this became public, Snipes couldn't back away fast enough. Apparently, he decided that allowing himself to be claimed as a real-life hero by the Nuwaubians was not a good career move. Through a spokesperson, Snipes denied having any affiliation with the Nuwaubians. The spokesperson claimed not to know who those people were, and she stated that Snipes's effort to buy property next to Tama-Re was a "pure coincidence."

There is no evidence to refute that claim. However, for those who don't put much stock into coincidences of that magnitude, it remains an open question why Snipes or his agents picked that particular piece of land.

The proposal was not taken lightly by Sills. To the sheriff, it would have created a migraine of nuclear proportions to have a military-style training camp next door to a group that he suspected would be willing and able to provide foot soldiers for an armed insurrection.

The owner of the property Snipes wanted hired an attorney to appeal the county's rejection of the zoning variances. But the litigation never went forward, the deal died, and the talk of celebrity investors abruptly ended.

Despite all the name-dropping and tub-thumping, this was also a frustrating time for York. He was not having much success in finding a new base of operations.

The Nuwaubians bought a building on Broad Street, the main thoroughfare of Athens, and began to renovate it. Their permits stated the building was to be used as a fraternal lodge. Later, the building permit was changed; the building was to become a bookstore. However, the requests for required inspections were never made, so the renovation was simply halted.

There was plenty of action at York's "mansion"; too much, in fact. York's neighbors complained that as many as fifty people seemed to be using or living in the house on the affluent cul-de-sac. A sheriff's deputy came to the house and told the Nuwaubians to curtail the business activity and the overcrowding. Things slacked off for a week or so, but then the arrivals of vanloads of children and adult workers from Tama-Re resumed, as did the mail-order businesses.

The flaunting of the warning did not go unnoticed by local officials. The combined city-county government opened an investigation of York for running a business in a residentially-zoned neighborhood. One morning, the assistant city attorney handling the case went outside her house and found a collection of dead animal parts on her doorstep.

Concurrent with his struggles in Athens, York attempted to get something going in Macon. He declared himself the "imperial grand potentate" of his own Masonic lodge, which was supposed to be part of his own Masonic order, which he called the International Supreme Council of Shriners, Inc. His lodge was later disavowed by existing black Masonic organizations.

Undeterred, York named the Macon chapter of his version of freemasonry the "Al Mahdi Shrine Temple No. 19," hanging on to the numerical designation of his "lodge" at Tama-Re, Lodge 19 of the Ancient Mystical Order of Melchizedek.

York's Masonic lodge joined with some established charitable groups in Macon for a canned food drive. He also staged a field day for local disabled children, and then made a $20,000 donation to the Make-A-Wish Foundation, claiming to have raised the money at his "Olympics."

In his new role as a Macon philanthropist, York put out a press release stating that he would deliberately exclude Putnam County from his largesse. His charity came tinged with bitterness, as he couldn't resist taking a swipe at his old nemeses.

"We will raise thousands of dollars from all over the world for the benefit of physically disabled children," the release stated. "It's a loss for the residents of Putnam County, Sheriff Sills and Francis Ford, with their seemingly racist actions to interfere with the county receiving thousands of dollars. In actuality, the county is dying."

That self-promoting spate of generosity and venom was essentially the beginning and end of York's good works in Macon.

Acting as the head of his Masonic group, York attempted to buy an abandoned Shrine Temple in downtown Macon. A purchase price of $800,000 was agreed upon, and York put up a total of $75,000 in earnest money. However, York was unable to leverage the rest of the money. The deal fell through and York lost his deposit. In response, York dispatched a group of his followers to picket the bank that had turned down his loan application.

York also attempted to open a new church in downtown Macon. He started preliminary negotiations to buy a church building from a Protestant congregation that had moved to a new facility in the suburbs. He even paid for some billboards around town, inviting local people to come worship at the new church, which he called the Holy Seed Baptist Synagogue, Inc.

A brochure for the wildly ecumenical church was printed, advertising services that were to include bar mitzvahs, baptisms, holy communion, etiquette and poise classes for young women, and classes in freemasonry.

However, the billboards went up and the flyers went out before the sale was anywhere near complete. Officials of the church that owned the building said they had cut off the negotiations even before the billboards went up, sending another York deal down in flames.

These forays may have attracted some new followers for York, but they never took root. At the same time, things weren't going so well at Tama-Re. Attendance at the Savior's Day festival for 2000 was measured in the hundreds, not the thousands. By the end of 2001, York had placed the Athens mansion up for sale, and he started spending most of his time back in Putnam County.

All through this period, Sills was having trouble finding much traction for his efforts to obtain federal support

"I never had any trouble with the federal agents," Sills said. "I always had trouble with the federal bureaucracy."

In the fall of 1998, Sills got a phone call that seemed to portend an aggressive federal presence in the Nuwaubian case. It was from an Assistant United States Attorney in Atlanta, who told him that she had a major counterfeiting conspiracy case that appeared to have a strong connection to Putnam County.

More than twenty-eight defendants had been indicted and arrested for stealing or counterfeiting corporate checks in one state and then cashing them in another. Six of the defendants had listed their home address as 404 Shadydale Road, which was Tama-Re. Sills was able to confirm that the six men were known to him as Nuwaubians.

The indictment included a RICO (racketeering) count, which enabled the prosecutor to seize any goods or property that had been part of the criminal enterprise. The prosecutor told Sills that she intended to move to seize Tama-Re.

Weeks passed, but nothing happened. Sills attempted to find out why, but his calls to the prosecutor were not returned. Then, a friendly FBI agent told him that a ruling had come down from on high – the seizure was not to be pursued. The agent also told Sills that he would not be winning any friends at the top of the food chain if he pursued the issue.

The defendants in the case copped deals and entered guilty pleas. The prosecutor racked up her conviction numbers but never looked further into the

Nuwaubian connection to the group of defendants in her case, which was quickly and permanently closed.

Racial and religious politics were the root cause of the federal temerity in these matters, Sills believed.

The last time federal authorities cracked down on a religious cult, the fiery tragedy of Waco and the Branch Davidians resulted. The last thing anyone in the U.S. Department of Justice wanted was another Waco. The fact that the Nuwaubians were a black-led organization with an almost entirely black membership, and that they were making strident protestations that they were the victims of racial persecution by a white sheriff in the rural South, could only have added to the inertia of the top officials of the Democratic administration in power at the time, he believed.

In late 1999, the Nuwaubians were able to take their complaints against Sills to Beverly Martin, then the United States Attorney in Macon. She responded by ordering an FBI investigation of Sills. Later, Sills viewed the case file on that investigation, which found nothing to support the Nuwaubians' allegations. The file included a letter from Martin, who noted that while the Nuwaubians had made convincing arguments against the sheriff, the charges were groundless; she apologized to the FBI for wasting their time.

What helped end the period of frustration and public-relations diversions was the return of a former prince of the cult, York's son Malik. His road from Brooklyn to Georgia was much longer and more winding than his father's.

After breaking away from Ansaru Allah Community in 1990, Malik first moved in with his sister, Afifah, who was then in the marriage arranged by their father. However, Malik brought the father's wrath with him.

Malik said Afifah was then receiving rental income from a Philadelphia apartment complex that York had put in her name. After York learned that Malik was with his sister, he sent crews to gut the Philadelphia apartment building and evict the tenants, thus depriving Afifah of her income, Malik said.

"I knew I had to leave," Malik said.

Then came a time when Malik drifted between the straight world and the underworld. He had already enrolled in Columbia University and his tuition had been paid, but he had no money and no place to live. Each day was an improvisation.

"Sometimes, you got to do the A-train," he said, meaning that there were nights he slept on the subway.

One night, Malik recalled that he was walking aimlessly in the Times Square area. He must have looked like he needed shelter, because he was approached by a nun who worked at Covenant House, which was then a home for runaways. She invited him to the shelter, which was not far from where he was loitering.

"We have a fresh bed for you," she told him, and he went in with her. For Malik, a lifelong Muslim, living at the shelter operated by Catholic clergy was a cultural stretch. As it turned out, though, it wasn't too difficult for him to talk to the religious people. At first, they didn't believe his story; they didn't get many Columbia students at Covenant House. One of the nuns confirmed that he was an officially registered student.

Malik never graduated from Columbia, but he did find his calling there. He organized some parties, as a way for the study-weary students to unwind. He brought emerging hip-hop performers in for the parties, and the successes led to his becoming a music promoter.

As a budding entrepreneur, he looked for venture capital wherever he could find it, sometimes in not-so-legal directions. He had friends who were burglars, and on occasion he joined them. What turned him away from crime was the realization that if he continued, he'd probably wind up in jail or dead.

He dropped out of college and focused on the party promotions, amassing enough money for an apartment of his own. He still needed to supplement his income with jobs like selling clothes, running an X-rated bookstore, and as a junior marketing executive for a soft-drink corporation. He said he was doing well at that last job, until his employers discovered that he had submitted a resume with some false entries, and he was dismissed.

During this time, he visited his mother regularly. He met and made friends with one of her neighbors, who was then a budding rap singer named Biggie Smalls.

By 1994, he had gone full-time into the music scene. But one of the parties he was promoting collapsed, and he became the target of lawsuits filed by vendors and artists he had been unable to pay. "I made some big money, but then I lost every dime," Malik said.

He tried moving to Philadelphia and starting over. A few months later, he got a call from his old friend Biggie Smalls, who was then red hot. "It's time," Smalls told him, and Malik went back to New York, to ride the crest of the hip hop wave.

He became one of the early managers of the rap star known as L'il Kim and was involved with producing her big hit "Junior Mafia."

"I was hanging out with the Masters of the Universe," Malik said.

During those years, Malik told few people that he was the son of a man who demanded to be treated as a god. Rather, he tried to sever all connections with his past and with the people he'd grown up with. If he happened to see someone he recognized from Ansaru Allah, he would cross the street to avoid making contact. He invented a background story to tell his friends, and it did not include growing up in a cult.

Then, around 1998, bits of his old life started to surface, like debris from an old shipwreck. He learned from his sister that their father had moved with his followers to a farm in Georgia, where York had started running a new, Egyptian-themed scam.

One night, Malik was in a nightclub, and he was approached by a man who identified himself as a federal agent. The agent asked him, "What's going on with your father?" Malik didn't know, but he figured it was time for him to find out.

So, Malik went to Tama-Re. His first impression was how wasteful and cheap-looking it all seemed. It reminded him of the way his father had squandered millions building his private palace at Camp Jazzir in upstate New York.

Malik confronted his father with what he'd learned from Afifah and other former cult members. He wanted to know if York had made concubines of the girls Malik had grown up with in Ansaru Allah. He also asked about the pictures he saw around his father's chambers, the ones showing York with groups of young children. Some of those children were ones Malik recognized from the time when they were toddlers and infants in the Brooklyn community.

Rather than try to deny it, the father seemed to almost boast of his depravity to the son.

"I'm the Prince of Darkness," York said to Malik. He admitted that his fondness for the children had become a sickness, but he claimed that he was gaining control of his pedophilic tendencies.

Malik said he didn't believe a word of it. He questioned his father about all the changes in the community. What happened to all the Muslim beliefs and practices, the daily prayers? And what was with all this new Egyptian stuff?

York told him that all the stuff, new and old, was just props for the scam.

"I don't believe in any of this shit," York told his son. "If I had to dress up like a nun, if I had to be a Jew, I'd do it for this kind of money."

And, speaking of money, York said, would Malik be interested in making an investment in the new enterprises?

At this point, Malik said, it was clear to him that his father wasn't interested in listening to anything he might have to say. That assessment was confirmed when he prepared to leave, and his father handed him a copy of *The Holy Tablets.*

"This will put you up to speed with where we're at," York told him.

Malik left convinced that his father was totally out of control. He was also determined to do something for the children of the cult. A little more than a year later, he moved to Atlanta and attempted to keep his music ventures going while commuting back to New York. The move cost him professionally, he said, but he was more concerned that the child-cherishing community he'd grown up in had become a community where children were being sexually exploited.

He put out the word that he would take in refugees from the cult at a house he rented in the Atlanta suburbs. His sister, Afifah, moved down to open a beauty salon and to help him de-program the former Nuwaubians who came to Malik's house.

The number of departing cult members who passed through Malik's halfway house reached as high as thirteen at one time. Malik and Afifah helped them acquire or re-gain basic survival skills, such as getting a driver's license, filling out a job application, or creating a resume.' The lack of an accredited education was a problem for many of them, but some of the women who'd worked in York's office had marketable computer skills.

On Memorial Day weekend of 2001, Malik drove with a group of the former Nuwaubian women for a weekend in Miami. The shared holiday brought back a touch of the closeness they'd had growing up as children in the isolated community of Ansaru Allah. On the way back, they started reminiscing; Malik told them of the hard times he endured after leaving the group.

Some of the young women started crying. They'd been told a different version of Malik's story, that he'd deserted them, that he despised them. Then the women started pouring out the ugly details of what had happened to them since they left.

A short time later, Sills took a phone call from someone who said he needed to speak directly with the sheriff. "I know the whole deal on York. I'm ready to tell everything," said the caller, identifying himself as a son of Dwight York.

At that point, Sills had never met Malik, the prodigal son. Nevertheless, the caller certainly had his attention. Arrangements were made to meet the next day at the FBI offices in Atlanta.

When Malik showed up for the meeting, he brought with him a major breakthrough in the case, in the person of one of York's most favored concubines, the young woman called Basheera.

Basheera's story was that she had been born into the cult in Brooklyn, and at the age of thirteen, she was ushered into York's chambers for her first sexual experience.

The older woman who was training her to be York's concubine was performing oral sex on York, when York snapped at Basheera to come and do what the other woman was doing. "Am I just a guinea pig here!" York said to her. "You're just sitting there, you know. Take your shirt off. Don't be scared. I'm not going to bite you."

Basheera would go on to become one of York's Backstreet Girls in

Bushwick. She later achieved high status among the concubines, rising to the unofficial rank of "wife No. 2." She bore two children by York.

She made the move to the camp in upstate New York, where she worked in York's offices and was trusted with handling the money. The main reason York left Sullivan County was money, she said. Building inspectors came to the large home he'd built, and then the valuation of his property was reassessed, leaving York with a tax bill of about $200,000, she said. "He said the white man was coming after him again," she said. "He said he wanted to get away from everybody."

After putting her on the list of the first people to go down to Georgia with him, York told Basheera to fetch some things from his quarters, in particular, two suitcases filled with cash and a box of pornography tapes. Basheera recognized them as the ones he would show to the girls. She was pregnant with her second child by York when the move was made.

In Georgia, Basheera was given greater responsibility in handling York's finances. She also started doing what the older women had done to her in Brooklyn, that is, grooming the children for having sex with York. As York's child trainer and procurer, she knew whom he was having sex with. She witnessed many of these encounters. She testified that, at York's instructions, she videotaped at least two such encounters, one of which was of a five-year-old girl performing oral sex on York. Those tapes were destroyed, she said.

By the time she reached her mid-twenties, she started becoming disillusioned with life as a concubine. She hadn't had a chance to go to college, but it wouldn't be that many years before her own children were college age.

"I was just fed up," she said. "I wanted a new life," she said. About this time, she went back to Brooklyn at a time when York's Sudanese wife was visiting some long-time members of the community. Basheera asked her about Sudanese sexual initiation practices, the ones she'd been told about when York started having sex with her, the ones she told the younger girls about when their time came.

She had asked the question, because to her, the Sudanese children looked somehow different, healthier, more innocent than the children at Tama-Re. The Sudanese wife was mildly shocked at her question and told her "No, that was like totally sinful, that children were never touched," Basheera said.

When she got back to Tama-Re, she started having vicious arguments with York, almost every day. When she threatened to leave, York would threaten her life. "He told me he was going to kill me or he was going to stab me in my knees so that I would never walk again," she said.

She left anyway. Officially, she had been expelled. Her mother had gotten tired of the Nuwaubian life and left earlier. Her father was expelled because of her transgressions. She went back to New York for awhile, and then she heard that Malik was in Atlanta helping former cult members. No one had to coax or persuade her to go to the authorities. She wanted to tell her story.

The story she told, the names she named, the details of the operation that she provided proved to be a major turning point in the case. No more zoning disputes. From this point forward, Sills said, the investigation was focused on child molestation.

"That's when the floodgates opened," Sills said.

Trespassers are warned to enter at their own risk.

Photo by W.A. Bridges, *Atlanta Journal-Constitution*

CHAPTER 9
Tribulations And A Trial (2000 - 2004)

"The acts with which they are charged are reprehensible acts. They are acts which have apparently been going on for a long period of time and which, in the view of this court, are likely to continue if defendant York is released from custody." – U.S. Magistrate Judge Claude Hicks.

The teenaged boy took a late-night stroll down his family's long driveway that ran through the woods and up to Shadydale Road. Something sprang from the darkness and knocked him to the ground. Before he could call out or fight back, the boy was gagged and cuffed.

The attacker was a man dressed in camouflage and with his face painted in the colors of the night. He was also one of Sheriff Howard Sills's "three marines," the deputies who were performing most of the around-the-clock surveillance on Dwight York. They watched from a spot in the woods on the bank of an abandoned railroad bed, close enough to the entrance to Tama-Re across the road that they could hear the gate guard cough.

In the spring of 2002, it was imperative to federal and county investigators that York not know how close he was to being arrested. Some of the witnesses who'd already come forward said York had threatened their lives, if they

Children's toys left behind after Nuwaubians were evicted from Tame-Re. Photo by Anderson Scott

went to the police. They had defied him, and if York found out, they'd be in serious danger.

At that time, there were at least fifty children living on Tama-Re, some of whom had been identified as molestation victims by the first group of witnesses. The police were concerned that York, if warned, would intimidate those children, or maybe just have them moved away.

All of which may have explained why the boy was lying trussed up on his own driveway. The deputies had him under control, but they also had a dilemma. What were they going to do with him now?

Sills had instructed his "three marines" to detain anyone who discovered the surveillance operation. No one, not even the deputies' wives, could know about their clandestine assignment. Now, though, the security had been accidentally breeched, simply because the driveway cut through the railroad bed, and the boy happened to pass by while the deputies were changing shifts at their observation post.

As soon as he received the radio call that one of York's neighbors had been taken into custody, Sills headed for Shadydale Road. He drove onto an adjacent property and walked through the woods about a quarter mile to the observation post, where the tricky situation awaited him.

The boy had done nothing wrong. Sills might have the legal authority to take him into some sort of protective custody, to preserve the secrecy of the operation; but that could easily backfire.

The boy's parents would likely protest, and rightfully so. The circumstances called for some country-style diplomacy.

Sills ordered the deputy to remove the restraints and gag from the boy. In return, the boy agreed to remain silent while they all walked back to his parents' house. Sills knew the family, and he knew they'd had a history of run-ins with the law. The boy's mother was Sills's age, and he'd known her most of his life. He decided to risk telling her the truth, then beg for her cooperation and silence.

"People are going to die if you say anything," he told the mother.

Then, he sweetened the pot, promising that their cooperation would not be forgotten. "You're gonna need me," he told the mother, counting on the tendency of the outlaw streak in the family's history to repeat itself.

The mother knew a good deal when she saw it. She accepted Sills's apology and gave her word that neither she nor her son would break the operational silence. They kept their promise, and so did the sheriff. Some of the family's later minor offenses were forgiven, and York remained ignorant of the fact that he was being closely watched.

York certainly did not behave like a man who thought the law might be closing in on him. In late 2001, he booked a banquet room at a fancy Manhattan hotel and invited a group of his children to a dinner party.

His daughter, Afifah, was one of those who attended. She had a faint hope that York might want to make things right with his children, most of whom he hadn't communicated with for years. She should have known better.

Instead of a family reunion, the party turned out to be a forum for York to spout his cynical outlook – and to ask his children for money. He was experiencing some cash flow problems. He had put his home in Athens up for sale and was spending more time on Tama-Re these days. What he didn't say was, according to some police informants, he was also planning to make one more big score on the upcoming Savior's Day, and then find someplace else to move to and start all over again. It was going to take some cash.

"Whoever has the most money will be in control," York told the gathering.

After the dinner, York worked the room, spending time with his male progeny. Then he came to Afifah, and offered her different advice from what he'd given his sons.

"You'll have to sleep your way to the top," York told her.

Afifah then confronted her father, telling him that he'd betrayed his children, just as he'd betrayed his followers.

"Those people are idiots," York said of the people who believed in him. "It's not my fault, it's their fault. They're dumb."

When Afifah asked him what had happened to the observances of the strict Islamic laws of the community she'd been raised in, York told her that he'd shifted to new costumes and a whole new religion.

"It's all about the packaging," York said.

In order that the investigation remain a surprise package to York, it had to progress slowly. The police did not simply start working to contact the list of possible victims given to them by Basheera in the summer of 2001. There was a serious concern that if word got back to York, he would flee. He had been arrested in the 1980s on charges of trying to leave the country on a false passport.

More importantly, police believed that secrecy offered the best protection for the witnesses. As long as York remained ignorant of the scope of the investigation and of who was cooperating, the witnesses would not be subjected to the kinds of threats and intimidation they had received from York, when they lived at Tama-Re.

So, Sills and the FBI agents told Basheera to spread the word quietly among the victim witnesses who'd already left York's land. They gave her the contact numbers for the agents working the case. "We knew if they came to us, they wouldn't be in as much danger," Sills said.

The investigation was now officially a joint effort among Putnam County and several federal agencies, primarily the FBI. "There were no more games," Sills said. He and Maxwell Wood, the recently-installed U.S. Attorney for the Middle District of Georgia, agreed, "We're both on this train; one car was carrying the state charges, and one car the federal," Sills said.

Where there had been mainly reluctance on the part of federal authorities, now there was cooperation. There was a different political party in power at that time; more importantly, though, there was a growing body of solid evidence of major crimes. York's racial politics card was being trumped by the statements of the children of his cult.

The witnesses started coming to the investigators. Practically every victim who was interviewed gave police more names. Now that they knew someone would listen, the children and their parents wanted to tell their stories. In situations where they thought it wouldn't compromise the secrecy of the investigation, agents approached people who'd left the cult and found more witnesses. Sills said the way the witnesses came forward, and their willingness to testify, separately and from the far corners of the country, was further confirmation of their veracity. FBI agents interviewed witnesses in New York, Georgia, Washington, D.C., California, Florida, Tennessee, and Hawaii.

Two female FBI agents – Joan Cronier, based in Atlanta, and Jalaine Ward, based in Macon, handled most of the victim interviews, particularly of the female witnesses.

In a 2006 interview, Cronier said Basheera, the first major witness, gave a matter-of-fact recounting of the shocking events she'd seen and, in some instances, participated in. "She didn't realize that was wrong," Cronier said. "That was her life."

Basheera's story was soon supported, when agents interviewed Badra, another former concubine of York's, who had actually called the FBI in Washington, D.C., several days before Basheera came to the FBI offices in Atlanta, Cronier said.

Even though the witnesses were now willing to cooperate, telling their stories wasn't easy for them, Cronier said. "The victims were still conflicted," she said. "They were free, but they were struggling with their feelings. Some of them were women who had had his (York's) children."

Despite such conflicts, the witnesses never broke the secrecy of the investigation, she said. "It was amazing that we didn't bump into someone who went straight back to him," Cronier said.

The momentum of the case accelerated as the body of solid evidence grew, in contrast to the frustrations experienced during the earlier federal and local investigations of York, Ward said. Even so, she knew it was not growing as fast as she would have liked. All the investigators were aware that while the case was being built, more children were being molested. "We knew what was going on there. We knew it had to get done and get done soon," said Ward. She said she'd first heard reports of possible molestations by York at Tama-Re from a witness in one of the earlier, discontinued investigations; but that report was second or third-hand, not the type of direct evidence they were gathering now. And as strong as all the new evidence appeared to be, it all had to be reviewed, evaluated, and corroborated, Ward said. This time, there could be no errors of the kind that had turned Waco into such a tragedy.

Until this period, she said, the prevailing attitude was that York's cult was "just a peculiar religious organization in our backyard – and we don't need to stir it up."

With each succeeding interview, the strength of the case grew, she said. "The stories were consistent," she said, even though the witnesses came forward at different times and from widely different places.

Still, the details were hard to hear, even for an experienced investigator. "It broke my heart," Ward said.

The rapid development of the case against York was halted by the terrorist attacks of September 11, 2001. The FBI agents were reassigned for months, but when the York investigation was resumed, they came back with additional legal firepower.

Due to the immense scope of the case – literally thousands of incidents of child molestation had been alleged by this time – the federal component of the team was joined by the Department of Justice's Child Exploitation Unit, based in the nation's capital.

With more players came more time spent around an increasingly crowded conference table for strategic planning meetings. To Sills, the feds were spending too much time worrying about procedural matters; and there was the unspoken fear that the arrest of a black religious leader would generate a backlash among civil rights activists. Sills's frustration levels were rising again.

Even after a federal grand jury returned sealed indictments against York and Kathy Johnson in the early spring of 2002, investigators were not ready to spring the trap. There was general agreement that the arrests must be made rapidly and cleanly, and that meant assembling a massive force. Of course, that meant more tactical planning and more coordination of an increasingly large number of schedules.

At one planning meeting, there were about sixty or seventy people present. Fed up with the delays and the hand-wringing, Sills declared an end to the preliminaries. Savior's Day was fast approaching, and the danger of losing the operational secrecy was growing every day.

"Look, we've got two weeks," Sills announced to his federal partners. "There are kids out there being molested every day. Either you go in with me, or I'm going in on my own."

Sills's comment did not have an impact on the timing of the raid; the Feds held to their timetable. The next day, Sills received a phone call from the FBI agent in charge of the federal component of the operation. A date of May 8 was set for the arrest.

The plan was to hit Tama-Re with an overwhelming force. One of the top priorities was to arrest York when he was away from his property, thus eliminating the frightening prospect that his followers would form an armed resistance to protect him. Immediately after the arrest, hundreds of local and federal agents would swarm onto Tama-Re to execute a warrant allowing them to search for evidence.

On the federal end of the operation, the FBI furnished nine search teams, each consisting of about twenty agents, for the various buildings on Tama-Re, as well as another team for the search of York's house in Athens. All those teams had to meet regularly to plan the raid. Ward also requested a hostage negotiation team, in case of resistance that included the taking of hostages. That request was granted. Ward said she "wore out I-75" traveling between Macon and Atlanta during this planning phase.

On the local end of the operation, it was necessary for Sills to do much of the detail work. There simply wasn't much of a federal presence in Putnam County, and if a large number of federal agents started moving in, there was a good chance they would be spotted and York would be alerted.

So, Sills started going around town asking for favors. He had to make an unexplained request to take over a fire tower used by state foresters, in order to use it as a repeater station for the federal agents' communications requirements. Washington had to be kept informed at all times.

He also went to an official of the area's rural electric cooperative and told him, "I may need the electricity cut off on the west side of the county." That part of the county included agribusinesses that comprised the cooperative's largest customers, but the director agreed. Sills could only tell him that the mysterious outage request involved something that was very important, and that it would only last a short time.

A command post for the operation was set up in a little-used state agricultural complex in a rural part of the county, a few miles from Tama-Re. The manager was told he could not report this usage to his superiors, largely because Sills was concerned that if word of the operation got to the upper levels of the state bureaucracy, it might also reach York.

The retreat lodges at Rock Eagle, a large state preserve surrounding a prehistoric Native American burial site were to be used as a possible overnight facility to bring some of the children living at Tama-Re. At that point, Sills and investigators with the district attorney who would prosecute the state's case believed that the children then living at Tama-Re should be interviewed, to determine how many of them had been molested.

Motel rooms had to be found for the eighty or so members of an FBI SWAT team who would be taking part in the operation. The motel couldn't be too close to Eatonton, and a cover story had to be concocted for the simultaneous arrival of the large group made up mostly of men with short haircuts and carrying large duffel bags.

The task force would also need physicians to accompany the agents making the raid. Sills went to a sheriff of a nearby county who lined up four military-connected doctors.

The planning got down to the level of porta-potties. To arrange for this operational necessity, Sills went to a friend in the construction business. On the day of the raid, the builder showed up, driving a flatbed truck with a load of porta-potties.

"So many people did what I asked, no questions," Sills said. "And they kept their mouths shut."

The secrecy blanket covered most of Sills's own deputies. They knew a big operation was in the works, but they were not informed what it was. All leaves and vacations were cancelled. All deputies were ordered to take extra training sessions on the firing range.

Still, the secrecy held for what Sills believes was the largest covert operation in Georgia law enforcement history. "That was the most amazing thing, that the secret was kept as well as it was," Sills said.

But on the night before the strike, the cover that had held intact for months was very nearly blown.

At his command post, Sills received a call from the FBI agent commanding the operation.

"Howard, I just wanted to let you know, we got a call from CBS in Miami," the agent said. Someone at the television station was working on a story and wanted to know why an entire FBI SWAT team from Miami had just checked in to a motel in Conyers, Georgia. The agent had no idea how the television station had learned of the deployment or how much else they might know.

All Sills knew was if the operation made the news, York would almost certainly batten down the hatches at Tama-Re. All the effort that had gone into keeping the operation a secret would have been wasted. The planned surgical strike could turn into a siege. The worst-case scenario, Waco II, seemed to be a present danger.

Worse, there wasn't a thing Sills could do to stop it. If he called the television station and pleaded with them to hold the story, two things could happen – he might receive cooperation, or his call might convince the news editors at the station that they were onto a big story, possibly making it even more likely that they'd put it on the air.

The situation called for a stiff drink.

Sills told a deputy to go out and get him a bottle of Jim Beam. The somewhat startled deputy needed to have the directive repeated.

"You know what Jim Beam is, don't you?" Sills barked. His mission clarified, the deputy left and soon returned with the whiskey.

Sills planted the bottle between his legs on his chair, and took a few long pulls.

"I couldn't believe the whole thing was falling apart," he said.

Dawn broke, but news of the raid did not. There was nothing about the police mobilization on television or in the newspapers. The previous night's

Federal and local agents seal off entrance to Tama-Re, as hundreds of other agents search the grounds of Tama-Re on May 8, 2002, the day York was arrested. Photo by Ben Gray, *Atlanta Journal-Constitution*

queries had not developed into the published news story that everyone in the investigation dreaded. Hopefully, it would all be over by the end of the day, and then, the news media would be welcome to the story.

For logistical purposes, a target time of 1400 hours, or 2 p.m., was set for the raid. They could only hope that York would make a move out of Tama-Re before then. The surveillance had established that there was no real pattern to York's movements.

All day, a strike force of nearly one hundred federal agents plus about twice that number of Sills' deputies and deputies on loan from other counties waited on ready alert.

Finally, with only about a half hour left before the deadline time, a black Lincoln Navigator pulled out of Tama-Re. York usually rode in an SUV just like that one. The deputy at the surveillance post in the woods called the command center to report the vehicle movement.

Was it York?

The deputy couldn't be sure. There were at least two people in the Navigator, but the windows were tinted too darkly to make a positive identification.

While the Navigator was being tracked by a high-flying helicopter, a debate crackled back and forth over the police airwaves. Should they stop the car? If York wasn't inside, would whoever was inside somehow alert him?

Sills voted to stop the SUV. If it wasn't York, they could always apologize. If it was, the show would be on.

The Navigator was pulled over near the Putnam-Baldwin County line, about fifteen miles south of Eatonton, into a supermarket parking lot nearby. The FBI agents who stopped the SUV reported that they had a man and a woman in custody, but they weren't totally sure who they had. None of them knew York. Minutes later, FBI agents Ward and Cronier arrived at the arrest scene and confirmed that the two people taken into custody were Dwight York and Kathy Johnson.

The green light for the raid was issued. At the command post in Putnam County, most of the components of the raiding party formed up according to plan and waited to be joined by other agents who had been waiting at another staging area. That group included two APCs (armored personnel carriers).

However, that last group breezed right on by the command post and headed straight for Tama-Re on their own. Sills jumped into his SUV and raced after them. Fortunately, the APCs had a top speed of slightly more than thirty miles per hour, so Sills did not have to go too far to catch up with them and stop them.

Then, the raiding caravan formed up in the proper order. The APCs were in the lead, followed by a couple of SUVs fitted with ramming bars, then there were about a half dozen black SUVs loaded with FBI agents, then Sills and his deputies, then the deputies from the other counties.

All roads leading to Tama-Re were blocked, and the phone lines were cut.

As the raiding party's caravan came into view of Tama-Re, the people on the property scattered. If they'd had any plans to resist, there wouldn't be time to put them into effect.

The lead component of the raiding party crashed through the main gate. Sills was with another group that entered through a gate across a driveway a short distance from the main gate. The progress of the raid was monitored by FBI officials in a helicopter hovering overhead.

Within five minutes, Tama-Re was secure. No one resisted, no one was hurt, and no one was arrested.

The search process took several hours. During that time, the one hundred or so people who were at Tama-Re at the time, most of them women and children, were brought to a grassy area near the center of the compound.

Ward said some of the FBI agents told her that some of the adults were ordering the children not to accept any of the food or drink being offered them. She circulated among the hot, hungry children, saying, "Please take the food. There's nothing in it that can hurt you." After that, the children opened the food parcels and ate, she said.

The FBI agents found many of the items that the witnesses had reported seeing in York's quarters, including the sexually explicit Pink Panther doll, the pillows and blankets they had described, as well as the white robes that York had sometimes made them wear, when they were called to him.

They also confiscated eleven firearms found in York's house, and about twenty more found in the men's barn.

A suitcase of cash was found in York's chambers. Along with the cash he was carrying when he was arrested, the police confiscated a total of about $400,000.

As the daylight faded, the federal agents in charge told everyone to start wrapping things up. That upset some of the district attorney's personnel, who would be charged with prosecuting the state charges. They wanted more time to confiscate evidence. One investigator searching York's bedroom found a box of dildos and vibrators right where some of the witnesses said they would be. He also found the barber's chair that the witnesses had described.

More troubling was that there would be no time to interview more of the children on the compound. The district attorney's investigators had wanted to take the children to the lodge at Rock Eagle, where they could be questioned away from the others in the group; but that wasn't going to happen.

However, the lead FBI agents had received a call from one of the witnesses, who told them that groups of Nuwaubian men were trying to plan a counterattack. It was time to call it a day.

As the evening faded into twilight, Sills came over to the small group of media representatives who had gathered outside the gate. He reported the arrest of Dwight York and Kathy Johnson on four counts of transporting minors across state lines for the purposes of illegal sex. That was the first time the public was informed that the government believed York was a child molester.

It was also the end of what Wood called a "flawless" raid. Most of the federal agents were able to head home before dark. Sills credited the FBI for leading such a massive raid that came off without violence or injury. In retrospect, Sills said the contingent of local officers probably could not have conducted such a successful operation, had they gone in without the federal forces, as he had said he might.

Five children living on Tama-Re were taken into state custody during the raid, because they had been named as possible victims by earlier witnesses. Four of those children were later found to have evidence of sexually-transmitted diseases.

About a week after the arrest, York appeared in federal court in Macon for a bond hearing. This time, he wore no costumes, no jewelry, just an inmate's jumpsuit and shackles. He wasn't being praised or prayed to. Rather, for the first time in thirty-five years, York was being publicly accused of being a criminal.

He was clearly uncomfortable. He remained subdued and silent for the most part, though he did manage a few smiles for his black-clad followers who packed the spectator benches.

Since the arrests were made on the federal charges, the bond hearing was a federal process. The specific charges involved the trips York had made with the children to hotels near Disney World. To make his argument that bail should be granted to him, York hired one of Atlanta's best-known defense attorneys, Ed Garland.

Throughout the hearing, whenever Garland referred to his client, he used the honorific title "Reverend," apparently granting York clerical status strictly on the basis of York's bogus claims. To the government, however, the defendant was plain old Dwight York.

As is typical in such hearings, the government presented one of its investigators as its primary witness. In this case, FBI agent Jalaine Ward was called to testify in support of the government's contention that York should not be granted bail.

In her testimony, Ward depicted York as a rapacious sexual predator and the sole ruler of the Nuwaubian cult. "York makes all the rules," she said. "His followers refer to him as their god."

She stated that the government's case so far consisted of statements from eighteen cooperative witnesses, who had named a total of about thirty-five underage victims of molestation by York. York began abusing one of the victims when she was four years old, Ward stated.

Ward gave a terse condensation of the victims' description of life within the cult. Families who joined were separated, once they were selected to live on York's land. The young children were groomed for sex with York by teenagers and young women who had been similarly groomed, mostly as they entered adolescence. She stated the victims were mostly girls, though a few were boys. Sometimes, adult concubines participated in the sex acts with York and the children, and sometimes they made videos of the crimes for York's viewing pleasure.

Ward told the court how the children would try to avoid York, by feigning illness or hiding. She also laid the foundation for the federal charges, testifying about how York "rewarded" the children with the Disney trips and then molested them in the fancy hotels where they stayed.

For the first time, some of the financial details of York's empire were revealed publicly. Around the time of the arrest, a network of from ten to twelve of York's bookstores was in operation in various cities, Ward stated. The operators of the bookstores brought about $14,000 to York every two weeks, she said. At the classes conducted at the bookstores and at Tama-Re, another four thousand was collected weekly, she stated.

The largest of the annual Savior's Day festivals, the one in 1998, brought in about $500,000 to York, Ward testified. In the next two years, the estimated proceeds dropped roughly in half.

Prosecutors argued that York's huge stashes of cash, plus his prior conviction on charges of passport fraud, made him a high risk for flight.

During his cross-examination of Ward, Garland gave a sort of preview of York's defense strategy. He questioned her about other cases, where there had been allegations that child witnesses had been coached into making their allegations. Garland's questions also implied that he believed York had been framed by angry ex-members of the cult or by investigators with an agenda.

"All the interviews were conducted in a very professional manner," Ward stated. Most of the underage victims were interviewed with a parent present, and the investigators did not use any pictures, dolls, or other props to help the witnesses express what had happened to them, she said.

"The children were old enough to know their body parts and intelligent enough to tell their stories," Ward stated.

Then, Garland called a series of character witnesses for York.

Brooks, the state legislator from Atlanta, testified that he believed York had a "good reputation." He stated that he knew York to be a successful businessman with "high entrepreneurship." Brooks testified he believed York was "developing a viable, stable community" through the Nuwaubian movement.

Brooks claimed he served as a mediator in the dispute between York's cult and Putnam County officials, after having been summoned by Joe Beasley, the regional director of Jesse Jackson's Rainbow/PUSH Coalition.

He stopped short, however, of making the kind of claims he had made publicly before, when he'd claimed that York was the victim of racial harassment. He offered no testimony alleging that Sills, or anyone else in Putnam County, had a vendetta against York.

Brooks also shied away from making statements about York's teachings or lifestyle. "I don't know much about religion," Brooks stated.

During his visits to Tama-Re, Brooks said he never witnessed anything close to sexual abuse of children. However, he conceded under cross-examination that if such crimes were being committed, they would almost certainly not take place in the presence of guests.

"I don't expect Dr. York or anyone to share that with me," Brooks stated.

Another character witness, Amadou Varmah, testified that he operated one of York's bookstores in Macon. He brought along a boxful of York's books, which Garland introduced as evidence.

Varmah stated that York's writings and teachings advocated non-violence and denounced racism. "He teaches a Christian doctrine; you have to have good conduct," Varmah stated.

He added that he trusted York with his own children. "They've been in his presence alone, and they love him," Varmah stated.

Among the other character witnesses were two officers of the Macon Police Department.

In his closing argument, Garland read passages from some of York's books, attempting to depict his client as peace-loving and benevolent. He also argued that in other cases, prominent people had been subjected to "false allegations generated by politics, envy, or hate." Child molestation cases were particularly susceptible to such injustices, he said.

But, just in case the judge saw some merit in the allegations against

Dwight York gives an encouraging gesture to his followers after a 2002 pre-trial hearing in Eatonton.

Photo by John Spink, *Atlanta Journal-Constitution*

York, Garland offered to make a deal. If the judge would agree to set bail, York would agree to wear a monitoring bracelet on his ankle and to surrender his passport. He would also give his word that he would not return to Tama-Re and would stay away from children.

Don't buy it, Department of Justice attorney Stephanie Thacker said in her closing argument.

Besides having a documented history of trying to travel on a fake passport, York had hundreds of thousands of dollars in cash in his possession when he was arrested. More importantly, keeping York in jail was the only way to stop him from molesting children, she said. Not long before his arrest, York had been observed by surveillance agents squiring a group of girls out for dinner. Some of those girls had been named by other witnesses as ones whom York had regularly molested, she said.

"This man they were taught to see as a leader, a god-like father" was the same man who "engaged in a long-term, consistent pattern of molestation," Thacker said. "The children are at risk, have been so, and continue to be."

U.S. Magistrate Judge Claude Hicks chose not to spend any time perusing the box of York's books. In fact, he took a verbal swipe at Garland for trying to use them as a criminal defense for their author.

"It's not my intent to denigrate or make fun of this philosophy or theology," Hicks said. However, he went on to note, "some of the most hated autocrats this world had ever known" have also written books or tracts that exhorted their followers to do good things.

Also, Hicks cited other religious figures – specifically, Jimmy Swaggart, Jim Bakker, and Jim Jones – who had an ugly track record of acting contrary to the doctrines they preached.

But this hearing wasn't about books or other notorious figures in religious history. It was about whether York should be allowed to get out of jail. Hicks had heard more than enough to make a ruling on that issue.

"The acts with which they are charged are reprehensible acts. They are acts which have apparently been going on for a long period of time and which, in the view of this court, are likely to continue if defendant York is released from custody," Hicks stated.

Bond was denied for York. However, Hicks said he saw Kathy Johnson as being in "another category." He set her bond at $75,000. Johnson cried softly as she listened to the terms of her release, the first of which was that she was not to come in contact with anyone under the age of eighteen.

Maybe she was crying because she was being cut off from her two children, one of whom had been fathered by York and the other named in witness statements to investigators as one of York's molestation victims.

Maybe she was happy to be getting out of jail herself.

Or maybe it was beginning to dawn on her that Dwight York, the man she'd served as a faithful concubine for about twenty years, was now looking at doing long and hard jail time.

Now, the state's case could be assembled as the second rail of the prosecution train. The federal case was built on four trips to Disney World. By contrast, the state's case was massive. The alleged molestation had been going on for years at Tama-Re, involving dozens of child victims.

Each allegation that York had fondled or had any form of sexual relations with a child was an accusation of a major felony. State prosecutors were limited to acts that occurred more recently than seven years before the indictment. Even so, they could have charged York with thousands of counts.

The job of working with the witnesses and sorting through all the details of the crimes fell to a small group, assistant district attorney Dawn Baskin, the district attorney's chief investigator Mark Robinson, and Putnam County Sheriff's Detective Tracey Bowen.

Baskin's first priority was to satisfy herself that the children were telling the truth.

"In this case, we just could not risk having any bad information going into the indictment," she said.

She had prosecuted child abuse cases before, so she knew what to look for. What she heard and saw sometimes shocked and outraged her, but it also convinced her that the case was built on solid ground.

First, these children were reticent about speaking of the details of what had happened to them. The information had to be elicited slowly and carefully. Speaking of one of the victims, Baskin said, "If you didn't ask her the right questions, she wouldn't tell."

Had the children been part of any sort of conspiracy, they would most likely have been eager to speak their part of a coordinated script, Baskin said.

More telling was the children's ability to recall details. Once they started responding to the proper questions, they displayed remarkable memories of their surroundings and of what had happened to them.

"They recalled sights, smells, feelings," Baskin said. They remembered things like seeing rat droppings and insects in their food, or the fact that York had painted over the cabinetry. They remembered details like the furnishings in York's bedroom, or the barber's chair where York liked to seat himself and receive oral sex.

One girl remembered the time when the floor of the bathroom gave way, and she fell through as she was showering.

Baskin saw this type of recollection as a strong confirmation of the witness's veracity.

"If a child is making the story up, typically she can't give you all the sensations, because she hasn't experienced it," Baskin said.

Mark Robinson, who is also Baskin's husband, was the primary contact for some of the male witnesses. To gauge their veracity, Robinson said he used his investigative training, supplemented by his experience as a parent.

"I have children. You just know who's telling the truth and who's not," Robinson said. From the way these witnesses reluctantly told their painful stories, he said, "It was obvious they were telling the truth."

Listening to their stories was painful for him as well. "Once, I just had to get up and leave the room," Robinson said.

Tracey Bowen said she reached her emotional limit after a three-hour interview with one of the female victims. "I just went home, laid down on my bed and cried," Bowen said.

They literally papered the walls of their "war room" with pictures of the witnesses, in an effort to keep the case properly organized. On one wall were the pictures of the children who could fall into the category of victim witnesses for the indictment they were preparing. On another wall were potential witnesses who came under the heading of "similar transactions," that is, they could testify to having been abused by York, but those incidents occurred before the time period specified in the indictment.

At one point, Baskin found herself preparing an indictment with more than five hundred counts. Her boss, District Atttorney Fred Bright, had to tell her to cut it way down. There was a serious concern that the jury might be overwhelmed by the collective weight of the accusations and might have trouble believing that molestation on such an incredible scale had actually occurred.

Also, there was a fear that the jurors might be inclined to give the defendant a pass, out of anger that the children's parents had not been charged along with York. For example, in the 2005 molestation trial of rock star Michael Jackson, many observers believed the jury's disgust with the behavior of the alleged victim's mother was a factor in Jackson's acquittal. In the York case, Baskin worried that jurors would want to hold some of the parents accountable for not intervening and protecting their children.

There seemed to be at least a partial explanation for this. York selected his child victims from families where the parents would be the least likely to protest. The adults in some of those families were among York's longest and most loyal supporters. Several had been with him for decades. If any of the children spoke of what was happening, York wanted the parents to be in the position of choosing to believe him or believe their children. He had a good idea which way they would go.

"There was a circle of adults that York kept around him," Baskin said. "He went after their kids, because he knew those parents would be the least likely to believe their own children."

From the people who gave him the most, York took the most.

When the Putnam County grand jury convened in the summer of 2002, more than ten victim witnesses were brought in from around the country to testify in the case against Dwight York. This was an extraordinary step; normally, such extensive testimony would be saved for the trial. However, state prosecutors wanted the grand jurors not just to hear summaries, but to hear the stories of the children firsthand. According to people who were part of the process, the testimony deeply moved the grand jurors, one of whom became physically ill from listening to one witness' graphic testimony.

The grand jury returned an indictment naming York in 120 counts of child molestation. Kathy Johnson and three of York's other concubines were also charged in one-to-four of the counts. Later, after more witnesses came forward, the indictment was amended, now listing 177 counts against York.

The public release of the indictment brought with it a new level of pressure. The names of the victims were now part of the public record, and that distressed some of them.

One of the witnesses had been placed in psychiatric care before the indictment, because she'd been haunted by thoughts of suicide. What would happen to her and the others, now that everyone, including the loyal Nuwaubians, knew who they were?

One of the male witnesses, Rafiq, signed a recantation statement. He went to a party where some of his old associates were present. Some friends and relatives insisted that he get in their car and take a ride with them. They asked how he was doing. He answered that he was under a lot of pressure, and he just wanted it all to end.

A relative told Rafiq that it would all end, if Rafiq would just sign a prepared statement saying that he had lied to the police. The relative also intimated that if Rafiq persisted in his testimony against York, his mother might suffer financially; she might even lose her house. At that moment, it sounded like a good deal to Rafiq, so he signed the statement.

The next day, Rafiq wrote a letter to his mother Sah'ira, telling her what he'd done and saying he'd made a big mistake. She counseled him to try to set things straight.

Rafiq was brought to a meeting at a restaurant with York's attorneys and their investigators. The attorneys summoned Rafiq to their table and asked him to tell them what had happened to him. Rafiq answered them truthfully, beginning to tell the same story he'd told the police. At this point, the defense investigators quickly cut him off. They knew the recantation statement was useless to them.

One of the female victims became terrified by some fallout from the legal process. She had given her diary to the police. Baskin described the diary as containing mostly the typical teenaged ramblings. Although it put dates on some of her encounters with York, it did not really contain much that could be used in the investigation. Much of it was the girl's observations on other boys to whom she was attracted.

However, under the rules of discovery, a copy of the diary had to be turned over to the defense. Soon after that happened, excerpts from the diary were posted on a Nuwaubian website.

During this same period, Basheera received a message from someone using York's email account. "Look what you've done!" the writer of the message ranted, calling her a series of ugly names. "You'll get yours!"

Baskin wasn't immune from the intimidation tactics. Although she thought that few people were aware that she was then engaged to marry Robinson, the Nuwaubians found out and later posted their wedding pictures on their website, along with pictures of Robinson's children.

The federal agents and prosecutors became targets of the pre-trial intimidation as well. Ward said she received word that York may have wanted to eliminate both her and Richard Moultrie, one of the lead federal prosecuting attorneys. During a search of York's jail cell, pictures of Ward and Moultrie were found hidden. Both of their faces had been marked with large "X"s, she said.

There were other personal costs, she added. During the closing stages of the investigation, she was dealing with her father's impending death from cancer.

In some ways, the intimidation tactics served mostly to strengthen the resolve of the victims, Baskin said. They formed their own communications network, reinforcing and encouraging each other, when they learned that any of the group was coming under pressure.

Meanwhile, York not only took on the role of persecuted shepherd, he seemed to relish it. At a series of pre-trial hearings, York treated the courtroom like his personal stage. Dressed in a suit and tie, he moved smilingly among the crowded defense tables, giving comforting smiles and touches to the women charged with aiding and participating in his molestations.

He also played to the crowds of loyalists who packed the spectator sections for most of the hearings. Once or twice as he left the courtroom, York turned around, raised his shackled hands and flashed the "Victory" sign to his supporters.

Via an email network that kept his scattered supporters defiant and hopeful – and that he used to solicit contributions for his legal expenses – that it was not he, the Master Teacher, that people were seeing on television and in the newspapers, being led in shackles into the courtrooms. No, the real Doc, or Baba, or Malachi, was actually free, somewhere in a galaxy far away. The person in jail was really just a clone, whom York had created and then left behind to take the heat.

Whoever it was sitting in the defendant's chair, he was giving every indication that he was going to fight the charges and that he was confident he would win. Defense attorneys scored points in their argument that the women indicted along with York should be severed from his case and tried separately. The number of charges they faced was a tiny fraction of the number lodged against York. Any jury would be prejudiced against the women, after listening to victim after victim testify against York.

This presented a serious problem for the prosecution. It was going to be difficult enough, logistically and emotionally, to bring in all the young victims for York's trial. To have to do it all over again in separate trials for the women would be a nightmare.

Then, York simplified everything by copping a plea.

Even as the adversarial roles were being played out in court, York's attorneys were trying to cut a deal with prosecutors. No one should have been surprised.

Garland's reputation had been built on making great deals for his clients. He had represented star pro football linebacker Ray Lewis, after Lewis was charged with murder following a post-Super Bowl stabbing outside an Atlanta nightclub. A man who'd had a run-in with members of Lewis's entourage inside the club was stabbed to death, after the fight was renewed in the parking lot.

The interior of Lewis's limousine was smeared with blood, but Lewis refused to cooperate with police. He was charged with obstruction of the investigation and jailed; later the murder charge was added.

Garland was able to negotiate the charges against Lewis down to obstruction, in return for Lewis's promise to testify as a prosecution witness against the two members of his posse who were still charged with the murder. Lewis testified that he hadn't seen the actual stabbing. The two defendants were acquitted, and Lewis went on to become the Most Valuable Player of the National Football League the next season.

The deal Garland cut for York was nearly as sweet.

Under the terms of the agreement, York would plead guilty, and one sentence of fifteen years would cover both the state and federal charges. He stood a good chance of getting out of prison around his seventieth birthday.

Prosecutors made the deal on the grounds that an admission of guilt was worth giving York a chance at freedom. They were worried about a hung jury; all it would take was for one juror to refuse to convict York, and they'd have to start all over again. Besides, some of the witnesses were being pressured by relatives loyal to York to change their stories.

There was also a fear that the overall story was too bizarre to be believed. "The scope of this case was so overwhelming, there was a concern that a jury would find it unbelievable that something like this could go on for so long," Baskin said.

So, the deal brought a measure of relief to both sides. York was required to appear in both the federal and state courts to enter his pleas. The pleading in the federal case went quietly and smoothly on January 23, 2003. The next day, a repeat performance was set for the courtroom in the county courthouse in Eatonton.

This time, there was a surfeit of drama.

It was the same place, but a radically different atmosphere, from the day about two-and-a-half years earlier, when York also faced the immediate prospect of jail. York wore no bejeweled costume this time, only an orange prison jumpsuit. The only shiny things in his ensemble were his shackles.

There were no chanting protesters this time. Only a handful of loyalists came to the hearing. During the previous night's trip from court back to jail, Sills had asked York to put out the word to his people to avoid turning the hearing into a demonstration. Whether York actually did that, or whether his people simply did not want to witness his admission of guilt, the courtroom spectator section was nearly empty.

Regardless of how many people showed up, the prosecution wanted to make sure that the public record included a detailed accounting of York's crimes.

District Attorney Fred Bright read each one of the charges, which had been reduced in number to seventy-seven under the terms of the plea bargain. Even with Bright's monotone recitation, listening to the shameful litany of York's perversions was a soul-darkening experience. It took Bright about an hour to name the children and specify the types of sex acts that York had performed on or with them. He listed the separate charges for the times when the children had been physically injured in the acts.

By the end, the extent of the Master Teacher's descent into real-life pornography had been exposed. He was the director and star of his own blue movie of a life, except that, unlike most garden-variety porn, his performers were children essentially powerless to refuse his casting calls.

When the judge summoned him to enter his plea, York shuffled forward, shoulders hunched and head bowed. There would be no strutting or oratory on this day. He spoke one word in a voice barely above a whisper: "Guilty."

Not long after this, there was a hearing in Putnam County juvenile court, regarding the custody of three children who'd been taken into state custody after the raid on Tama-Re.

Their father, Karim, wanted them back. Karim, who'd spent thirty years as one of York's most loyal followers, had left the cult in 1997. He had become disillusioned by York's ever-changing belief systems. He also realized that some younger men were supplanting him in positions of confidence within the group. Some of them accused him of keeping money he'd earned in outside real estate work, rather than giving it to York. Karim knew that he had personally offered the money to York, who had told him to keep it. When the money became the source of an accusation of disloyalty against him – and York did nothing to set the matter straight – Karim knew the end had come.

He moved to Atlanta, leaving his children with their mother, who elected to stay at Tama-Re with York. In the years that followed, Karim was frequently denied permission to see his children, when he came to Tama-Re.

So, he only learned of York's arrest when the rest of the public did. By this time, he had found regular work in Atlanta, divorced his first wife, and married Nuha, the nurse who had joined Ansaru Allah Community in the 1970s but left the cult shortly after the move to Georgia.

As much as news of the charges against York shocked him, Karim was even more shocked to learn that his own children had been made wards of the state, because they had been named as victims of York's molestations.

At the custody hearing, Karim had to fight for custody of his own children. As he listened to the reports of what had happened to them at the hands of the man he had loved and trusted, Karim broke down and wept.

Sills was able to share the news of York's admission with his mentor and surrogate father, George Lawrence. Not long after that, though, Lawrence succumbed to cancer.

After York entered his guilty plea, his attorney, Manny Arora, declared that justice had been served in the plea agreement. In light of what the sentence might have been, Arora said, York was satisfied with the recommendation of fifteen years. Arora described York as "distraught, apologetic, and accepting of responsibility."

Well, not quite. A few weeks later, the deal fell apart, after a federal judge decided that it was simply too sweet.

The way the federal process works, once a guilty plea has been entered, a pre-sentencing investigation is conducted and a report issued by officials of the penal system. In this case, after receiving the required report, U.S. District Court Judge Hugh Lawson informed the parties that he could not buy into the deal. The sentencing report was never released publicly, but it clearly must have concluded that fifteen years was far too light a sentence for someone who had pleaded guilty to a staggering amount of major crimes.

Legally, the case reverted to the point where it had stood nearly a year earlier, right after York had been arrested. Lawson called a hearing in July.

The show was back on. York's loyalists were back out in force, some wearing Indian-style garb, and some pounding drums on the street outside the courthouse. York was trying again to claim he was a Native American chief and thus not subject to the jurisdiction of the court.

Inside the courtroom, Lawson struggled to have York express an understanding of his legal options. York could either keep his guilty plea in effect, in which case he would certainly receive a longer sentence than what his attorneys had negotiated for him. Or, he could change his plea back to innocent, and exercise his right to have a jury trial.

Rather than make a choice, York made the federal courtroom into another stage for one of his bizarre performances. He insisted on speaking for himself.

"In all due respect to your court," York declared to Lawson, "I'm a sovereign. I'm a Native American. I'm a Moorish Cherokee, and I cannot get a fair trial, if I'm being tried by settlers or Confederates."

Lawson persisted in trying to get a straight answer out of York, repeating his options and demanding that York make a decision about his plea. York persisted in playing Chief Black Eagle Thunderbird.

Then, Lawson switched his questions to York's lawyers. He would display none of the patience toward them that he had afforded York. Lawson demanded the defense attorneys tell him whether there was any legal basis for the claims York was making, and he threatened them with sanctions, if they tried to play York's silly games.

Arora promptly responded that there was "no legal merit" to York's stunt.

Finally, York stated that he wanted to change his plea to not guilty.

At this point, Lawson ordered that York should be transported to North Carolina for a competency examination at a federal psychiatric facility. Not long after the hearing, Lawson, probably with great relief, recused himself from the case.

York was competent enough to stand trial, and competent enough to fire his attorneys. He would go through a total of eight attorneys before the case was ended.

The annual Christmas parade in Brunswick, Georgia, is always a colorful little event. For the 2003 event, there was a late importation of a band of people wearing Indian and Shriner costumes – York followers using the parade as a forum to protest their leader's innocence.

More than fifty of the Nuwaubians formed a unit to march in the parade, and along the route, other Nuwaubians passed out fliers proclaiming York's innocence.

They'd popped up in Brunswick, a small city on Georgia's coast, because that is where York's trial was to be held, beginning in mid-January 2004. Brunswick has a reviving downtown district, but much of the rest of town hasn't changed much since the '50s. Before he was fired by York, Garland had suggested Brunswick as the best site for a change in venue. The city is quite close to some of Georgia's finest coastal resorts.

So, the Nuwaubians used the Christmas parade to introduce themselves to the pool of people from whom York's jury would be selected. The defense attorneys had been the ones to move for a change of venue, but apparently the Nuwaubians were not averse to generating a little pre-trial publicity themselves.

Prosecutors objected to the flagrant attempt to influence potential jurors, but they really didn't want to have the trial moved or delayed.

When the curtain finally went up on January 13, the security presence was heavy and grim. Inside and outside the federal courthouse, about four hundred police officers were stationed, braced for riot control. Some of the police were armed with automatic weapons, and others wore protective face masks.

The presiding judge, U.S. District Court Judge Ashley Royal, had taken the extraordinary step of barring spectators from the courtroom. Prosecutors had successfully argued that their young witnesses would be intimidated, if they were required to testify about York's crimes in front of a courtroom packed with glowering, black-robed Nuwaubians, some of whom would likely be related to the witnesses and still deeply loyal to York.

A separate courtroom was set up with a grainy, closed-circuit television, for members of the public who wanted to view the York trial. On the first day of the trial, twenty to thirty Nuwaubians showed up in the viewing room. Members of the media were allowed in the courtroom where York was being tried.

Royal also ordered extraordinary security measures for the jury. None of the parties in the case would know their names. They were also instructed not to drive themselves to the courthouse. Instead, they were to be picked up at secret locations by U.S. marshals, who would then drive them to court.

The victim witnesses were to be identified only by their initials, but that did not diminish the power of their testimony.

The first witness was Jokara. She was nineteen at the time of the trial, though she looked no older than sixteen. She was asked to start telling her story by stating what had happened to her when she was eight.

The ages were important to Richard Moultrie, the Assistant U.S. Attorney leading the prosecution trial team.

The age of eight was a milestone in Jokara's life, she testified. That was when York first started molesting her.

"He pulled down my pants. When he was finished, he gave me candy. I was crying," Jokara testified in a barely audible voice, telling the story of the sexual abuse by York that continued for nearly a decade. She was the first of the children to testify in open court against York.

To reinforce her story of being assaulted as a child, Moultrie showed Jokara a photograph taken at her eighth birthday party. In the picture, Jokara was among a group of girls all wearing birthday hats. Moultrie then passed the birthday picture to the jury members; he wanted them to see what an eight-year-old concubine looked like.

The cross-examination consisted mostly of an attack on Jokara's character by York's trial attorney, Adrian Patrick. He tried to get her to admit that she had once stolen some money from York's office. Unshaken, Jokara said that one of her friends might have done that; but so what? They were often hungry. The jurors were left to ponder what connection there might be between the allegations of petty theft and Jokara's hours of testimony about molestation.

Jokara clicked off a list of about ten other persons she had witnessed York molesting when they were children. For her and the others, York "took away our childhoods," she stated.

It went on that way for most of the first week of the trial and well into the second. Twelve other victims told their stories in graphic, numbing detail. Throughout all this testimony, the Pink Panther doll that had been confiscated from York's chamber sat like silent spectator in the courtroom, propped up at the evidence table.

The prosecution also introduced testimony from two women who had handled York's finances, in support of the racketeering charges that had been added to the amended federal indictment. After York exercised his right to change his plea, the government had exercised its right to up the ante.

The racketeering counts alleged there was a direct connection between the money and the sex. York was charged with using most of the cult revenues to support a lifestyle that included the freedom and power to rule the cult without question and to indulge his sexual depravities with impunity. A conviction would give the government the right to seize any and all property that York had gained through his racketeering. In effect, that meant that Tama-Re was on the table.

Basheera testified that she had been placed in charge of York's finance department from 1999 until she left the community in 2001.

Any of the cash that came in from the bookstore operators in denomination of fifty dollars and higher went directly into York's suitcases, she stated. The rest went into accounts that were used to pay for food and for other operating expenses at Tama-Re.

Other revenues were generated by renewal fees for the visitor passports to Tama-Re, at a rate of twenty-five dollars per passport holder per year. It cost twenty-seven dollars per year in dues to be a member of York's Ancient and Mystic Order of Melchizidek.

Also, just as he had done in Brooklyn, York sent male Nuwaubians out to cities to panhandle or to sell trinkets or books. They were expected to bring him one hundred dollars per day.

Basheera also confirmed York's plan for a political takeover of Putnam County. She said York instructed some of the women workers to call all the bookstore operators in early 2000, instructing them to come to Putnam County to register as voters. The plan turned into "a mess," she said, because too many of the Nuwaubians used the same addresses to register, and they were caught.

The proceeds from the Savior's Day festivals were treated as York's personal birthday present, she said, with all the cash going straight to York.

Sometimes, when York made major purchases, he dipped into his suitcase stash; but he added some financial sleight of hand. York would give some of his followers stacks of cash amounting to thousands of dollars. The followers would use the cash to buy money orders, which were then deposited as donations into one of York's business accounts. This way, York could make the purchases -- $75,000 for a large statue of the Sphinx for the grounds of Tama-Re, $80,000 for a bus, or $25,000 for printing equipment – without having to declare the money used for the purchases as his personal income.

Badra testified that she also worked in York's finance department. York would allow money that came in from the mail-order sales of incense or cosmetics to go to operational accounts. However, he claimed all the money from book sales as his own.

It was part of her job, she said, to make cash deposits in banks, usually going out to several different banks two or three times per week. York instructed her to make deposits of less than $10,000 in cash, so that he could avoid filling out the required forms for larger cash deposits. Sometimes, she said, she took large amounts of cash in lower-denomination bills to the bank for conversion to larger bills, which would then go directly to York's suitcases.

Mostly, she said, York grabbed all the money he could. "Every money that came in, we were just told, that's his money. We weren't allowed to use it to pay the bills or anything. He just said right out, 'That's my money,'" she said.

Whatever York didn't take went toward sustaining the rest of the community, she said. There was a rotating schedule for kitchen chores, but there wasn't always food to eat. "Mostly, it was rice and beans, but there were times when we ate relish," Badra said.

The testimony of York's own accountant established York as a slavemaster who didn't need to chain his slaves. In the years 1996 to 2002, York's reported income averaged about $1 million annually, the accountant testified. After claiming deductions of about $5 million for that period, York showed a net income of about $775,000, on which he paid about $300,000 in taxes, the accountant stated.

Nowhere in those deductions, however, were there any claims for wages paid – because York didn't pay anybody, even though many of his workers routinely put in twelve-hour days and longer. In return for their labors, they were given squalid living quarters and food, or relish, as the case may be.

York's defense was primarily based on name-calling.

"They're all liars," claimed defense witness Evelyn Rivera, a member of York's cults for more than two decades. "I knew them as children. They all lie." Other than this accusation, she offered no testimony to refute the statements

The defense was allowed to raise a conspiracy theory to explain why so many witnesses were accusing York of having molested them. It was all cooked up by York's revenge-minded son Malik, the defense maintained.

Leah Mabry, one of York's daughters, testified that Malik had a "vendetta" against York. She stated that Malik had tried to recruit her into his conspiracy, but she offered no insights into how Malik had orchestrated the testimony of so many witnesses, most of whom he'd never met. As Mabry left the stand, she blew a kiss to York.

The defense was free to try to subpoena Malik to testify at the trial, but they chose not to. That was probably the prudent move, since if Malik had been allowed to testify, he could have told the jury some ugly stories, like the one where his father turned a teenaged girlfriend of Malik's into one of his concubines.

Malik could not add much to the prosecution's case, since he had left the community years before the time period covered by the indictment.

Other than the phantom conspiracy theory, the defense called a parade of York's followers to testify to all the good things that York had brought to their lives. They praised him as an inspirational leader who did things like elevate their self-esteem. They could not offer any evidence to refute the prosecution's case, because they were nowhere around when the crimes were being committed.

Defense attorneys told the court they planned to call a psychologist who would offer expert testimony about other cases, where children may have been coached into making allegations of sexual abuse. However, they never called their expert.

Basheera's father, a York loyalist, testified that he thought his daughter was probably lying. Under cross-examination, the father admitted that he had approved of his daughter becoming pregnant by York when she was seventeen. "She asked me for permission to be part of his family, and I granted that," the father stated.

Six young women who'd been named as victims in the state's indictment testified as defense witnesses. They stated that their previous statements to prosecution investigators were lies and they claimed they had only been saying what the police wanted them to say.

One of those was a girl who'd vanished shortly after being interviewed by investigators at her school in Athens. She gave a voluntary statement describing the same sorts of molestations as the other victims. That same night, her family moved, and prosecutors were unable to find her, until she appeared as a defense witness. Now, the girl testified that she had lied to police and that York had never molested her. Her parents had remained loyal to York, she stated.

In his closing argument, defense attorney Patrick made some frequency estimates of York's sexual activity, as a way of showing that the government's case was preposterous. He put up a chart with an estimate of twelve thousand alleged

A window of many symbols adorned York's quarters at Tama-Re.
Photo by Bill Osinski, *Atlanta Journal-Constitution*

incidents of molestation in the seven years covered by the indictment. That worked out to about 150 molestations per month, or three to four a day. No normal middle-aged man would be physically capable of such an excessive level of sex.

That was precisely the point the prosecution had been trying to make. York was not a normal man. As depicted in the testimony of the girls and boys he molested, York was a man who summoned women and children to have sex with him day and night, whenever he pleased. His sexual stamina was apparently chemically assisted. Police found evidence that York was taking regular doses of the male hormone testosterone.

In his closing argument, Moultrie called on the jurors to ignore the unsupported conspiracy theory and concentrate on the testimony of the young people who'd given such graphic descriptions of their repeated molestations as children. He asked them to recall how painful and difficult their time on the witness stand had been for them. He asked them to consider how hard it must have been to know that some of their own parents had disregarded their reports of the abuse and instead of comforting them or apologizing to them, had called their children liars.

The only conspiracy at this trial was the one among the York supporters, who had pressured some of the victims to deny their earlier accusations of abuse by York, Moultrie said. Those denials had all been made under pressure from family members who remained loyal to York, he said.

Moultrie asked for the jurors to return a guilty verdict, in order to help the molested children put their "horrible nightmare" behind them.

The jury quickly complied. After deliberating a total of about seven hours at the end of a three-week trial, they convicted York on all counts.

After the verdict, Malik York said, facetiously, that he was "flattered" that his father's attorneys apparently thought he was brilliant enough to have engineered such a vast conspiracy.

Regarding the verdict itself, Malik said, "Justice for the innocents has finally been done."

U.S. Attorney Max Wood said the verdict would help strip York of all the grandiose religious and secular titles York had falsely claimed throughout his life. "He is Dwight York, a con man from Brooklyn, New York," Wood said.

In the end, the trial had been a rather anti-climactic melodrama. Although the Brunswick jury was unaware of it, York had previously admitted his guilt in another courtroom. Also, York had chosen not to try to charm the jury. He did not take the stand.

In the controlled venue of the courtroom, York could not use the tactics he'd frequently used before. He couldn't pass out the windy, lie-laced rebuttal newsletters or pamphlets that he'd used both in Brooklyn and in Georgia. Instead, he had to sit at the defense table and listen to the children tell of all the repugnant things he had done to them.

There was, however, one more opportunity for York to take the stage. This was at his sentencing, in a Macon federal courtroom in April 2004.

"Today is a very sad day," York said, speaking, as usual, primarily for and about himself. He was delivering the customary defendant's speech before pronouncement of the sentence.

York's sorrow was confined to his own condition. He knew he was about to be sent to prison for a long time. He refused to use any of his precious spotlight time to express any sadness for all the years of pain he had inflicted on children who'd been taught to worship him. He certainly wasn't sad for all the thousands of his followers, whose deep belief in him he had betrayed.

Even to his last public statement, York insisted that he was the one who was suffering. He was sick, he claimed, and he wasn't receiving proper treatment in jail. A classic sociopath to the end, York was totally focused on his own distress.

"I'm in a strange situation. My life is on the line," York whined. The guilty verdict had "hurt me and hurt America," he stated, not offering any of his wisdom as to how America might muddle along without him.

York still considered himself an important, persecuted spiritual leader. "This is a religious case," he said. "This is not a child molestation case. This is not a RICO case."

He claimed his constitutional right to make a living had been violated, not bothering to mention any of his own violations. Then, he once again tried to claim that he was a leader of his race.

"It's convenient to y'all to get a man of my stature off the streets," York sputtered.

Next, York attacked practically every aspect of the investigation and trial. He claimed the prosecution had presented "no real evidence" against him. The witnesses against him had been coerced, the jury had been improperly selected, and the judge was prejudiced against him.

"We never got a fair trial," York blurted out, with an impertinence that suggested his old days as a reincarnated god, the days when he needed only to express his slightest wish and his subjects would scurry to make it come true.

The man who had maintained a harem for decades, indulging in any and every sexual whim, the man who had paraded in front of his concubines and their children he had fathered, was now reduced to portraying himself pathetically

Tama-Re in ruins. Photo by Anderson Scott

as an ailing man with failing potency. "It was physically impossible for me to have sex that much," he claimed.

As his tenuously coherent diatribe fizzled to an end, York tried playing the name game one more time. He claimed to be a Freemason, then claimed to be an Indian chief, namely, Black Eagle Thunderbird. Finally, he claimed to be a citizen of Liberia with some sort of diplomatic immunity that was supposed to shield him from what was about to happen.

It was, however, far too late for any more games. Judge Royal paused a moment to make sure that York was finished. Then, without further comment, he sentenced York to 135 years in a federal penitentiary.

CHAPTER 10
Epilogue To Evil

I know there is evil in this world, but I have never seen it on the scale that I have in this matter. – Putnam County Sheriff Howard Sills

One of the strangest things about this sorrowful saga is that there seemed to be so few winners at the end. Justice prevailed, but a sense of triumph has been very hard to find.

York was treated harshly by the justice system, but not nearly as harshly as he had treated so many of those who believed in him.

Yet, for those who finally stopped his decades-long run of criminality and perversion, there have been few fruits from their often-courageous efforts.

By and large, the women, girls, and boys who defied York's threats and provided the key evidence against him have faded away. A few seem to be doing well in their new lives. Some of them are still struggling. Some are under psychiatric care.

With the exception of Sills, the local officials in Putnam County who stood up against the Nuwaubians have paid a steep price politically. There was a subtle, and somewhat odd, backlash against them. It was as if some of York's racist smears against them stuck, even though York was exposed as a criminal.

The events of this story exposed a racial fault line that is still wide and deep. Whites who have earned the right to claim credit for ridding society of a monstrous predator are reluctant to do so, apparently due to some lingering fear of being perceived as anti-black. On the other hand, blacks who should be furious that so many black children were molested for so long are instead curiously silent.

The moral of this story is that racial stereotypes are, even in the twenty-first century, often stronger than the truth.

No one has suggested putting up a plaque on the Putnam County Courthouse green to commemorate the Nuwaubian affair. Unlike Wasco County, Oregon, where the people have honored the public officials who did their job and stopped a cult from taking over the county, the people of Putnam County seemed somewhat embarrassed by the whole business. Certainly, the crimes were repulsive, but it would seem to be worth remembering that a coalition of black and white people in a small Southern county stood together and stopped a man who'd fooled and eluded authorities in the nation's largest city for more than twenty-five years.

Despite what that coalition did, some say that race relations in Putnam County are more strained now than before Dwight York came to town.

"There should have been some coming together, but there hasn't," said Maryann Tanner.

Tanner's efforts to purge the county's voter registration rolls of fraudulently-registered Nuwaubians were ultimately upheld by the federal courts. However, those efforts also placed her at odds with members of the county commission who had sought a rapprochement with the Nuwaubians and had accepted their political support.

In 2005, the commission eliminated Tanner's job, creating the office of Supervisor of Elections. Out of work, Tanner was hired by Sills as a dispatcher.

Sandra Adams recalled that the Nuwaubians got away with calling her names that, had they been spoken against her by whites, would most certainly have touched off a racial firestorm. She said she got angry at the defamations, but she refused to respond in kind. "I know who I am, and I know what I am and what I am not," Adams said.

The Nuwaubians' attacks on Putnam County blacks who opposed them were vicious and based in ignorance, she said. "This is a small town in the Deep South, and the prevailing attitude of the blacks who fled is that this is still a racist environment," Adams said. "They don't know the progress that's happened since they've been gone."

However, she added, that progress has been threatened, both by the Nuwaubians and by the nationally-known civil rights activists who came to Tama-Re to support them.

"They never came to us," Adams said. "For them to claim to be national leaders and only get one side of the story, I resented that greatly."

What makes her even angrier, she said, is that the visiting activists were most likely paid for their appearances. "Jesse Jackson, all he wants is the dollar. He doesn't care what color it is," Adams said.

Adams said too many people seem to be overlooking the central fact that there was no interracial aspect to the crimes York committed on Tama-Re. "This was black-on-black crime. White people didn't do this. York did this to black babies," she said.

People should be angry with York, not with the officials who put him in jail. Adams knew where her anger should be directed. On the day when York pleaded guilty in Eatonton, Adams was one of the few people in the spectator seats. "I was sitting there with the rage building inside me," she said. "I was thinking, 'God, is there a way I can leap over that railing and get in one good blow."

Somehow, the notion of just who was the villain in this story has escaped some others in Putnam County. It's as if the racial animosity that York worked so hard to re-kindle is still smoldering, Adams said.

"It has divided this community," she said. "People are a lot more racial. They think more in terms of black and white."

Even now, there are blacks in Putnam County who mutter about what they saw as racially-motivated mistreatment of York, saying things like, "They set him up," she said.

The politics of race was an underlying theme in the 2004 campaign that ended with Sandra Adams losing her seat on the county commission. Adams's district had been re-drawn, making it majority black. Another black woman, Janie Reid, won a commission seat in the same election.

Reid said the Nuwaubian issue was a factor in both races, in that Adams sought to portray her as being at least unofficially affiliated with the group.

"Some people may have gotten bent out of shape, because I treated them like human beings," Reid said. In the early 1990s, when York first moved to Putnam County, Reid worked in the county tax office. She said York stopped in for normal business, and was pleasant to her.

She visited Tama-Re a total of three times, but she was never a member of the Nuwaubian community, she said. She said she was aware of the name calling and accusations made by the Nuwaubians against some of the public officials; but if the charges were false, why didn't the officials sue them?

Georgia Smith in downtown Eatonton. Photo by W. A. Bridges, *Atlanta Journal-Constitution*

The way the Nuwaubians were treated by some local officials made some blacks upset, she said. "From the beginning, there was talk that if they weren't black, they wouldn't be going through all this," she said.

Reid compared the Nuwaubians and their desire to do what they wanted on their property to the wealthy residents, mostly white, who live in gated communities on Lake Oconee. "What's the difference?" she said.

Zoning was a relatively new concept when the zoning laws were applied against the Nuwaubians, and some people believe that those laws were selectively enforced against the Nuwaubians, she said.

Reid said she was appalled by the charges of sexual abuse brought against York, but she also had some reservations about the way the case was handled and about whether York had truly committed all those crimes.

That lingering skepticism is a residue of the times – and they weren't all that long ago – when there was clear and blatant racial inequality in Putnam County, and in the rest of the South for that matter. Some blacks looked at the Nuwaubian situation and could only see a replay of the bad old days.

"It's opened up old wounds," said Georgia Smith. "People don't want to talk about it, but it's there."

Some people thought she was out of line for being so vocal in her opposition to York, she said. "I was told more than once, 'Leave him alone. He's just a black man trying to have something.' But I had a gut feeling something was wrong. I'd say, 'What's wrong with you? Don't you see what's going on?'" she said.

The criticism hasn't bothered Smith. She still heads the Mothers Against Crime group that she founded. Indeed, she is one of the private citizens of Putnam County, white or black, who will publicly proclaim her pride in doing her part to rid her county of Dwight York.

It's been a nightmare, but we did something New York couldn't do," Smith said. "We stayed on it, and we didn't back up. This little town didn't back up."

There have been few curtain calls for the other players in the Georgia scenes of the Nuwaubian melodrama.

Former Governor Roy Barnes is now a private attorney practicing in the Atlanta suburb of Marietta. His former chief counsel, Penny Brown-Reynolds, is a judge in Atlanta.

Bobby Kahn, Barnes' former chief of staff, was the chairman of the Democratic Party of Georgia until he was succeeded by Jane Kidd in January 2007.

Tyrone Brooks continues to represent his Atlanta district in the Georgia state legislature.

Ed Coughenour lives in North Carolina and works as a superintendent for a construction company.

Among the former Nuwaubians, Nasira lives in New York City, where she subsists primarily on Social Security payments. She is raising her youngest two daughters, the ones fathered by York. The younger of those suffers from Downs Syndrome.

Her oldest daughter, Aludra, lives with other relatives in Florida and works part-time for a shipping company. "I started my life at twenty-five years old, without a dime in my pocket, no high school diploma, no credit. It's so hard. Before being consumed by that place, I was always an "A" student," she said.

"I'm still very afraid of dealing with people I don't know," Aludra said. There have been times recently when she has accidentally encountered people who have remained loyal to York; most of those times, those people have harassed her. "So much persecution for standing up and telling the truth," she said.

"I know in my heart that we downplayed a lot of things that he did to us, because there is still some amount of guilt that we were doing the wrong thing for telling," Aludra said. "No matter what we do, where we go, we will always be different. There are hundreds of people (York loyalists) who go to bed every night wishing people like me harm and praying for bad things to happen to us – people I grew up with like sisters. I hate it."

Now in her early thirties, Aludra plans to enroll in college.

Nasira's other two children, Jokara and Rafiq, live near their mother. They support themselves and they attend school. Jokara said she found it quite difficult to adjust to life in the real world. For about six months after leaving Tama-Re, she said she would stop every time she passed a mirror. She thought she might catch a glimpse of the demons that York warned would beset once if she ever left him.

Nasira said she accepts part of the blame for not seeing what was happening to her three children on Tama-Re and not acting to stop it sooner. "I punish myself every day," she said.

Badra lives in Washington, D.C., and works for the federal government. Her daughter, Azizah, who endured years of molestation by York, attends an alternative high school and is under the care of a mental health professional.

Nevertheless, Badra said, their relationship has become very close. "It's a miracle that my daughter still talks to me," Badra said.

Ramillah, the molestation victim who called her father to help her escape from Tama-Re, now lives with relatives in Florida. Her civil suit against York has lapsed into inactivity. She is taking college courses in business via the internet, and she is raising her young child (not York's) as a single parent. Her father operates a thriving construction business and is trying to repair some of the damage York did to his family.

Malik lives in Atlanta and owns a recording company that specializes in hip-hop music. His sister, Afifah, operates a beauty salon, also in Atlanta.

There are still a few remnants of the Nuwaubian movement, small pockets of people who have remained loyal to York and who still work to raise money for him. At least two of the bookstores remain open, one in downtown Atlanta and the other on Bushwick Avenue, in the heart of the old Ansaru Allah Community. York's tracts can still be purchased there. Some of his followers occasionally put Nuwaubian memorabilia up for sale on internet auction sites; bidding for a mint-condition copy of *The Holy Tablets* signed by York recently reached three hundred dollars.

On occasion, the loyalists can still generate public demonstrations of their support for York. In June 2005, about fifty black-clad Nuwaubians held a march to the land that was once Tama-Re, which had been seized by the federal government a few months earlier and then sold to a developer who plans to tear down most of the structures before re-selling the property. The Nuwaubians protested what they called the destruction of church property.

In September 2005 about two hundred of York's followers appeared on the streets of Atlanta, while oral arguments in York's appeal were being heard by the U.S. 11th Circuit Court of Appeals. Inside the courtroom, the arguments focused not on York's claim that he was falsely convicted but on the defense attorney's contention that the racketeering counts should not have been included with the child molestation counts. Assistant U.S. Attorney Richard Moultrie responded that the sex and the money were inextricably linked: York used the money primarily to maintain his sexually excessive lifestyle.

On the sidewalks outside the courthouse, York's supporters were dressed in a variety of costumes, most of them with a Shrine-style theme. Many of the men wore fezes that said "Mahdi Shrine Temple" and others wore bright blue gloves.

After the hearing, the York loyalists tried to peddle their conspiracy theories to television and newspaper reporters.

About three months later, the appellate court, ruling without comment, turned down York's appeal and upheld his sentence.

The extent to which the loyalists refuse to see the gaping flaws in their leader's character is exemplified by Sakina Lewis, a woman who has followed York faithfully since the 1970s. She still operates the All Eyes On Egypt bookstore on Bushwick Avenue, in a building next door to York's old mosque.

Lewis will simply not accept any contention that York is a criminal, and she still gives him credit for just about all the good there is in her life.

"His life is my life," she said.

She refuses to use the word "belief" in connection with the tenets of York's ideology. "Belief" implies a doctrine that people accept on faith, she said, but York teaches only undisputable truths.

"It's got nothing to do with a belief. We're dealing with the facts. Truth is truth," Lewis said. In her world, and that of the other loyalists, there is no room for flexibility or interpretation, or for allowing that a reasonable person might see things differently and still have a valid point of view.

As for the legally-established truth that York molested at least dozens of children, Lewis simply denies that it ever happened. "I was at the trial. They didn't present any evidence," she said. "He was convicted on mere hearsay."

To her, the prosecution was more of a persecution. "They always make us out to be the bad guys. Why? We always get the railroad," she said.

Lewis wonders why people won't give York credit for all the good things he has done. For example, she cited the mayoral commendation York received about thirty-five years ago for appearing to keep drug dealers out of his neighborhood.

The loyalists cling to the expectation that York will be exonerated and their movement will survive. "It only takes two people to be a nation," Lewis said.

Other loyalists work to keep York's cause alive. Joe Beasley, the southern director of Jesse Jackson's Rainbow/PUSH Coalition, wrote a letter in 2005 on York's behalf to U.S. Secretary of State Condoleezza Rice, with a copy to U.S. Attorney General Alberto Gonzalez.

"I have followed the trail(sic) of Dr. York very closely, and in our view, justice did not prevail," Beasley wrote. He stated that York should be released from prison and allowed to go to his adopted country, Liberia. He assured Rice that the Liberian government was ready to accept him.

"I respectfully urge you," Beasley wrote to Rice, "to take an interest in this case and schedule a meeting, at your earliest time possible, to effectuate diplomatic negotiations for the immediate transfer of Dr. York to the Republic of Liberia, West Africa."

The letter was posted on a pro-York website, along with a picture of York in a costume straight out of a Gilbert and Sullivan light opera. The caption identifies York as "Consul General: Dr. Malachi Z. York." In the picture, York is wearing a bejeweled cap, a prince-like necklace and medallion, white gloves with fringed wrist coverings, and a ceremonial sword at his side.

The posting claims that York has renounced his American citizenship and is now a citizen of Liberia. It identifies him in terms of his cultural heritage as "Maku: Chief Black Thunderbird of the Yamassee Native American Moors of the Creek Nation (Indigenous Nubuns of African Descent)." It also claims that York "has spent most of his adult life dedicated to the upliftment of the African American Negro in the United States of America."

Another of York's followers sent him a letter that included a drawing of what was called a Liberian Secret Service badge. The idea was to sell the badges to other loyalists.

In 2006 York's supporters leased a billboard on US 441, just outside of Eatonton. On it, they placed a large photo of York in one of his elaborate, Masonic-style costumes. There is also a plug on the billboard for a website, www. heisinnocent.com. Browsers of that site are informed how they can contribute to York's continuing legal defense efforts.

It is just this sort of preposterous twaddle that makes any reference to York as a "Master Teacher" – or criminal mastermind, or master anything, for that matter – sound downright silly.

Dwight York was a pompous, uneducated poseur. To call him a religious leader is to blaspheme the whole notion of religion as a force for good. To call him a legitimate voice of the black community is to demean all those who have suffered and fought for the cause of racial justice.

The street toughs in Brooklyn had him pegged, when they called him "the pimp imam."

As a singer and entertainer, he was embarrassingly bad and a consistent failure. He built lavish recording studios for himself wherever he moved, but he never produced successful music. He purported to be the author of hundreds of books, but many of them were borrowed heavily, or flat-out plagiarized, from existing books.

He dressed the part of a potentate, with flowing, shimmering robes, gold and jewelry galore, while the girls who dared to deny him sex were given no clean clothes. While he conducted orgies in his Jacuzzi, one of his young concubines who had displeased him fell through the rotted floor of her shower.

Perhaps worst of all, York had little but contempt for his followers. They gave him all they had, even their children, and he called them "idiots."

Give the devil his due. York was a gifted manipulator. He could convince his followers that he was a supernatural being who could take them to a faraway galaxy. He could convince the children he was molesting that he was the only one who loved them. He convinced some of their parents to ignore their children's complaints, accuse the children of lying, and believe him instead.

He convinced high officials of the largest city of the United States that he was cleaning up a tough neighborhood, when he was actually using the trappings of an orderly, strict, religious community as a cover for his wide-ranging criminal enterprises.

And through all the years, whatever he called himself and his cult, York was able to inspire a deep, atavistic devotion among his followers.

However, none of York's personal qualities, good or wicked, can fully answer the key question of how he was able to last as long as he did. To get away with everything from molesting children in secret to possibly having a rival murdered in the streets, York had to have help, a lot of help.

Deliberately or unwittingly provided, that help came from a succession of people in authority who could have stopped him, or at least impeded him, but did not.

An early case in point was the handling of the investigation into the murder of Horace Green in 1979. Had the police officials who imposed the "hands off policy" limiting the pursuit of investigations into Black Muslim communities been more attentive or discerning, they might have seen that aside from the issue of its validity, the policy should never have been applied to York. He was no more a Muslim in his soul than Douglas Fairbanks Jr. was the *Thief of Baghdad*.

Nevertheless, York's Muslim façade succeeded in thwarting Detective Bill

Clark from properly investigating the Horace Green murder and from connecting the killing back to York. A few years later, the same policy nearly prevented New Jersey Detective Jack Eutsey from pinning another brutal murder on Green's suspected killer.

The office of former New York Mayor Ed Koch took an active interest in the Green murder, offering a reward for information in the case. Had anyone informed Koch or his aides that the same group Koch had commended for patrolling their neighborhood was also possibly harboring Green's killer, maybe the murder investigation could have been directed where it belonged.

Instead, the murder of Horace Green was allowed to become a statement killing. No one in York's sector of Bushwick challenged his control after that.

Other crimes later attributed to Ansaru Allah were not fully investigated when they occurred. The 1993 FBI report on York's cult cited several cases of arson, where the initial reports stated that members of Ansaru Allah were seen near the torched buildings. Those reports were apparently never pursued.

In the late 1980s *The Ansaar Cult* was published, exposing York as a phony Muslim who kept a harem for his sexual pleasure and claimed most of his followers' possessions. No one outside the Muslim world paid much attention, and the Muslims who were outraged by York apparently did not do much to bring York to the attention of outside authorities.

The FBI 1993 intelligence report attributed numerous serious crimes to York, but none of its findings were shared with local police. The crimes were state crimes, not federal, but that does not excuse allowing them to go uninvestigated and unpunished. Certainly, one phone call could have re-opened the Horace Green case. Had that happened, York might never have made it to Georgia.

Once in Georgia, York succeeded in obtaining something similar to the immunity he'd enjoyed in New York. High-ranking state officials apparently accepted the notion – with no supporting evidence other than the complaints of York's political allies – that York was the victim of racial discrimination by the backward folks in Putnam County.

Despite the official denials that anyone in the governor's office had sanctioned or commissioned the near-disastrous foray of the Georgia Rangers into Putnam County, someone certainly sent the gun-packing trouble magnets down there. Ed Coughenour, the leader of the Rangers, admitted to making a bunch of stupid moves throughout the episode; but there is an undeniable core of reasonableness to his assertion that he would never have moved into the middle of a racially-charged standoff, unless he had been convinced that he was being backed by the power of the office of the governor.

According to the GBI investigation of that case, Governor Barnes was given Ed Coughenour's obviously bogus crime-fighter business card on the day of his ride with Tyrone Brooks. That was also the day before the Rangers hit Putnam County in force. Rather than heed the red flags that should have been flapping in his face, Barnes did nothing to stop the strange mission.

Elected officials had plenty of company in the see-no-evil corps. Public school officials in Brooklyn could have enforced attendance rules on York's community, thus making it harder for York to use his marching, praying children as window dressing. School officials in Georgia should have questioned why fifty or more children were being home-schooled at the same address. The administrators of the hospitals where the Nuwaubian women, some of them obviously underage, were delivering babies under such strange circumstances — including the menacing presence of unrelated male guards and the mothers' refusals to give the father's name — should have asked questions.

Then there were the academics who looked at York's community, but did not study it critically. There were journalists both in New York and in Georgia who settled for writing only about the surface-level appearance of York's group.

Regrets have been hard to find in any of those quarters.

Dawn Baskin, who is now in private practice, expressed sorrow for the human costs of the delays. During the months that the case against York was being methodically put together, Baskin said she often thought of the children who were being molested while the justice system plodded towards putting York away. "I just wish we could have moved faster," she said.

Outrage has been even harder to find than regrets. Even now, some whites in Putnam County will speak privately about their relief at having a scourge removed from their county, yet they are reluctant to speak out publicly, for fear of being perceived as antagonistic to blacks.

And where are the black voices of protest, which should be raised in righteous anger over a case of prolonged, systematic, and despicable exploitation of black children? In an interview with this author, Joe Beasley, the southern regional director of the Rainbow-Push Coalition, continued to insist that Sheriff Sills is "crazy as hell." He also said he was "committed to keeping the Nuwaubian movement alive," adding that "somebody else could take Dr. York's place." Neither Jesse Jackson nor Al Sharpton has returned to Georgia to lead a protest, or to apologize for their previous support for York. Neither Jackson nor Sharpton responded to requests for comment for this book.

Why are there no rallies for the victims?

Conventional wisdom – "wisdom" is probably too kind a word in this context – about race was turned upside down in this case. A rural, white-dominated county in Middle Georgia was invaded by a militant black cult determined to operate as a sovereign nation, in which its leader wanted to be free to flaunt civil and moral law.

The result was a rather awkward sociological waltz, with twenty-first century political correctness staggering around the floor in the embrace of the skeletal remains of Civil-Rights-era activism.

The villain in this ungodly tale has come to a fitting end, due to some courageous children and to the combined efforts of a dedicated, thick-skinned sheriff and his deputies, working in concert with a massive effort by the FBI. Dwight York is now an inmate at the "supermax" security federal prison in Florence, Colorado, a place sometimes called "the Alcatraz of the Rockies." He will almost certainly spend the rest of his life there.

Still, the story also tells us how much more we need to grow as a society, before race relations can mature past the stage of legal tolerance and toward mutual acceptance. We are not at the place in our history where the vision of Dr. Martin Luther King Jr. is close to reality, a place where people are judged on the content of their character and not the color of their skin.

Hardly anyone has studied York and his cult more deeply, from a behavioral perspective, than FBI agent Jalaine Ward. To her, York was nothing more or less than "an indiscriminate sexual predator," she said, adding, "He was the black Koresh."

Howard Sills gave perhaps the best overall summation, when he said, "I know that evil exists in the world, but I have never seen evil on the scale that I have seen in this matter."

Eventually, all traces of Tama-Re would be obliterated. In the summer of 2005, after the land had been sold, Sills allowed himself a moment to savor the triumph over the evil that had permeated this place.

He sat in the cab of a front-end loader and lit up a six-inch cigar. He revved up the engine and lowered the bucket, then shoved the machine into gear and smashed the machine's metal claw into the arched entrance to Tama-Re. Like all of York's lies, the drivit exploded into dust.

NOTES

Chapter 1 - Pyramids In The Cow Pasture

York, Dwight – comments made to media representatives, including this
 author, June 1998

Alima – interviews with the author

Chapter 2 - A Cult Grows In Brooklyn

York, Dwight – self-published books, including *Rebuttal To The
 Slanderers, Is God A Wimp?,The Fallacy Of Easter, Santa Or
 Satan?, Was Christ Really Crucified?, Who, What, And Where Is
 The Devil?, Islamic Marriage Ceremony And Polygamy,
 Christianity: The Political Religion, The Sex Life Of A Muslim,
 Slave Trade, Holy War (Jihad), Did The Hog Come For Mankind?,
 Leviathan 666, The Man Of Miracles In This Day And Time.*

Breslin, Jimmy – column for *Newsday*, 1989

Green, Cora – interview with the author

Clark, Bill – interviews with the author

Koch, Ed – interview with the author

Lincoln, C. Eric – *The Black Muslims in America*

Wolfe, Tom – *Radical Chic & Mau-Mauing The Flak Catchers* (Farrar, Strauss & Giroux, Nov., 1970)

Federal Bureau of Investigation, Intelligence Report, 1993, "The Ansaru Allah Community"

Karim, interviews with the author

Ali, Noble Drew – *The Holy Koran,* with other archival materials at the Shomberg Center for African-American Studies, New York City

Haddad, Yvonne Yazbeck, and Smith, Jane Idelman – *Mission To America: Five Islamic Sectarian Communities In America* (University of Florida Press, 1993)

Clegg, Claude A. – *An Original Man* (St. Martin's Press, 1997)

Malik, interviews with the author

Eutsey, Jack – interviews with the author

Chapter 3 - Bushwick Babylon

Afifah – interviews with the author

Malik – interviews with the author

Mullins, Phil – interviews with the author

Karim – interviews with the author

Halaat – interviews with the author

Philips, Bilal – *The Ansaar Cult* (Tawheed Publications, 1988)

York, Dwight – *Rebuttal To The Slanderers,* self-published), and promotional materials for various musical enterprises

Nasira – interviews with the author and investigative and court documents

Aludra – ibid

Asad – interviews with the author

Alima – ibid

Badra – ibid

Chapter 4 – The Artificial Nuwaubian

O'Connor, Flannery – *O'Connor, Collected Works* (Library of America, 1988), including exerpts from *Wise Blood, The Artificial Nigger, A View Of The Woods, Everything That Rises Must Converge*

Harris, Joel Harris – *Uncle Remus, His Songs And Sayings* (reprinted by Cherokee Publishing Company, 1981)

Harris, Julia Collier – *The Life And Letters Of Joel Harris Harris* (reprinted by Studio Designs Printing, Milledgeville, Ga.)

Walker, Alice – *In Search Of Our Mothers' Gardens* (Harcourt, 1983); *The Third Life Of Grange Copeland* (Harcourt, 1970)

Danielle, Chris – *Living By Grace*

Rozier, John – *Black Boss* (University of Georgia Press, 1982)

Sterling, Dorothy – *The Trouble They Seen*

Greer, Evelyn – interviews with the author

Timmons, Edgar – interview with the author

Green, Melissa Fay – *Praying For Sheetrock*

Jones, Charles – interviews with the author

Atlanta Journal-Constitution, articles by the author on Harris Neck and Hancock County

York, Dwight – *The Holy Tablets*, self-published

Samarra – interviews with the author and investigative document

Temple, Robert – *The Sirius Mystery* (Destiny Books, 1998 edition)

Bauval, Robert and Gilbert, Adrian – *The Orion Mystery* (Three Rivers Press, 1994)

Hurtak, J.J. – *The Keys Of Enoch,* (Academy For Future Science, 1977)

Sitchin, Zecharia – *The Wars Of Gods And Men* (Bear & Co., 1990)

Chapter 5 - The Little Town That Wouldn't

Adams, Sandra – interviews with the author

Adams, Dean – ibid

Sills, Howard – ibid

Tanner, Marianne – ibid

Layson, Sheila – ibid

Layson, Steve – ibid

Ford, Frank – ibid

Adams, Dorothy – ibid

Lassen, Arne – ibid

Smith, Georgia – ibid

Portland Oregonian – series on Rajneeshee cult by Leslie Zaitz

Newsletter and flier articles circulated by members of United
    Nuwaubian Nation of Moors

Kilgore, Gus – interviews with the author

Atlanta Journal-Constitution – articles written by this author on the
    Nuwaubian conflict

Chapter 6 - True Believers, False God

Areebah – investigative and court documents

Jokara – investigative and court documents

Azizah – interview with the author and investigative and court
    documents

Rafiq – investigative and court documents

Ramillah – interviews with the author and investigative and court
    documents

Letters to "Doc" – investigative documents

Conditions in Girls' House – investigative documents

Hill, Marc – interviews with the author

Hodge, Derrick and Shanda – interviews with the author

Ba'ith, Sahar – interviews with the author

Seabrooks, Diallo – interviews with the author

Rohan, Robert – interviews with the author and *Holding York Responsible* (Responsible Enterprise, 2005)

Fauset, Arthur Huff – *Black Gods Of The Metropolis* (University of Pennsylvania Press, 1944)

Arnn, Philip – interview with the author

Moser, Bob – interview with the author

Singer, Margaret Thaler – *Cults In Our Midst* (Jossey-Bass 2003)

Lifton, Robert Jay – "Cult Formation" (essay in *The Harvard Mental Health Letter*)

Conway, Flo and Siegelman, Jim – *Snapping*

Ross, Rick – interviews with the author

Chapter 7 - Savior Daze Showdown

Sills, Howard – interviews with the author

Georgia Bureau of Intelligence – report on the "Georgia Rangers" incident

Atlanta Journal-Constitution – articles written by this author

Brooks, Tyrone – interviews with the author and statement to GBI

Coughenour, Ed – interviews with the author

Barnes, Roy – interview with the author and written responses to queries

Kahn, Bobby – interview with the author and statement to GBI

Ford, Frank – interviews with the author

Chapter 8 - Exodus From The Egypt Of The West

Ramillah – interviews with the author

Asad – interviews with the author

Aludra – interviews with the author and investigative and court documents

Nasira – interviews with the author

Azizah – interview with the author and investigative and court documents

Badra – interviews with the author and investigative and court documents

Areebah – investigative and court documents

Visits of Al Sharpton and Rev. Jesse Jackson taken from accounts of Nuwaubian promotional materials and from local news reports

McGowan, William – *Coloring The News* (Encounter Books, 2002)

Snipes, Wesley – statements through spokesman to this author

Diehl, Tom – interview with the author

Ward, Jalaine – interview with the author

Cronier, Joan – interview with the author

Malik – interviews with the author

Basheera – investigative and court documents

Chapter 9 - Tribulations And A Trial

Sills, Howard – interviews with the author

Hicks, Claude – statements in court

Afifah – interviews with the author

Wood, Maxwell – interview with the author

Ward, Jalaine – interview with the author, hearing testimony

Brooks, Tyrone – court testimony

Varmah, Amadou – court testimony

Garland, Ed – court statements

Tucker, Stephanie – court statements

Baskin, Dawn – interview with the author

Robinson, Mark – interview with the author

Bowen, Tracy – interview with the author

York, Dwight – court statements

Basheera's statement – court documents

Bright, Fred – court statements

Karim – interview with the author

Lawson, Hugh – court statements

Moultrie, Richard – court statements and interview with the author
    Atlanta Journal-Constitution – articles on York trial
York, Dwight – court statements at sentencing

Chapter 10 – Epilogue To Evil
Sills, Howard – interviews with the author
Tanner, Marianne – interviews with the author
Adams, Sandra – interviews with the author
Smith, Georgia – interviews with the author
Reid, Janie – interview with the author
Aludra – interviews with the author
Nasira – interviews with the author
Badra – interviews with the author
Lewis, Sakina – interview with the author